Outlandish

Walking Europe's Unlikely Landscapes

NICK HUNT

First published in Great Britain in 2021 by John Murray (Publishers)
First published in the United States of America in 2021
by Nicholas Brealey Publishing
Imprints of John Murray Press
An Hachette UK company

This paperback edition published in 2022

I

Maps drawn by Rosie Collins

A CIP catalogue record for this title is available from the British Library

Paperback ISBN 978-1-529-38741-4
UK Ebook ISBN 978-1-529-38740-7
US Ebook ISBN 978-1-529-38138-2

Typeset in Bembo MT by Palimpsest Book Production Limited,
Falkirk, Stirlingshire

Printed and bound in Great Britain by Clays Ltd, Elcograf S.p.A.

John Murray Press policy is to use papers that are natural, renewable and
recyclable products and made from wood grown in sustainable forests.
The logging and manufacturing processes are expected to conform
to the environmental regulations of the country of origin.

John Murray (Publishers)   Nicholas Brealey Publishing
Carmelite House   Hachette Book Group
50 Victoria Embankment   Market Place Centre, 53 State Street
London EC4Y 0DZ   Boston, MA 02109, USA

www.johnmurraypress.co.uk
www.nbuspublishing.com

Nick Hunt has walked and written across much of Europe. Twice shortlisted for the Stanford Dolman Travel Book of the Year Award, he is the acclaimed author of *Walking the Woods and the Water* and *Where the Wild Winds Are*, and his articles have appeared in numerous publications. He is also an editor and co-director of the Dark Mountain Project. He currently lives in Bristol

Praise for *Outlandish*

'If on the surface *Outlandish* is, like much travel writing, a search for anomalies – places out of place – it becomes a reckoning with what has been squandered, and with an environmental future that often seems too horrifying to face . . . In this beautiful, disquieting book, Hunt helps us to look them in the eye' Will Atkins, *Financial Times*

'If travel writing is your ticket out of dreadful headlines, you will love *Outlandish*. Ready yourself to be transported to a puzzling, preternatural world of standing eagles and pagan gods, reindeer herds and polytunnel pampas – all, more or less, on your doorstep . . . *Outlandish* cements Hunt's reputation as a stellar writer about nature as well as travel' Oliver Balch, *Literary Review*

'Hunt is a fine descriptive writer' Sara Wheeler, *The Spectator*

'Proving that you don't need to travel long haul to find adventure, Hunt sets out to explore four of Europe's strangest environments . . . As well as sublime evocation of landscapes, there are encounters with the people who live in these extreme places' Tom Robbins, *Financial Times*

'Nick Hunt's bold exploration of our hidden continent makes you fall in wonder with the earth again. Passionate, learned, surprising and revelatory, this is a journey for our times – into "places of power" beyond human influence, where timelines get tangled like the last of the ancient forests'

Kapka Kassabova

'Nick Hunt is splendid company: kind, acute and wise, with an unerring eye for eloquent detail and a philosopher's view of the big picture. Don't miss this walk with him through portals you'd never stumble across yourself, and on into the thrilling surprise of a wholly improbable Europe'

Charles Foster, author of *Being a Beast*

'Hunt himself regards *Outlandish* as "a book of fantasy", but it is more than that. It is also a wave of a warning flag, elegantly told with plenty of proper travel and entertaining encounters – plus a fair few dreams – along the way'

Tom Chesshyre, *Critic*

'The eternal beauty of travel writing is, of course, that you don't have to go anywhere to voyage the world. With books like Nick Hunt's *Outlandish* . . . you won't have to budge from your armchair to sustainably broaden your mind'

Caroline Sanderson, *Bookseller*

'A wise and beautiful book, glowing with atmosphere and passion for the world that's slipping between our careless fingers, Nick Hunt's *Outlandish* shines a light on Europe's past and offers an eerie glance towards its future'   Nick Jubber

'Nick Hunt discovers something intense and otherworldly in Europe's wild fringes – a wonderful and deeply absorbing book'

Philip Marsden

'Nick Hunt's powerful imagery and vivid storytelling make for an original and unique travel book. *Outlandish* is beautifully written, enriching and informative, ensuring each chapter, each page, is a journey of its own where his curiosity takes the reader with him to somewhere new entirely'

Geordie Stewart

'A deep dive into some of Europe's most extreme and unexpected landscapes. Fascinating, illuminating, and filled with revelations. Makes the world seem bigger and brighter than you had imagined, which is all you could ever hope for from a travel book'

Neil Ansell

'Vivid, moving, profound and sometimes very funny . . . *Outlandish* is a truly stunning work of non-fiction and an important addition to writing that explores the deep connections between ourselves and our place on earth'

Joanna Pocock, author of *Surrender*

'Hunt paints with words, the canvas is large and there are many vivid colours. The texture of each challenging environment comes rippling through each page as we can sniff the air, suss out the skyline, test the ground and set off in any direction we choose'

James Crowden

'*Outlandish* is filled with boundless energy and insatiable curiosity yet it is gloriously gentle, too, carefully and elegantly steering us towards new ways of seeing our world'

Caroline Eden, author of *Black Sea*

'Precise, moving and exacting in its prose, this embodied and emotional journey gives the near world a fresh urgency, and makes it suddenly curious'

Helen Jukes, author of *A Honeybee Heart Has Five Openings*

Also by Nick Hunt

Walking the Woods and the Water
Where the Wild Winds Are
The Parakeeting of London

For Archer

Contents

Altogether elsewhere, vast
Herds of reindeer move across
Miles and miles of golden moss,
Silently and very fast.

W.H. Auden,
from 'The Fall of Rome'

INTRODUCTION
Outlands

The place that is sometimes called 'England's only desert' can be reached by a miniature railway line that runs to a nuclear power station on one of the largest expanses of shingle beach in Europe. Across the pebbled coastal plain a tiny, gleaming steam engine chugs bravely and ridiculously past weather-beaten huts and abandoned fishing boats, to deposit its passengers near the foot of a black lighthouse. The power station hums inland, too brutally large to understand. Ahead, the shingle foreshore lilts towards the sea. Sections of board-walk lead visitors out across the stones, past rusted bits of winching gear and outcrops of sea kale; in summer, the pebblescape is red with poppies. Stepping off the wooden boards, stones crunch with every step. The shingle is composed of flint. If you bring your boots down hard, your footsteps might strike sparks.

The English desert of Dungeness draws a million people a year, pilgrims to its weirdness. Why go to the Sahara when you can visit Kent? The headland noses out from the south-east coast towards Boulogne-sur-Mer, thirty miles across the sea. It is out on a limb, on its way to nowhere.

We did not arrive by train, my partner Caroline and I, but by cycling eastwards along the sand-duned coast from Rye, inland through the town of Lydd, and then back towards the sea. Despite the cloudless, glaring sky, what felt like a gale-force wind tore against us all the way, dragging the breath from our lungs if we faced directly into it, so that we progressed like drunks, teetering and gasping. At times the wind was so intense that it almost forced us to retreat, or into the shelter of barriers raised against the sea, but soon there was no shelter left. Ahead lay only pebbles. The emptiness seemed immense and we became extremely small. Distances were hard to gauge, proportions misaligned.

We stayed for a week in Dungeness in one of the iconic huts – it belonged to the family of a friend – and spent our days walking the foreshore and our evenings watching the sun collapse in a wobbling orange ball, like a shot-down UFO. The sky was not the English sky but the sky of a greater continent, with a clearer quality of light. Our discoveries got stranger. Astonishingly for what looks, at first glance, like a desolate place, this headland provides a habitat for a third of Britain's plant species, many of them rare; the ceaseless sifting of the sea sorts the pebbles into troughs and ridges that trap rainwater, creating small pockets of life. Sculptures of driftwood and scrap metal protrude along the shore, the creations of artists drawn here by the legacy of Derek Jarman, the avant-garde film director who coaxed a garden from the stones. And in one strange spot offshore, hidden pipes discharge hot water from the nuclear power station (actually two nuclear power stations, Dungeness A and Dungeness B) into patches dubbed 'the boils', where the warmer temperature attracts tiny sea creatures which, in turn, attract shoals of fish and wheeling seagulls. The waste water is – apparently – clean, but it is hard to overcome suspicions of mutant energies. A common description of this coast is 'post-apocalyptic'.

One evening at sunset, with crimson light pouring over a scene of wind-whipped marram grass and the skeletons of boats, I experienced a moment of dislocation; suddenly I was not in England but in a North American wasteland, some time in an imagined future that felt dreamily familiar, surrounded by the flotsam and jetsam of a collapsed culture. The light; the rusted metal cables; the plants like deformed cabbages; the presence of the power stations with their mysterious blinking lights; the landscape's sheer *outlandishness*: it was briefly enough to jolt me free from time and place. 'Outlandish' comes from the Old English *ūtland*, which means 'foreign country', and that was this desert's uncanny effect. It made my country foreign.

Dungeness – disappointingly – is not actually a desert. In less taxonomic times the word was more cultural than geographical, meaning simply a place that was deserted (from the Latin *desertum*) but scientific classification has now fixed the term in place and there are climatological parameters that this headland does not fit. To qualify as a true desert an area must receive less than 250 millimetres of precipitation a year. Dungeness gets more than that – the sea kale, sea holly, orchids, vetch, broom, sorrel, sage, bugloss, poppies and six hundred other species of plant are proof – too much rain falls even here, in one of Britain's driest places. In 2015 the Met Office, in response to a newspaper claim, officially refuted the myth of the shingle's desert status.

Nevertheless, for a moment there, I found myself transported.

This book is about places like that. Places that transport. Portals.

After our week in Dungeness, the experience stayed with me. It had been like falling into the clear light of another world, a place that was 'altogether elsewhere', like the line in that Auden poem that had always tugged at me. But it was not elsewhere, not far away at all. What was it about the thought of a desert – even a not-really-desert – nestled in the south-east corner of England that was so exhilarating? England should not possess a desert, or anything remotely resembling one; the very hint of such a thing felt dangerous and subversive. Deserts surely belong in places that are remote and far away from this green and pleasant land, or from this over-civilised time. There should be no place for them here. And yet here one (almost) is.

Following on from that Kentish desert was a West Country rainforest; another place that tipped me unexpectedly into elsewhere. On a cold February day I went in search of Wistman's Wood, a sliver of ancient oak woodland on Dartmoor, and discovered a dwarf jungle of contorted green limbs clustered with mosses, lichens, ferns and other epiphytes – plants that grow on other plants, a common indicator of rainforests – which felt like stepping into a primordial other-world. Patches of temperate rainforest can also be found in riverine valleys in the north-west of Wales, on the Atlantic coasts of Scotland and Ireland, and in Cornwall and Cumbria (sometimes they are romantically called 'Celtic rainforests'), part of a coastal temperate rainforest biome that reaches east to Japan and west to the Pacific seaboard of North America. As with deserts, rainforests seem to belong to somewhere far away, but their existence should hardly be surprising in a place where it rains all the time. 'Learning that Britain is a rainforest nation astounds us only because we have so little left', writes the journalist George Monbiot; once, the dripping canopy covered the most part of these islands.

Casting around for the feeling these moments most reminded me of – the Dungeness desert and the Devon jungle – what came to my mind was snow, the meagrest sprinkling of which has the ability to transform the everyday into the extraordinary: a lawn into a frosted steppe, a suburban park into a taiga.

At the beginning of 2019 I yearned for more of that feeling. The year before, devastating fires had swept across the world, burning millions of square miles in places where they hadn't burned before, or never on such a scale, from the

Mediterranean to the Arctic Circle. (I couldn't have imagined it then, but the Amazon was to go up in flames a year later.) In the Arctic and the Antarctic, as well as across the world's mountain ranges, glaciers and ice caps were melting at an unprecedented rate. Climate breakdown – which, until then, had felt like a distant future emergency, alarming in an intellectual but not a tangible way – was suddenly made real to me in a way it hadn't been before. The perfect archetypal landscapes I had believed in as a child – the mountains capped with snow and ice; the dense dark forests stretching away, impenetrable and vast; the endless plains of yellow grass and golden moss seething in the wind – were not immutable features of the world, somehow immune from change. Glaciers were melting into slush and rainforests desiccating into savanna; from continent to continent, distances were becoming less vast and empty horizons were being filled in with the clutter of the Anthropocene. As I stumbled upon these English outlands, the greater outlands of the world were vanishing or being changed beyond all recognition.

As a travel writer increasingly aware of the damage that travel can do – mainly, of course, the chemical violence done to the stratosphere by flying – I was looking for transformative journeys that lay closer to home. My previous books had been about walking and Europe, and in both of them I had experienced states of outlandishness. Often those states had not occurred in remote wildernesses but in close proximity to towns, roads and agriculture, and this proximity somehow increased, rather than diminished, their magic. It seemed a version of the Celtic conception of the otherworld, which exists alongside our own, and can be accessed in certain locations, or in certain frames of mind. As the Welsh mystic Arthur Machen wrote of early twentieth-century London: 'He who cannot find wonder, mystery, awe, the sense of a new world and an undiscovered realm in the places by the Gray's Inn

Road will never find those secrets elsewhere, not in the heart of Africa, not in the fabled hidden cities of Tibet.'

While I wanted to venture a little further abroad than the Gray's Inn Road, the idea that wonder, mystery, awe, new worlds and undiscovered realms might lie a train ride away, rather than on a carbon-intensive flight to the far side of the globe, opened up possibilities for a different type of travel. What other unlikely landscapes might be lurking out there, ready to snatch the unwary traveller into the outlandish?

Europe is sometimes referred to as the world's only desert-free continent (there are frozen deserts at the poles) but a bit of research revealed examples of other desert-like places where you would least expect to find them. In the south of Romania – in my mind so richly green – desertification catalysed by communist-era deforestation has created an area popularly known as the Oltenian Sahara, which grows larger every year. Serbia has its Deliblatska, a region of sandy hills that once formed the bed of a sea; before tree-planting programmes in the nineteenth century, sand was reported being blown as far west as Vienna. And in the heart of Poland lies the anomaly of Błędów, another semi-desert that owes its existence to human greed. Centuries of deforestation caused the topsoil to erode and exposed a bed of ancient sand (though local legend blames the devil, who dumped the sand in order to bury a nearby silver mine). During the Second World War, Germany's Afrika Korps trained there. Poland became a practice ground for deployment in the Sahara.

Again, none of these are deserts in the strict scientific sense – mainland Europe has only one true desert, which I explore in this book – but learning of the existence of these geological oddities expanded the imaginative horizons of the continent; suddenly it felt larger, somehow older and infinitely more unknown. Following this outlandish thread, I discovered that there are fjords in Ireland (three of them, all in the west);

bizarrely eroded 'badlands' in the south of France and Italy, respectively known as *calanques* and *calanchi*; and western Europe's only steppe is stranded in Provence. The thing that drew together such wildly different topographies was the fact that each of them seemed to belong to another part of the world, or even to another historical or geological era. Fjords should be Scandinavian (or, at a pinch, Chilean); badlands are associated with the North American frontier; steppes are properly situated in the grassland tracts of Mongolia, Central Asia and southern Russia. All of them are exclaves, which is normally a geopolitical term describing a region that belongs to another country but is not connected to it by land, and finds itself alone, surrounded by alien territory.

I began to think of Europe's outlands – these portals to elsewhere – as exclaves not only of place, but of deep time.

Of all the outlandish places I learned about, four in particular called to me, and became the four chapters of this book: a patch of arctic tundra in Scotland; the continent's largest surviving remnant of primeval forest in Poland and Belarus; Europe's only true desert in Spain; the grassland steppes of Hungary. As well as their surface connotations of geology and ecology, all of them had deep, and often surprising, cultural links with faraway regions of the world – the Arctic, the Siberian tundra, the badlands of North America, the Sahara, the steppes of Central Asia – and the act of stepping into them, and the alchemy of walking, were a means of being transported without setting foot outside this small, supposedly tame continent (which, especially to a walker, is neither small nor tame). These journeys through snowstorms and burning sun, mountains and deserts, forests and plains, were also walks through time. They did not only lead me backward into pre-human history, glacial landscapes and great migrations – by way of Paleolithic cave art, reindeer nomads, desert wanderers, shamans, Slavic forest gods, ibex,

European bison, Wild West fantasists, eco-activists, horseback archers, Big Grey Men and other unlikely spirits of place – but forward, into a future whose map we are only just starting to glimpse.

Perhaps the result is not a nature book, or even a travel book, so much as a book of fantasy: four small pilgrimages into the imagination.

~

In fading light we walked to where the stony plain met the waves, past hunched fishermen and the cannibalised wrecks of boats. The lighthouse beam probed the sky with the power of a hundred thousand candles. As night came on, the almost-desert merged with the greying sea.

We found ourselves in an open space that expanded on and on, populated by the blinking lights of trawlers floating off the coast and the right-angled monoliths of Dungeness A and Dungeness B shimmering inland. Beneath our boots the shingle shifted like a bed of atoms. Thousands of years stretched between the flints whose striking once sparked fire and the nuclear power station whose waste will last for centuries more, a monument both to eternity and to extreme fragility. For a moment in the dark we stood between the past and the future; between what lay beneath our feet and what looms on the horizon.

SCOTLAND'S ARCTIC

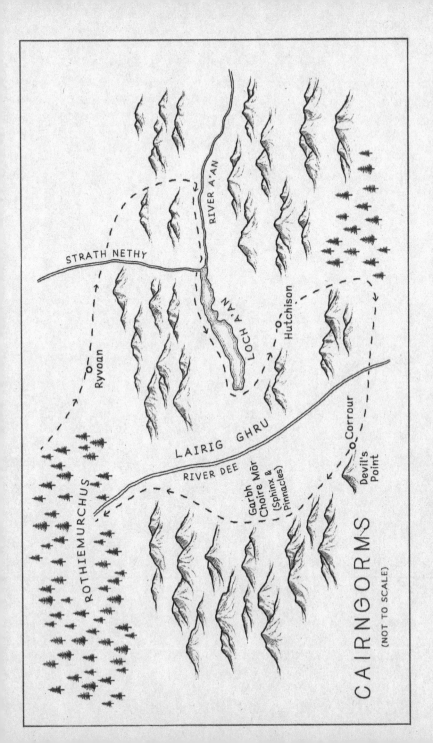

Once all of this was ice. A solid river. It ran south for hundreds of miles, deep into what was not yet England, west across a buried sea to what would one day be Ireland. But mostly it ran north and east, a sloping frozen shoulder enveloping the granite bones of mountain ranges, an ice-limb that connected this rock to the vast Eurasian continent. You could walk it for a thousand miles and still not see its end.

It was not flat but deep, in places three miles thick. It was not pure but cluttered with boulders and the rubble of rocks, holding them above the earth as if suspended in time. It was not still but constantly moving, flowing under the weight of itself, faster on top and slower below, sliding and scouring at a rate of inches every year. The ice at its surface was years old. The ice at its base, millions.

Centuries – millennia – of snowfall augmented its mass with compacted layers fused as hard as stone. Its sides heaved mountain walls apart, and rocks embedded in its base raked the earth like teeth, leaving jagged scars. In these lands it deposited lochs; further north, fjords. As the world took shape beyond its foot, the landmasses feeling out their forms, its icy bulk advanced and retreated, advanced and retreated, advanced and retreated, like the outflows and inflows of a frozen breath. When it breathed out, life shrank back.

When it breathed in, humans came.

To the earliest Paleolithic hunter-gatherers venturing north, that great machine of ice must have seemed the limit of everything. But the ice withdrew its reach and the earth rebounded back. Migrating human populations followed migrating animal herds in the wake of migrating glaciers, discovering new lands beneath, like people cautiously setting forth on a recently drained seabed. But as one door opened up, another door was closed.

The North Sea, long since solid, became a sea once again. The ice-shelves split, broke into bergs, and the waters rose. Britain was re-islanded, severed from the continent to which it had been joined by ice, orphaned from the north.

One patch of the frozen past was left, an island upon an island.

Somewhere, in the depths of time, a figure emerges from the gloom. The Cailleach, the divine hag, milking her herd of deer. She is known as the Queen of Winter, bringer of ice and snow, with teeth as slow as glaciers, who gnawed at the mountainsides to make the waters flow.

~

Aviemore does not live up to the poetry of its name. Knowing nothing about the place, I imagined something wistful, wild. Instead, a blare of electric light splashed across wet tarmac. Through beating wipers I look out at a row of discount retail outlets dedicated to mountainwear and commercialised outdoorsiness. I expected to see snow but there is mild, persistent rain.

I have come to Scotland looking for the Arctic.

Dougie Strang, my friend and guide, eases the car into the kerb and we get out and stretch our legs. We have driven two hundred miles north from his home near Lockerbie. We will walk into the mountains tonight but first we need to fuel ourselves, so I follow him through drizzling mist to the Old Bridge Inn.

The pub is richly carpeted with improbably large dogs, six or seven ungainly breeds splayed across the floor. In this warm canine menagerie we find ourselves a corner. We order food and beer and Dougie spreads out a map.

The Cairngorms mountain range unfolds across the table.

It is wrinkled, whorled and strange to me, a language I do not know how to speak. Its *coires* and *choires*, *lairigs* and *beinns*, *allts* and *gleanns*, *lochans* and *carns*: the Gaelic is as alien as Hungarian or Polish. But Dougie knows the territory, linguistically and physically. Linguistically from a long-standing interest in Gaelic language and myth, and physically from childhood expeditions with the Boys' Brigade – he hated the marching and the uniforms, but fell in love with hill-walking – and a subsequent forty-year entanglement with these mountains. He is slight, with reddish stubble and kind, lucent, fox-like eyes. He is tracing possible routes for the next few days.

'We can walk together to Strath Nethy then go different ways. If you take the high road to Bynack More you can cross the river at the Fords of A'an, if the water's low enough. I'll stay low and follow the Nethy to the loch. Either we meet at the Shelter Stone or up at the Hutchison Hut . . .'

While we plan, the boyish young Englishman at the next table eavesdrops slightly anxiously. It turns out that he is heading back south after a week of winter skills training – I imagine ice axe and crampon use, avalanche survival techniques, sawing off frostbitten digits and that kind of thing – in which he was disappointed, as there was no winter. This time last year, he says, it was white from the summits to the glens. Now everything is brown. Aviemore is a ski resort without snow, unseasonally out of season.

'When I was a child, the daffodils didn't come out until

April. This year I saw them on New Year's Day,' he says, smiling helplessly.

I can't help thinking, as we leave, that he practically *is* a child; he looks about fifteen years old. Far too young, it seems, to remember things being different back then, in the cooler climate of his youth. But solastalgia, like everything else, is speeding up these days.

The Latin word *sōlācium*, 'consolation', spliced with the Greek *algia*, 'pain': the philosopher Glenn Albrecht's term for the existential anguish for an environment that has gone. Like the grid references and the Gaelic place-names on the map, it is a word we will navigate by over the next few days.

We put the winterwear sales behind us and drive on, into the hopeful darkness beyond the last lights of the town. Dougie parks by the side of the road near the Reindeer Centre at Glenmore. The drizzle has mostly stopped as we finalise our supplies: enough food to last three days – home-made stew, various dhals, miso soup and porridge oats – tactical layers of warm clothing, waterproofs, whisky, first-aid kits and a bag of coal split two ways. Before locking the car, Dougie leaves a note: *Tuesday 15th Jan. Off to Ryvoan, then Hutchison, then Corrour. Back on Friday 18th.*

I am quietly thrilled by this. It is as if we were about to step briefly out of time.

There is a special feeling to walking into mountains at night, like approaching a herd of sleeping cattle. We cannot see them but can guess at them looming somewhere close at hand, their bulk only hinted at, shapes darker than the dark. There is a path along a stream, its sound an abstract bubbling, and bouts of damp, disturbed air rushing through pine branches. Dougie has a fragment of myth in his mouth – the last Pict vanishing north in the tracks of the last reindeer, facing backward as they go – and these words run inside my mind as we walk. He doesn't say what it means and I don't want to ask. It is suitably enigmatic for now. The image replaces Aviemore, and that is enough.

Within the hour, just as my back starts growing accustomed to the particular weights and pressures of my rucksack, a negotiation of small discomforts, we see the roof of Ryvoan standing black against the sky. This bothy is where we will sleep tonight. The door is unlocked. There is no one inside. It is a cube of bare stone. Dougie lights the stove using nothing but firelighters and chips of shining coal, no need for kindling – a trick I haven't seen before, which should be taught on all winter skills courses – and nurses the flame until it takes. We sit here getting the warmth in our hands. The stove resembles the helmet of a mean and stupid knight.

We are just considering going to bed when three tall climbers stumble in, which is always a possibility when sleeping in a bothy. They, too, are looking for snow and have been disappointed. In such close proximity their personalities seem very large, filling the space and nudging Dougie and me into the corners. One, with a surfer's flowing blond hair, is a mathematician writing his dissertation on ice climbing angles; after settling in he devotes his evening to doing difficult yoga moves. One is four days out of the army – boredom and budget cuts made him quit – and spends a long time, unprompted, telling us about the relative turret sizes of various models of tank and the types of terrain that each can cross. The third, who is the quietest and most serious-seeming of the three, talks about the time he discovered a frozen body, five years missing, on the side of a mountain near Glencoe. The conversation turns to death.

This is another possibility when sleeping in a bothy. Everyone seems to know someone who knows someone who has died, of falling or freezing or foolishness or all of these combined. This prompts Dougie to tell his tale, which I have heard before – and am always happy to hear again

– about the man he once knew who tripped and slithered helplessly, in full view of his horrified friends, down a glistening bank of snow and was launched into empty space above an almost certainly fatal drop on to the slopes below. As he disappeared over the edge he yelled, 'Geronimo!' He broke dozens of bones in his body but, incredibly, survived. He never climbed again but his almost-last word made him famous in his town.

I do not tell my story because there is no space for it, but last winter I almost had my own Geronimo moment. Descending the summit of Scafell Pike in thick fog with an adventurous friend, my feet slipped from under me and I found myself sliding on hard snow. At first it was almost fun until I realised I could not stop, that I was picking up speed, and that the slope below me ended in nothingness. All I had was a hazel stick that I managed to jab into the snow; I lost my grip but it slowed my momentum just enough to bring me to a halt. I looked back up at my friend's shocked face. 'Be really careful there!' I shouted. He nodded gravely, took one step, and did exactly the same thing as me. As he hurtled towards me I had an instant to decide what was least worst: to let him go and hope he managed to stop as I had done, or to grab hold of his leg. I grabbed hold of his leg. That set me off again, and then both of us were sliding faster and faster towards the edge, clinging on to one another in grim, astonished silence. At the very last moment, he managed to jam his boot against a rock. We stopped.

Neither of us would have shouted anything as we fell.

If I'd had an ice axe instead of a stick, what almost happened wouldn't have happened. That is why I have one now, price-tag-new, strapped to the side of my rucksack, its sharp and serrated head wrapped in a canvas bag. I don't have crampons but I have spikes that slip over the top of my boots to provide grip on snow and ice. Against everything suggested by the pattering rain outside, my hope is that I will need them.

I am glad of Dougie's company in this first outland of my walks. People die in the Cairngorms every year, mostly at this time of year, and that horrible slither down Scafell Pike has left a humbling impression. It still makes me twitch when I think of it, an elongated aftershock, a reminder of how suddenly things can go wrong. I am appropriately daunted by the Cairngorms' massiveness: not only by the mountains themselves, whose summits I feel no need to 'bag', but by the vast, exposed plateau – a thousand metres above sea level and stretching for hundreds of square miles – that forms the highest and the coldest upland in the British Isles. There is also another instinct behind my seeking company. It has something to do with the fact that this place, for all its Gaelicness – and, as I hope to discover, its improbable Arcticness – is a part of the island on which I live. It is not so far from home. For reasons I don't quite understand, this makes me more nervous of it.

It is as if my actions here were somehow better witnessed.

Dougie, as a veteran of month-long solo walks through the Highlands, is someone who understands the clarity and the happiness of walking in solitude, with no other ego to amplify one's own. With this in mind he has planned a route that gives us both some space. Our paths will begin together, divide and then run separately, merging again at crucial points, like interweaving threads. We will always be close enough but far enough away.

We are close enough tonight, at least, with five of us in the bothy. The mismatched climbers snore, sprawled across the floor like the dogs back in the Old Bridge Inn. Rain thwacks the corrugated roof. The knight's helmet dims and cools. We wake early to a band of pale lemon sky.

I step outside. To the north and south, mountains breach like whales.

~

A *strath* is a broad river valley, unlike a glen, which is steep and deep: my first Gaelic teaching of the day. We are walking to Strath Nethy. The land around us is saturated, purple-brown, like swollen grapes, with grazes of bare scree where the mountains' skin has slipped away. And snow. Yes, there is snow, but only very little. It is smeared high up Creag nan Gall, the nearest summit to the south, pallid and unhealthy-looking, as if it should be wiped away. Rain falls in bitter showers.

What did I expect to see?

Unbroken, frozen whiteness.

In terms of their climate, flora and fauna, the Cairngorms are not really part of Britain. This plateau, with its glacial valleys and its blunt, eroded summits, is defined, uniquely on our island, as 'arctic-alpine tundra', which means it is closer to Scandinavia, Greenland, northern Canada or Siberia than to any other place with which it shares a landmass. The climate is drier here, less boggy and midge-infested than in the neighbouring Western Highlands, and prone to greater extremes of cold: the lowest temperature ever recorded in the British Isles – minus 27.2 degrees Celsius – was measured at nearby Braemar in 1982. The tundra supports ptarmigan, Lapland bunting, snow bunting, dotterel and other Arctic-dwelling birds (on rare occasions, even visiting snowy owls have been spotted here) and plants like alpine milkvetch, alpine cinquefoil and mountain everlasting. Cloudberry and bearberry are redolent of Scandinavia. Hundreds of species of mosses and lichens texture the rocks and trees.

This is a biome out of place, seven hundred miles south

of its native range. It is an exclave of the Arctic stranded in north-east Scotland.

'Arctic' derives from a civilisation that probably never went anywhere near it; it comes from the Greek word *arktikos*, which means 'near the bear'. This refers to Ursa Minor, the Little Bear, the constellation whose brightest point is the North or Pole Star, but it is tempting to imagine that it was a reference to actual bears, a map-maker's warning along the lines of 'Here be monsters'. In terms of physical location it is normally taken to mean the area north of the Arctic Circle, which – as an arbitrary line on the map, the position of which is dependent on the tilt of the earth's ever-shifting axis – is apparently moving northwards at a rate of fifteen metres a year; and therefore drifting ever further away from Scotland. This latitudinal retreat, entirely theoretical, is like a cartographic echo of the retreat of the glaciers.

An alternative way of defining the Arctic is by its average temperature, which must not rise above ten degrees Celsius in the summer. Or it can simply refer to what lies north of – or above – the treeline. Where the forest ends, the tundra begins; defined as cold, barren upland, tundra covers a fifth of the world's land surface, mostly in a skirt around the North Pole but also in the Alps, the Andes, the Himalayas and other mountain ranges. (As the word 'alpine', uncapitalised, can refer to montane environments that have nothing to do with the Alps, 'arctic' is also a term that has broken loose of geography. For many people, it is simply a word for 'extremely cold'.)

In the taxonomic zeal of the late nineteenth century the parameters of tundra – both Arctic and arctic – were set by the Köppen climate classification, a system still widely used today. The Russian-born botanist and geographer Wladimir Köppen – who, in photographs, resembles Leon Trotsky's craggier twin – simplified the world's climates into five basic groups: tropical (A), arid (B), temperate (C), continental (D) and polar (E). Each of these groups is then divided into smaller groups, also with a corresponding letter: tropical into savanna wet (w), savanna dry (s), rainforest (f) and monsoon (m); arid into desert (W) and steppe (S); temperate and continental into dry summer (s), dry winter (w) and 'without dry season' (f); polar into tundra (T) and ice cap (F), also called 'eternal winter'. Finally these are subdivided into even smaller groups: hot (h), cold (k), hot summer (a), warm summer (b), cold summer (c) and very cold winter (d).

According to this abstract code, the Cairngorm plateau is ET (polar tundra), with patches of Dfc (continental subarctic).

Clearly this is a horrible way to describe a living landscape.

But on a Köppen-Geiger map – developed by Rudolph Geiger, the German climatologist who continued Köppen's work – this codification of the world becomes strangely evocative. Picture a global thermogram with colours flowing across the continents in garish bands, oscillating with temperature: red across North Africa, Australia and the Middle East (BWh: arid, desert, hot); deep blue in the Amazon (Af: tropical, rainforest); yellow across a swathe of southern Europe (Csa: temperate, savanna dry, hot summer). Most of Britain is a gentle green (Cfb: temperate, without dry season, cold summer) apart from the aberration of the Cairngorms tucked away in the north-east, a darker green and a stony grey that matches Scandinavia; a swooping bridgehead to the wider, colder north.

The word 'tundra' filters into English from Russian, and into Russian from Kildin Sámi, the indigenous language of the Kola Peninsula bordering the White Sea. A prosaic description – 'flat, treeless tract' – but the word is thrilling. Since childhood those syllables, the double-thump of a shaman's drum, have conjured in my mind a sense of unbounded space, vast silences and distances and stabs of loneliness. It evokes fields of snow stretching to the horizon, distant herds migrating through expanses of nothingness. Tundra is often accompanied, or underlaid, by permafrost – soil and sediment that stays frozen for over two consecutive years, and often for millennia – which, in my imagination, meant the same as 'permanence': an environment safe from change, a frozen fastness that had always existed and always would exist. The continual presence of ice and snow was a proof of eternity; perhaps as close as I ever got to believing in an afterlife.

One of my relatives once touched such an eternity; not the eternal snows of the north, but of the world's highest mountain. My great-uncle John Hunt – a name that last night's climbing trio would almost certainly have known – was the leader of the first successful Everest expedition in 1953, when the Sherpa mountaineer Tenzing Norgay and the New Zealand beekeeper Edmund Hillary planted the Union Jack on the highest point on earth. His tallness is what I remember most – he seemed halfway up a mountain already – and the long strides of his legs as he hiked into his eighties. Those legs had carried him, I knew, to a secret world above the clouds, a semi-mythical, dreamlike realm of icefalls and unmelting snow, a place that no human had glimpsed before and surely few would see again; those who attempted it must go, like him, in hobnailed boots and oxygen tanks requiring almost superhuman strength to lift, ice axes against which mine would look like an item of cutlery. He himself might have been changed by his ascent to the home of gods, but the mountain would not – could not – have been changed by his visitation; once the snow had filled his tracks or the icy wind blown them away, the place had returned to its sanctity as if he had never set foot there.

Growing older I saw the photographs of alpinists queuing in their hundreds to be shepherded up that same ascent, a backlog of brightly clad commuters 8,800 metres high. I heard about the cadmium and arsenic deposits in the snow, a legacy of Asian smog, the discarded oxygen tanks, the trash and the scores of frozen corpses littered on the slopes. My great-uncle could never have imagined where his steps up the mountain would lead, or how many people would follow them, in the globalised world of mass travel – of mass adventure – that was to come; let alone the invisible creep of warming temperatures. The legendary Khumbu Icefall, the crevasse-riddled glacier that forms the first part of the climb, is melting dangerously now; the 2014 ice avalanche killed sixteen Sherpas. The mountain that Tibetans call Chomolungma, 'Holy Mother', and Nepalis call Sagarmāthā, 'Goddess of the Sky', is now referred to as 'the world's highest garbage dump'. Learning about the degradation of this once unreachable place was like losing a part of my childhood. An end to eternity.

As Dougie and I make our way from Ryvoan, the mildness of the winter we walk through – the brownness of the mountaintops – brings me a similar feeling of disturbance. Dougie shares it too. Like everyone else we have read the reports, turned away from the news when it got too much, observed with our eyes and felt with our bodies the change, like the winter skills student with his talk of daffodils. In this age of climate crisis, all definitions are breaking down. The retrenchment of the Arctic is not just a line of latitude; if the word is taken to mean summer temperatures of below ten degrees, what happens when it surpasses that? The northernmost regions of the world are heating at twice the rate of anywhere else on the planet. The Arctic will not be arctic soon, as the Alpine will not be alpine. In Siberia, millennia-old permafrost is melting seventy years earlier than the worst-case predictions. No longer perma. No longer frost. An end to permanence.

The colour bands are rippling. The ET and Dfc are becoming Csa.

For now, though, we walk on. What else can anyone do? Ahead of us runs the Nethy, the quick, shallow stream where we will part ways. A pair of black grouse erupts above the heather. Dougie points out juniper, blaeberry, the recent regrowth of Scots pine, where the forest is gradually spreading from its strongholds in the glens: a hopeful sign of regeneration against the zeitgeist of decline. To the south lies Cairn Gorm, the mountain that gives the range its name – though it is not its highest peak – floating like a magical island, distant and unreachable. Its ridges seep with light. The rain has broken and the sky floods with winter gold.

Then, just before we part, two strange silver ghosts emerge beyond the Nethy.

At first I think they are dogs. Then deer. But they are not quite deer. They are squat yet elegant, forms I am not familiar with.

'Reindeer,' Dougie says.

And with that, the outlandish portal opens. The tundra becomes real.

They approach on soft, splayed feet and cross the little bridge, expressing no more than mild interest in our presence. They are joined by a third, a fourth. They become a herd. We stand quietly and watch as they bend their mouths to the montane grass, chewing rhythmically. Snowy ruffs sway at their necks. The silver-greyness of their hair is the colour of cooling metal. We count their antlers, furred like moss: two have two; one one; one none. Their sodden pelts are as matted as the land they eat.

In his years of walking in these mountains Dougie has never seen them before. We must be lucky.

The story of their presence here seems, at first, unlikely. These velvet-faced, solemn beasts are descended from the herd brought here in the 1950s, after a Swedish Sámi reindeer herder and a Swedish-American anthropologist, Mikel Utsi and Ethel Lindgren, happened to be visiting Scotland on their honeymoon. From the railway bridge at Aviemore, Utsi looked towards the Cairngorms and saw reindeer pastures. The mottled plateau reminded him of tundra in the north of Sweden, carpeted with the slow-growing lichens – in particular branching reindeer lichen, also known as reindeer moss – that other ruminants turn up their noses at, but which form a crucial part of a reindeer's winter diet. Five years later the couple, with backing from the recently formed Reindeer Council of the United Kingdom, persuaded the Ministry of Agriculture to grant them several hundred acres of land in Rothiemurchus Forest.

The first eight pioneers arrived from Sweden on a ship called the SS *Sarek*, after which one of them was named. It was a rough North Sea crossing; Utsi's eye was accidentally gored by an antler on the way, so he arrived wearing a piratical-looking eyepatch. One reindeer calf died during its six-and-a-half-week quarantine in Edinburgh, but the others survived and were trucked north to their new enclosure. The first year in Scotland was hard, with the animals sickly and weak, but once the colony was established it was strengthened by a second influx from Scandinavia, followed by a third, a fourth. In 1954 the Forestry Commission leased out a further thousand acres on the northern slopes of the Cairngorms, and in that same year the reindeer gained the freedom to roam beyond their enclosure, escaping the midges, mosquitoes and horseflies that had tormented them at lower altitude. Now there are 150 scattered across the plateau.

The names of the early females have a jingling Christmas feel: Inge, Pelle, Assa, Ina, Maja, Tilla, Nuolja, Vilda . . . In 1955 two more males arrived, with the lusty names Fritzen and Ruski. Technically they are not wild but owned – after Utsi's and Lindgren's deaths the herd was purchased by Tilly and Alan Smith, who manage them today – but presumably that detail does not matter to the reindeer. The experiment has been so successful that, at the World Reindeer Herders Congress held in north-east China in 2013 – alongside Sámis, Soyots, Evenks, Chukchis, Komis, Nenets, Iñupiaqs and other indigenous herders from across the Northern Hemisphere – the Smiths accepted Scotland's recognition as the thirtieth member.

Call it reindeer diplomacy, a link to a wider northern world. This patch of arctic-alpine tundra, marooned between Inverness and Perth, has been drawn into a boreal heritage of reindeer husbandry that links Scotland to Finnish Lapland, Siberia, Mongolia, Kamchatka, Greenland and Alaska.

Or rather, it has been drawn *back*. For this was not an introduction but an overdue reintroduction.

The saga of reindeer in the Cairngorms is older than the 1950s. In his book of place-names, *Gathering*, the artist Alec Finlay writes of reindeer deep time: 'As far back as we know, a band of nomads camped out on the Geldie, near Caochanan Ruadha, and at Chest of Dee. Braving vast snowfields and the residue of glaciers, they followed a herd of migrating reindeer north, *c*. 8100 BC. The domestication of reindeer was an early form of pastoralism.'

Reindeer are the only type of deer to have been domesticated, though 'semi-domesticated' is a more accurate description. Across the circumpolar north (including North America, where they are called caribou, from a Mi'kmaq word meaning 'shoveller of snow'), they migrate in herds many thousands strong, and humans have learned less to control them than be drawn into their flow; like American plains buffalo, they are not so much farmed as followed. Although they can pull sleds like dogs – or, in the case of sturdier breeds, can even be ridden like antlered ponies – they are chiefly used by nomadic peoples to provide food and milk, while their skins and wondrous pelts are turned into clothes and shelter.

Like any life-giving creature in animist cultures, they also play a powerful role in spiritual beliefs. Reindeer are sacrificed and their skins and antlers worn in ceremonies or to help guide the deceased to the afterlife. Their urine, psychedelically infused from fly agaric mushrooms, is drunk for its hallucinogenic and visionary effects (second-hand stories of flying reindeer are probably the origin of Father Christmas's sleigh). To the beat of reindeer-skin drums, Siberian and Scandinavian shamans leave their physical bodies behind in order to journey between the worlds, voyaging with the herds and returning with insights and wisdom. Reindeer are venerated as powerful liminal beings, not only drawing together territories thousands of miles apart, and the winter to the summer, but providing a spiritual connection between beasts and people.

Britain, literally severed from the north when the ice melted and the sea level rose, could not provide enough space for thousands-strong herds to roam. Islanded reindeer, like islanded people, could not follow seasonal patterns of migration on the scale of their Arctic and Eurasian cousins. While deer were certainly worshipped in Scotland – the cervine trinity of red, roe and rein – there is less evidence for a tradition of reindeer husbandry such as that practised in the shamanic far north. There are, however, hints and clues, distorted through centuries of myth.

'On milk of deer I was reared/On milk of deer I was nurtured', goes the Highland lullaby 'Bainne nam Fiadh', 'Milk of Deer'. The Cailleach, the divine hag – bringer of winter, gnawer of mountains, the touch of whose staff freezes the ground – appears in folk-tales milking her herd of deer; shy of humans, ineffably eldritch, deer were traditionally regarded as fairy cattle. One theory suggests that knowledge of farming deer was not indigenous to Scotland but imported from Scandinavia; stories of a mysterious deer-herding culture might have crossed the North Sea in the longships of colonising Vikings, who would have had contact with Sámi tribes, and taken root in Scottish soil. If this is true, Utsi was merely cutting out the Norse middleman in reforging an ancient connection between Scots and Sámis.

Reindeer had probably vanished from Germany, Denmark and southern Sweden by the early Neolithic, pushed northwards by the warming climate and by the predations of humans. It is not known exactly when they disappeared in Scotland. 'By the 13th century they were sparse and by the 14th they were gone, chased from the last dells and glens, their beautiful fur adorning castle floors and their furred, coral-like horns on stone castle walls', writes Finlay, but this late date is contentious, as archaeological evidence points to a much earlier extinction. The only 'proof' of their existence into feudal times is found in the *Orkneyinga Saga*, written by the Viking Earls of Orkney, about a reindeer hunt in Caithness in the thirteenth century. Many scholars believe that the line actually refers to red deer, and that reindeer became extinct in Britain between eight and eleven thousand years earlier. The temporal ambiguity only adds to their mystery.

> how did we first come here?
> following behind the reindeer
> walking backwards into Spring

That fragment of myth emerges again. It is a poem from Finlay's book, dreamily misremembered by Dougie last night as we walked to Ryvoan; nothing to do with the last Pict, but about a much earlier human migration into Scotland. Legend tells of a fairy-man – perhaps a folk memory of a vanished indigenous population, or even a Sámi a long way from home – riding a deer with his face to its tail, warning Highlanders about approaching falls of snow. It feels significant, though, that Picts were prowling Dougie's mind; that ancient, enigmatic culture is another absence here. The early inhabitants of north-east Britain before they were displaced, or absorbed, by the Gaelic-speaking Scots – who confusingly might have come from Ireland – they left behind little but beautiful stones inscribed with salmon, wolves and stags, place-names scattered here and there, and a long-forgotten language written in Ogham script. Not much about them is known at all. The last trace of unified Pictish culture disappeared around the ninth century.

Unlike the reindeer, they have not come back.

Now Dougie and I go different ways, and the reindeer do as well. As they pad away they make a rhythmic clicking sound: tendons in their legs snapping over bones, designed so that they can follow one another in a blizzard.

This turns out to be a weather forecast, or a warning from the fairy-man. Minutes after they have gone, it begins to snow.

~

First the rain turns into sleet. When does one become the other? Is there a Köppenesque system to determine which is which, measured by proportions of water to slush to ice? Whatever, it is cold. I pull my hood snug around my face and fasten the ear-flaps of my hat, following the little path up the rise of Bynack Mòre. As I climb the track, the sleet gets thicker, wetter. It drives from the west in pale squalls interspersed by slashes of startlingly bright blue sky, as if the weather is undergoing a process of realignment. Looking back from the height I've gained I see a white, malevolent mist drifting across the strath, flapping like the ghost of a manta ray. The land is losing all its folds, its dimples filling in. I catch a last glimpse of Dougie very distantly below, a small figure sinking into a landscape that resembles something from the dawn of time, following the meanders of a liquid metal river.

There goes the last Pict, vanishing with the reindeer.

The sleet is now fierce snow, not tumbling gently like a Christmas card but whirling chaotically from every direction at once, flurrying inside my hood. It stings the underside of my face, flutters in my eyes. The air tastes like a wet knife. The blood in my fingers thumps with pain, even inside my gloves. Astonishingly quickly the snow has altered everything: part by part the views collapse and all I can see is driving static, dizzying in its patternlessness. Above, the gold-illuminated peak of Bynack More blinks out, and it is like losing sight of a headland from a boat at sea.

The right-hand side of my body is now a furred strip of snow. The intensity of the onslaught rapidly becomes alarming. There is a strong sensation of being untethered from the normal world that I was inhabiting just minutes ago. I have to reassure myself that I have a map and compass, the psychological crutch of my ice axe, that my friend is out there somewhere and he knows that I am too. But I cannot see how far I've come, or, with the land's shape hidden, where it is I have to go. Already the path ahead is fading and losing form, visible only as a furrow in the heather.

The reindeer make sense here now, for the land has assumed their colour. Everything is silver, grey, shades of dun, black and white, which makes it appear as if I were walking on reindeer pelts. During the hundreds of years in which the herds were absent from here, did the tundra feel their loss? Did the lichen miss them? When animals have been extirpated from the place in which they evolved, that place takes on their memory, a reminder of what it has lost. The ice is a morphic resonance of that silver-grey fur, the moss of branching velvet horns. Now that the herds have returned the two have been brought together again so that the reindeer are almost walking extensions of the land, parts that have gained sentience and detached themselves to wander.

With the snow encrusting me, I am becoming reindeered too. I am another walking extension, but much less well adapted.

The snow intensifies again, and again I am scared, a thump of fear in my belly and groin. Thick flakes batter my eyes so I can hardly see. This is a true blizzard now. Did the reindeer know this was coming? Surely their curious, sensitive noses smelled the warning in the air, their antlers picking up on some signal like antennae. Did they seek the shelter of the strath for that reason? There is no clicking tendon ahead of me, no herd to show me where to go, and the tactical solitude that Dougie so carefully curated for me slips, with rather embarrassing speed, into something more like fear.

Just as I am considering whether or not to attempt retracing my steps, to follow the reindeers' example and seek the protection of lower ground, the humped ridge of Bynack More re-emerges on my right. My eyes can reach further again. There is a kind of lull. I am in the summit's lee and the violence has gone out of the snow, as if it has established its dominance and can afford to relax somewhat. The flakes fall fatly, pillowing the land. Once more I can see the clear lines of the contours ahead, and – reassuringly – my route does not lead up but down. Pale light breaks through the clouds. I carry on.

To the east the tundra opens up, fed by vascular black streams. With the cover of snow it is hard to determine size or distance. The path goes south, gently bending westwards with the mountain's curve, several hundred metres below the Barns of Bynack. These are jutting outcrops of contorted granite blocks that have risen taller as the softer mountainside has shrunk away, elemental monoliths, slumped and heaped and folded. I wonder if there is some link between the word 'barns' and 'bairns'; if they are really the mountain's children, huddled on its shoulder. A localised storm is raging up there, icy spindrift boiling around them, and their flanks are grey with cold as if they were exhausted.

I sympathise. It is only midday but already I am tired, with the deep muscular ache that comes from fighting cold. Just as the glimpse of reindeer opened a portal to the tundra, that brush with fear has had the effect of giving me arctic eyes. The landscape around me is no longer Scottish but something grander and deadlier, requiring a different scale of respect. It does not feel bounded in the same way, but expanded without end.

Hopping a burn called Uisge Dubh Poll a' Choin – a noble name, and a lengthy one, for a stream crossed in two steps – I continue my descent into the valley. Bright rivers writhe down there. The sun is a golden ball. The land is studded with erratics, the displaced, unlikely rocks deposited by glaciers: scattered colonies of bairns to populate this terrain.

In an hour I reach the refuge at the Fords of A'an, just a pitched-roof wooden shed, and crawl inside to escape the icy hammering of the wind. The walls are covered in graffiti from others who have done the same. 'Looking for sexy fun?' someone has written next to a mobile number. Regarding the barren wastes outside, I can only admire their optimism.

Dougie was right: the fords across the A'an, bloated with rain and snow, are impassable. Having left the shelter of the hut I waste a quarter of an hour trying to pick out a route across thundering white noise but the stepping stones are perilous, greased with slicks of ice. Rather than continuing south I must follow the river westwards to the loch that shares its name. In English it is called the Avon.

'Avon' has the ring of home – I grew up in the West Country – but as rivers go they couldn't be more different. My Avon, muddy, broad and slow, was an artery of empire, slavery and industrialisation, a highway to the modern world; this A'an, rumbling through snow, looks as if it has not changed since the glaciers melted. But the name is ubiquitous throughout Britain: there are three in Scotland, at least seven in England (including a diminutive Aune in Devon) and an Afan in Wales. There are also two in Canada, two in New Zealand and five in Australia, as if the name were carried out on the tide of colonialism.

The modern Welsh for 'river', *afon*, provides the etymological clue: they all derive from the ancient Brittonic word *abona*, the source from which these namesakes flow. Once upon a time in Britain all rivers were the Avon.

Snow has filled the puddles, pools and lochans with cloudy ice, giving the impression of frogspawn. I follow the tautology of the River River west. For the rest of the day my body pushes into a biting headwind pouring down from the slope of Cairn Gorm, picking up the loch's deep chill on the way. At the bottom of this glacial valley, the cold feels like the memory of the great ice-tongue that lay here eleven and a half thousand years ago. Time itself feels cold. The going is an arduous slog over uneven ground, a tumble of peat hags and the stumps of long-vanished trees. The snow is replaced by a torrent of hail that stings like flung gravel. Wading upriver, uphill and uphail, I eventually reach the loch to find it much larger than I expected, its furthest shore invisible behind a seething mist of ice; white-capped waves are surging in a trapped and angry sea. After what seems like a very long time I still cannot see its end, only an indifferent haze. The distance eats my energy. My legs are getting clumsy.

Finally the loch peters out below the walls of a boulder-strewn moraine. Somewhere in that pile of heaped erratic blocks, some as big as cottages, must be the Shelter Stone: a great rock underneath which a refuge has been hollowed out and improved with a drystone wall, a summer camp for climbers. But darkness is threatening and my curiosity is spent. I look at my torn, sodden map. My stomach sort of clenches. The Hutchison Memorial Hut, where I will spend the night with Dougie, is at least as far again as the distance I walked from the start of Loch A'an, but up and down the other side of one of those precipitous walls. There is a winding path that I have little confidence about being able to find in the snow, let alone the fading light; in this litter of broken rocks I can't tell where it's meant to begin. Then, a thump of relief: a man's shape is up there. It must be Dougie. I call and wave. The figure stops, seems to regard me, then continues on its way. As I hurry after it, it disappears again. Stumbling on, I find myself on the crude impression of a path and climb as fast as I am able, not wanting to lose the trail. When I see the figure again it is somehow below me. In the twilight it has veered off the path and into the boulder field, where it seems to be searching for something, casting about in the gloom. It can't be Dougie! Not pausing to question why anyone would be wandering around down there – slightly horrified at the thought – I carry on uphill, panic fluttering in me now. Fear makes my footsteps imprecise. The path keeps vanishing. My instinct when getting lost is, illogically, to walk as quickly as I can and not stop to rationalise, and I know that I am falling back into this pattern but am being carried along by a dead-brained inertia. When I look back down to the rocks the figure has disappeared.

There are stories in these mountains of a Big Grey Man.

In Gaelic he is called Am Fear Liath Mòr. His full name in English is the Big Grey Man of Ben Macdui, after the mountain that he haunts – the highest point in the Cairngorms and the second-highest in the country – which lies not far away from here, feeding the headwaters of Loch A'an. Whether he is a ghost or a yeti-like humanoid is not entirely clear. The manner in which he makes his appearance depends on the observer.

An early account is from 1791, when the shepherd and writer James Hogg described, in the parlance of his time, 'a giant blackamoor, at least thirty feet high, and equally proportioned, and very near me. I was actually struck powerless with astonishment and terror.' A hundred years later, Professor J. Norman Collie – a respected Royal Society member as well as a noted mountaineer who gave his name to peaks in Canada and Skye – was frightened out of his wits while descending from Ben Macdui's peak, although he didn't go public with the story until 1925. At a meeting of the Cairngorm Club, he recounted:

> I was returning from the cairn on the summit in a mist when I began to think I heard something else than merely the noise of my own footsteps. For every few steps I took I heard a crunch, and then another crunch as if someone was walking after me, but taking steps three or four times the length of my own . . . As I walked on and the eerie crunch, crunch, sounded behind me, I was seized with terror and took to my heels, staggering blindly among the boulders for four or five miles nearly down to Rothiemurchus Forest.

This eerie crunching sound appears in numerous other accounts, as does the feeling of blind fear that causes otherwise sensible mountaineers to react in ways that endanger their safety more than any apparition. During the Second World War, the leader of the Cairngorms RAF Rescue Team almost ran off a cliff after being 'overwhelmed with panic' at hearing something approach in the mist: 'I tried to stop myself and found this extremely difficult to do. It was as if someone was pushing me. I managed to deflect my course, but with a great deal of difficulty.' In another wartime episode the naturalist Alexander Tewnion, climbing the mountain with a handgun in case he came across 'small game', actually opened fire on the summit of Ben Macdui.

> The atmosphere became dark and oppressive, a fierce, bitter wind whisked among the boulders, and an odd sound echoed through the mist – a loud footstep, it seemed. Then another, and another. A strange shape loomed up, receded, came charging at me! Without hesitation I whipped out the revolver and fired three times at the figure. When it still came on I turned and hared down the path, reaching Glen Derry in a time that I have never bettered.

From behind comes the sound of crunching steps. Something is catching up with me. From the dimness looms a face, not grey but purple from the cold.

'I thought I'd have a look for the Shelter Stone,' says Dougie. 'I couldn't find it.'

Great relief and gratitude: I have rejoined my herd. As we walk on together that third figure, the Grey Man of the Boulders, recedes like a dim ghost in my imagination.

Now we climb, bone-weary, over the final mountain. Snow comes heavily again, pouring down thicker than before. It is not the best time, and we are not in the best frame of mind, to encounter the first true ice, or the first true snowdrifts, of the day, but these things wearyingly await: the ice a peril for the ankles, hiding under dusted snow, and the snowdrifts deep enough to swallow our legs to the calf. Dougie's shape ahead of me comes and goes in grainy murk.

Down a long sloping hill, finally we see the hut. I would have taken it for an erratic if I hadn't known it was there. As I cross the last stream, a rock rolls like a wheel and plants my boot in icy water, which instantly pours through. We hobble to the hut, hooved in ice and snow.

There is a worrying number of ice axes and walking poles lined up outside the door. We can hardly open it for the bodies packed inside. Pushing in from the cold we find ten people in the tiny room – barely a quarter the size of Ryvoan – nine men and one woman, Royal Air Force reservists on a training exercise. They don't say what they're training for; presumably a crash landing in Krasnoyarsk or Nunavut. Somehow they make room as we pull off sodden clothes and try to put on dry ones, spilling the contents of our rucksacks and stepping on people's hands. They are welcoming, at least; not that there is any choice. Heat blasts from the stove and the air is thick with food smells, drying smells and body smells, a comforting human stench. It seems absurd, considering the vast expanse of empty space that lies a few metres away, that a dozen people are crammed so tight that we can hardly breathe. But the empty space is worse. This night would kill us all.

True to military stereotype they speak largely in TLAs (three-letter acronyms), a code that is incomprehensible to us. Perhaps our talk of reindeer cults might be incomprehensible to them. They discuss ETAs and objectives to fulfil: a zero-seven-hundred-hour start for the yomp up Ben Macdui, the distance measured in clicks. One of them they call 'the Worm', and I feel sorry for him, until he starts speaking about his ambition to become a pilot of Reaper drones. No more tramping up mountains for him: he will be in a control room somewhere with a joystick in his hands, raining down death on people he cannot see, hear or smell. Perhaps on people tramping up mountains, running for cover over open ground. In this hut we are very close and very far away.

The water in the stream is so cold that I can barely rinse our pans. Snow is still thumping down fatly on the mountain. It is minus nine degrees, lower with the wind chill, the kind of cold that scalds the skin. In my water bottle, an Arctic sea crashes icebergs against my teeth.

I sleep on top of a wooden bench while Dougie sleeps

underneath, bagged up on the floor, the most primitive of bunk beds. Twelve of us breathe the same air, whatever our dreams might be of.

~

In the morning the RAF up and leave with all the orderliness you'd expect of nine men and one woman cooking their breakfast, packing, unpacking and repacking their enormous rucksacks in confined dimensions. They donate us a breakfast ration pack, a glaucous mix of sausages and beans, which is surprisingly tasty.

The stream outside is beginning to close, as if putting up a defensive shell; thick, glassy lids of ice have grown like funguses. The day is calm but deadly cold, rose pink and electric blue.

We clothe ourselves for a hostile environment in which our bodies do not suffice. Gloves on our hands, scarves over our faces and metal spikes on our boots, ice axes readied like weapons against the temperature. Thinking of reindeer yet again – that silver pelt that is warm yet cool, the tubular, hollow hairs that insulate them perfectly – I understand the basic function of the hunt: to take someone else's skin that is better than our own, and pretend that it is ours. No wonder we made gods of them.

Crunching through unbroken white we continue down the valley, happy not to walk alone. When black grouse burst up suddenly from some snowy hiding place, Dougie says, 'Look – they puff their feathers out and thole it.' 'Thole' is a Scottish word meaning, roughly, 'to endure'. Through the drifted powder snow it is less a walk than a wade, for which our aluminium poles are pairs of stabilisers. There is verglas on the rocks, that slippy glaze of frozen rain, and neve, granular snow that pops and crunches pleasingly. Each footstep is an act of trust: one moment a step is firm and the next the surface plunges into unexpected pitfalls that threaten injury. We can never tell what's down there or how far we'll sink.

There is no path visible but the route is clear enough: downward into Glen Derry, where a soft, diffuse light reflects as from a golden bowl, burnishing our faces. Below are the rare forms of trees, pioneering Scots pines dotted up and down the glen, converging on its slopes like prehistoric creatures. Herds of dark, wind-stunted things roaming out across the plain. Festooned with snow, they resemble corals or peculiar growths of mould. It is lovely to see foliage after the empty mountain.

In one place fox prints appear beside the tracks of a mountain hare, the distinctive scrape of its long back leg. 'There's a story there,' says Dougie.

In forested Gleann Laoigh Bheag we catch sight of a red squirrel, a spark rúnning up the bending fuse of a resinous branch, then leave the trees behind and climb back into blankness. The path is a simple one, much downhill or on the flat, and tonight's destination doesn't seem too far away. This doesn't feel far enough: I want to thole it more. Dougie and I part ways once more and I take the high road, up the longer path that leads up Carn a'Mhaim. A field of snow rising steeply into a clear sky.

My first act once alone again is to trip and hit myself in the back of the head with my ice axe, almost Trotskying myself. It leaves a little clot of blood that freezes in my hair. At least I've used the ice axe.

With the pain buzzing there I climb without looking back, and then I look back. Those extra four hundred metres of height change everything. From the top of Carn a'Mhaim I am high enough to see the illusion I have been labouring in for much of the afternoon. The route that we have taken today has brought us to the bottom of my map, and, without thinking it through, I have until this point assumed that we were at the edge of the plateau, skirting its southern extent; as if what is not shown on my map does not exist. 'The map is not the territory', goes Alfred Korzybski's famous phrase, and from here I understand. *This* is the territory. With a lurch my centre shifts: all around are ranks of snow-frosted mountains stretching in every direction that I can see, peak after peak after peak, far more than seems possible. The scale is hard to comprehend. I am not at the edge of anything but at its very centre – at the centre of *everything* – and the realisation unbalances me. It feels as if a rug has been pulled away, as if a trick has been played. For a moment it feels exciting. And then – thump – the fear.

It will seem silly, looking back, as these things always do. I am not far from the path. I know where I am going. But, for a few moments, I am absolutely lost, unmoored in space and time, as if I have woken up in some astounding dream. There is nothing human in the circumference of what I can see, no sign that humans ever were. There is nothing to hold on to, no context and no history. I feel the psychedelic shock of dropping into the unknown, a silent terror that I will find no route to take me back. Stripped and de-personified, I try to locate small holds to reattach me to the world: there are my bootprints in the snow, which I can retrace if I choose, there is the pine-wooded glen we left an hour ago, with its icy stream and its snow-bent branches and its interlacing animal tracks. And to the west is the Devil's Point – I know, it says so on my map – a bleak buttress of grey stone standing a thousand metres tall, and the perfectly symmetrical glacial scoop of Glen Geusachan. These tricks work. I do not look at the vastness all around but at the things in front of me, the small points that I can name, define and put in their proper place. The horrifying centre shifts and I am on the edge again. There are two hours of daylight left. I know where I am.

I descend from Carn a'Mhaim the fast way, knowing I probably shouldn't: a steep fall of unstable scree with hidden pockets of deep snow, ankle-breaking territory. But the threat of injury feels easier than infinity. On the valley floor I sit for a while, eating oatcakes and semi-frozen cheese, and hurt my teeth with a mouthful of cold water. I rejoin Dougie's footsteps, cut precisely in the snow.

What happened up there? I am not sure. Already the feeling is mostly gone, as it always is once a risk has passed and the route home is clear. The memory is troubling and largely inexplicable. I had a glimpse into the portal, the outlandish place I came looking for – that unbroken, frozen whiteness stretching endlessly away – but the sight of it only frightened me. It felt a little like that Geronimo slither towards emptiness, a sense of shocked disbelief and nothing to stop my fall.

I walk on, stop, walk on again. My movements are a little drunk. The stones are slick with verglas, rippled, black, as hard as iron, and every step is a stamp, driving in my spikes. I leave a trail of tiny pick-marks, like some sharp-hoofed creature. The sun has trundled along the horizon through the hours of the day, barely managing to hold itself above the line of mountains. When it finally loses the struggle, sinking fatalistically, cold rushes from the ground as if it has been unleashed. The earth, the boulders and the rocks actively pump it out; the colours themselves seem to generate cold. Corrour bothy lies ahead, closer than I had imagined.

But I am not done today. I am too full of mountains. I briefly say hello to Dougie, who is comfortably settled in, dump my rucksack and take the track that leads up Coire Odhar. Something feels unresolved. My body can't stop walking. The Devil's Point on my left is festooned with vertical icefalls, long dribblings of frozen snot down the sheer grey rock. A full moon has risen, yellow, seemingly two-dimensional. From the *coire* – the Gaelic for 'corrie', a glacial hollow in a mountainside – a steep ridge runs further upwards to the Devil. My body is so tired that my breath sounds like someone else's voice, making barks and grunts I can't control. The snow is turning nighttime-blue, but something pulls me on.

From the top there is nothing but chilled air between me and the moon. All around, the snowbound tundra slides into dimness. The summit of Ben Macdui is lost in its own personal blizzard – the Big Grey Man raging up there – but everywhere else is uncannily calm. There is not a breath of wind. The last moments of the day plunge into electric blue, as if the spectrum is slowly flooding with argon gas. I do not feel as if I am at the top of something but suspended in its middle, floating in a band of shifting iridescent colour. A stray line comes to me: 'The air is part of the mountain, which does not come to an end with its rock and its soil.' It is Nan Shepherd.

The twentieth-century novelist, poet and teacher from Aberdeen, whose face now adorns one of the Scottish five-pound notes – with her hair loosely plaited, a headband and a small jewel set on her forehead, like an Indian chief – spent a lifetime walking the Cairngorms and was the author of *The Living Mountain*, which has become a kind of sacred text about these hills. It is less a description of a landscape than an act of becoming one with it, for Shepherd was a natural and unpretentious shaman. I think of that moment on Carn a'Mhaim – my fear of the white unknown – and how it might have been different for her, because she knew these mountains with the intimacy of companions. She was not making a linear journey of 'discovery', but returning cyclically, like Dougie, year after year. 'Yet often the mountain gives itself most completely', she wrote, 'when I have no destination, when I reach nowhere in particular, but have gone out merely to be with the mountain as one visits a friend with no intention but to be with him.'

Perhaps that goes some way towards explaining my profound disorientation up there: these mountains are not my friends, because I am a stranger to them. I am not seeing them from a place of habitual knowing. They do not belong to me, or, to put it a better way, I do not belong to them. My experience is dislocation rather than connection.

Famously Shepherd writes of walking *into*, rather than *up*, a mountain, as a way of knowing it. The phrasing is political. With a single line – 'To aim for the highest point is not the only way to climb a mountain' – she destroys the machismo of climbing culture with its colonial talk of bagging Munros and conquering peaks, of assaults against virgin summits. I think of the red, white and blue flag on the world's highest mountain, and of what its planting opened up. Shepherd never planted flags. It would have been like sticking them into her own body.

In *The Ascent of Everest*, completed six months after his return, my great-uncle wrote of a 'lingering regret that this great peak no longer remains inviolate to hold out its challenge'. But the book ends with the consolation: 'there are many other opportunities for adventure, whether they be sought among the hills, in the air, upon the sea, in the bowels of the earth, or on the ocean bed; and there is always the moon to reach.'

There was always another frontier. It was a different world.

We live in reduced times now. We have reached our conquering heights and are coming back down the mountain. With the last light vanishing, feeling that I am about to push my luck too far, I run back down from the Devil's Point, jumping from rock to rock. The descent seems charmed: the stones hold my steps, as if the moon were suspending me slightly in its gravity ('my eyes were in my feet', wrote Shepherd). I skitter on ice and smash through snow but feel uplifted, held. The snow is lucent with the glow of the lunar-reflected sun, so the route back down is bright, and I feel as if I could run for ever downward without stopping. At last I arrive at Corrour, where Dougie is just wondering whether or not to worry.

There are not ten acronym-speaking reservists in the bothy. There is only George, a gnome-like man of indeterminable age and a goatee that bristles like a broom, eating endless biscuits. He speaks in a rapid Glaswegian mumble, the words tumbling over each other, and even Dougie, who was born in Glasgow, doesn't catch half of what he says. He is the kind of person I can't imagine existing anywhere but in a bothy; a 'bothy-rat', as Dougie will later call him with affection. He rolls cigarettes from a battered tin and exhales the smoke into the stove, as if making propitiatory offerings to the hut that shelters him. As Dougie and I heat our stew, George tells us, through a gap-toothed mouth, what started his walking career: he was electrocuted. Up a ladder, doing up a house, he touched a live wire and received a continuous shock that lasted for fifteen minutes. 'I was stuck to the wire. For the first five minutes I couldn't speak, like being out of breath. Then I started yelling. My mates thought I was taking the mick. "I'm not taking the mick, I'm being electrocuted!" They knocked the wire away and I fell. I was paralysed for a month.'

Once he had regained the use of his legs he decided to walk the Cape Wrath Trail. Then he walked around the Isle of Arran with his possessions in a shopping trolley, listening to a wind-up radio. Then he carried on walking.

Hot toddies do the rounds along with chocolate biscuits.

Before sleep we step outside to see an eerie spectacle. The moon, much higher and smaller now, is at the centre of a vast black halo ringed with silver light that fills the whole southern sky, like nothing I have seen before. It is a moon-broch, an effect caused by lunar rays reflecting off clouds in the troposphere, but that doesn't explain anything. It is a beautiful bad omen, for its appearance is believed to presage ugly weather. Under that dark corona the tundra waits in silver light. The frozen corries and falls of scree bide their time, unbothered.

Back in the bothy George is rubbing Deep Heat into his legs, darning his socks with a needle and thread, twiddling with the dial of his wind-up radio, which picks up nothing.

In the morning my trousers, hung to dry, are as solid as frozen fish. I have to beat them against the wall before they bend.

Sunlight has not yet reached the floor of the Lairig Ghru.

~

The Lairig Ghru is the inverse space left behind by ice, the impact of the enormous damage wreaked by temperature. It is Britain's greatest glacial valley, slicing from north to south for almost thirty miles, and – along with its sister valley the Lairig an Laoigh to the east – is one of the two main passes that divide the Cairngorms three ways, into their high, exposed, tundra-supporting plateaus. Sunder. Cleave. These words come to mind: it looks like the cut of a terrible axe, its sharp edges smoothed by time. It is tempting to think of it being hewn by a single cataclysm, but it formed over millions of years, as an unstoppable estuary of ice shouldered its way through the landscape. How old is it? Unimaginably old, and it keeps getting older. It was long thought that it was made, like most of Britain's glacial breaches, during the Last Glacial Maximum that started 2.6 million years ago, but the British Geological Survey and Scottish Natural Heritage have claimed more recently that it might really date back 390–400 million years, all the way to the formation of the granite itself. The name 'Ghru' might – as Adam Watson, the great scholar of the Cairngorms, suggests – derive from *drùdhadh*, meaning 'oozing'. This would refer to the countless rivers and streams that drain into it, but, with that older date in mind, it conjures up an image of the ooze of semi-liquid rock, cooling like a giant porridge, riven by fracture lines. It is not only ice that has flowed, but the land itself.

To non-geologists like me – and perhaps even to geologists – there is not much difference in these numbers on any emotional level. To creatures whose average life expectancy is a mere eighty years, 2.6 million and 400 million are equally incomprehensible. It is easier to use that mythic shorthand, 'Once upon a time . . .'

Once upon a time the world was made of ice. The frost-giant Ymir, the first creature of creation, was slaughtered by the gods Odin, Vili and Ve, who used the severed parts of his body to populate the cosmos. His flesh became the earth, his blood the seas, his bones the mountains, his hair the plants and trees, the dome of his skull the heavens, and his brains the clouds. His eyebrows became Midgard, the middle realm of mankind. According to Norse mythology – climatologically and geologically coupled with this terrain – we are all children of the frost, ice-bairns, the orphans of glaciers.

Surely this is a cultural memory of a glacial time.

(On a more profane note, the Devil's Point that I climbed last night is a prudish Victorianism, as Dougie delights in telling me; its Gaelic name – diplomatically changed to avoid embarrassment during a royal visit – was Bod an Deamhain, or Devil's Penis. Perhaps that impressive granite bulge, upward-thrusting and veined with ice, is a monument to another part of Ymir's anatomy.)

Dougie and I have two options today, the final day of our

walk. Either we follow the pass, in the absence of the glacier, or we climb to Coire Odhar and follow the ridge in a westerly loop around the summits of five mountains: Cairn Toul, Sgor an Lochain Uaine ('Angel's Peak'), Carn na Criche, Einich Cairn and Braeriach, the third-highest point in the country. Both paths will lead us home, one way or another. The decision was always going to be dependent on the weather; even the relatively sheltered pass can be arduous in bad conditions, and the edge of the plateau, in a blizzard, would be perilous. But last night's omen has not come to pass. It is the clearest day.

The mountains are pink, yellow, blue, orange, every colour but white, flushed with the deceptive appearance of warmth. Eruptions of suspended cloud are muddled in their folds. From the punctuation marks of cloven prints in the snow it seems our bothy was surrounded by many deer last night – red not rein, Dougie thinks – and something else, too big for fox. 'Badger, some other beastie.' Breakfast is porridge with chopped ginger, heated on a camping stove. As George lopes south towards Braemar, an engine puffing out tobacco smoke, Dougie and I go vertical, into the high places.

It is hard going up. Our bodies are reluctant. Rucksackless and lunar-eyed, I almost ran up here last night, but this morning every step is an aching struggle. Plunging knee-deep in the snow feels like being partially consumed. Perhaps *this* is what Nan Shepherd meant by 'walking into the mountain'. In an especially deep drift I am hugged up to the waist in an embrace that does not want to let me go. By the time we reach the sun we are sweating in the cold.

There is no visible rock up here, only blinding fields of snow. To the west, the arctic-alpine tundra stretches into whiteness.

Neither of us has any need to get to the top of anything. Staying above a thousand metres we will skirt most of the peaks, using their contours to stay high, as if gliding on frozen thermals. My overwhelming first impression, though, is not of being high but of being fathoms deep on the floor of a strange sea. The snow is not uniform, not a sheet stretched out flat, but a baroque scrollwork of immaculate wind-sculpted drifts that becomes more complicated the more I look at it. With every step we destroy a microcosm of crystal growths, fluted rimey husks of ice, a miniature coral reef. Each fractal structure takes the form of a feathery, furred plume that repeats identically, ranging from the size of my little fingernail to the length of my hand, billions of them silently erupting from the snow. Wind-formed, these perfect sculptures grew up here all by themselves, with no intention of being seen by human eyes. I have a strong realisation that we are intruders in their world. There are things happening here that have nothing to do with people.

The gleaming ridgeline reaches north towards the hump of Cairn Toul. Clumsy in our many layers, we begin to thole it.

Navigation is easy, at least. We must keep the plateau to our left and the Lairig Ghru to our right, a gulf of space plunging to the black thread of the river. The River Dee: too sweet a name for anything in that grey, scarred bowl (the Gaelic name Uisge Dhè runs a little deeper). Nothing whatsoever moves in the vastness of the landscape. For the sake of the view it is tempting to step right to the edge, where a pillowy crest of snow offers a perfect platform. But Dougie cautions me away, for, as becomes apparent when looking back from further on, it is an overhang supported by nothing but air, a shelf over emptiness; a true Geronimo cornice. Dougie watches nervously as I take a swing and bury my ice axe deep, just once, to say I've done it. He has not needed his either, but they are talismans as well as tools; their real use on this walk has been psychological.

We round the summit of Cairn Toul just as the Angel's Peak ahead vanishes into seething cloud. Moments later the air around us changes its consistency and everything goes opaque, a blanket being drawn. The talismanic confidence of a metal stick with a spike at the end disappears rapidly as we trudge onward, blind, no longer able to see the drop that plunges to the side of us. Depth and distance vanish, all features gloom away. Following the compass reading is superstitious faith. Just as we are starting to be concerned – how much blinder will we get? – the Angel's Peak appears again, clarifies, reasserts itself. Just like that, the cloud is gone and the way is clear.

Well, not quite. A luminous haze has been cast across the plateau, soft-focusing the world. Both of us see something at the same time and its strangeness makes us stop: on the edge of the gulf is the outline of a man. He is not lying flat like a shadow but standing vertically, with elongated arms and legs, hands wide as if grasping. His head is at the centre of a halo, a glory of rainbow-coloured beams lancing out in all directions, but he has no substance to him. We can see right through his body.

Last night we saw a moonbroch and now we are seeing a Brocken spectre. Ethereal shadows ringed by light, they are oddly similar. This morning's manifestation, however, moves his arm when I move my arm, takes a step when I take a step, for he is my own shadow projected on to the air. Dougie is seeing a different spectre, a projection of himself.

The phenomenon takes its name from a mountain in northern Germany and is caused, in misty conditions, by the low sun scattering its rays through droplets of suspended water. It has often been suggested that these eerie apparitions are the source of Am Fear Liath Mòr, who, almost without exception, is sighted on misty days, when the angle of a low sun might cast an upright shadow. Certainly the illusion was behind the 'devil' that the shepherd James Hogg encountered, as his initial terror gave way to childlike playfulness: 'I took off my bonnet, and scratched my head bitterly with both hands; when, to my astonishment and delight, the de'il also took off his bonnet and scratched his head with both hands . . . I laughed at him till I actually fell down upon the sward; the de'il also fell down and laughed at me.' But some of the more lurid accounts – a giant with an 'air of insolent strength', a being with pointed ears and talons, or a massive-headed creature with shortish brown hair – cannot possibly come from atmospheric illusions. Neither can those crunching steps. Certainly mountains are full of strange noises – rockfalls, distorted echoes and wind, easily twisted by exhaustion, adrenalin and imagination into something more sinister – but the majority of these reports come from veteran climbers who, you might think, would be accustomed to the acoustics of lonely places. Dismissing every reported encounter as a trick of the light or a random noise falls a long way short of being a satisfying explanation.

Grey Man sightings are not confined to the slopes of Ben Macdui, but are common across Scotland and the Celtic world. The figure of the Bodach, 'Old Man', often appears as a male counterpart to the deer-milking Cailleach – both ancestral trickster figures to be feared and respected – while the Bodach Glas, or Dark Grey Man, is a portent of impending death. He is far from being alone: from the trolls of Scandinavia to what the Irish call the *sídhe*, the otherworldly fairy-folk who inhabit Neolithic barrows, shadowy humanoids appear in the collective minds of cultures everywhere. Dwarves, ogres, imps, giants, goblins, leprechauns, pixies, elves: we populate every mythology with monstrous versions of ourselves, recognisable in their humanity but not fully human. As is suggested by the association of fairies with prehistoric burial mounds – or that backward-facing fairy-man warning of snow on his departing deer – these might be submerged memories of the people who came before, cultures and ethnicities that were displaced by subsequent waves of invasion and settlement. Perhaps Picts or ancient Sámis have a presence in these tales, or perhaps people more distant still, those who first came to these lands with the melting of the ice.

There is another possibility, yet more atavistic. Neanderthals, our larger-brained but much maligned evolutionary cousins, with whom anatomically modern humans shared Europe and parts of Asia for many thousands of years, only vanished as a species forty thousand years ago, which is the blink of an eye in evolutionary terms. Further back, the world produced dozens of highly similar species of humanoid that resembled us in almost every way, only with a longer jawbone here, a flatter cranium there. *Homo erectus*, *Homo ergaster*, *Homo floresiensis* – the 'hobbit people' that survived on the island of Flores into Paleolithic times – *Homo denisova*, *Homo naledi*, only unearthed in the last decade: every few years, it seems, more variants of ourselves are disinterred, peering back at their extant cousins from the fossil record. They are like us but not like us, close but unimaginably far away. Do our glimpses of them now represent a remembering?

When I was a child John Hunt told me of seeing the footprints of the yeti in the snow around his tent on the ascent of Everest: abominable heels and toes padding across the mountain. He also – or did I embellish this? – heard weird howls at night carried on the wind. I kept the tale in the same state of suspended disbelief as I did Father Christmas, the Holy Ghost and other confabulations, half real and half absurd. I never knew whether he was joking or not, and I still don't know.

Alexander Tewnion, that gun-toting naturalist from the summit of Ben Macdui, wrote that he went on to return to the site of the terrifying incident many times afterwards, alone, with an easy mind. His account contains a poetic insight into his subsequent lack of fear: 'For on that day I am convinced I shot the only Fear Liath Mhor my imagination will ever see.'

Perhaps each of us gets only one, and when it's gone, it's gone.

At present we are safe from apparitions, whatever they might mean to us. The mist has cleared and the only crunching footsteps are our own. After we have finished playing with our respective spectres – or perhaps they are playing with us – we cross a dazzling white expanse, astronauts trudging through the element of extreme cold, breathing out icy smoke. It is not yet midday.

Again and again my eyes are drawn to the plateau on my left, its rumpled enormity: the tundra lying deep in snow, white on white on white. But on my right, looking down, lies the hollow of Garbh Choire Mòr. This serrated, concave bowl – its name translates as Big Rough Corrie – is an important landmark for me.

Down there lurks another throwback from the cold, deep past.

～

The Sphinx is a long-lying patch of snow that clings to the corrie's northern flank far beyond the winter. Now, of course, it is just snow, merging into anonymous whiteness, hiding in plain sight. But as the rest of the slope melts away this single, stubborn lump – which a Big Grey Man could cross in three steps – remains in place, refusing to melt, hanging on against the odds. In summer it is visible as a scrape of grubby white, getting dirtier by the week with scattered soil, atmospheric pollution and the bootprints of curious climbers who make pilgrimages to walk on it. It becomes less white than grey.

In winter, if it lasts that long, it is renewed.

It has vanished only eight times since anyone bothered recording it, which was three hundred years ago. On its first disappearance, in 1933, the Scottish Mountaineering Club declared the event to be so unusual that it was 'unlikely to happen again'. But it did, in 1953, 1959, 1996, 2003, 2006, 2017 and 2018. For the past dozen years these vanishings have been recorded by volunteers undertaking an annual snow-patch survey across Scotland, measuring length, width and depth and offering forecasts about longevity; foremost among these 'snow patchers' is an expert called Iain Cameron, who gives an annual report to the Royal Meteorological Society, monitoring these icy anomalies as bellwethers of winter health. According to him, there are only two instances in recorded history when the Sphinx has been outlasted: in 1953 by Pinnacles, a neighbouring patch in Garbh Choire Mòr (both the Sphinx and Pinnacles take their names from nearby climbing routes), and in 2018 by a nameless blob on Aonach Beag in the Western Highlands. But of the dozens of long-lying snow patches in Scotland's mountains, the Sphinx, digging in its claws, is the most tenacious.

Dougie has written about a visit, in the company of his youngest daughter, to another famous snow patch also in the Cairngorms. In the summer of 2018 they climbed to the Laird's Tablecloth in Ear-choire Sneachdach ('Snowy East Corrie') on the flank of Beinn a'Bhuird, not far from where we are today. 'The snow field sloped upwards ahead of us, the size of a five-a-side football pitch. When we reached its edge, four stones, protruding from the middle of it, stood up and loped away: mountain hares, that had been sitting stone-still in bowls they'd scraped in the snow.' Like the Sphinx, the Laird's Tablecloth used to stay frozen throughout the year, a dependable landmark from lower ground, but it started disappearing in the twentieth century. The lairds that give the patch its name are the chiefs of Clan Farquharson, owners of the 108,000-acre Invercauld Estate that stretches from the southernmost Cairngorms to Balmoral. Legend says that the family will lose its tenure of the land, which it has held since 1632, if the snow of the Tablecloth ever melts. As Dougie writes:

> So far, in this hot century, it has disappeared before the end of every summer, but the Farquharsons still own Invercauld. When pressed on the current lack of snow, the current Laird will admit only that 'the tablecloth might be dirty, and in need of a wash to bring out its whiteness!' It's a good response, given with a twinkle in the eye; but accelerating climate change means there might soon be years when there's no snow at all in Ear-choire Sneachdach, even in winter.

Snow patches such as these are not only scraps of winter but scraps of history, of deep time. Obvious symbols of endurance, of bloody-minded obstinacy, they are also thermometers that self-destruct as the planet warms. When their last smudges have dripped away, the national thaw will be complete. The British Isles will be entirely free of snow in summer.

The Farquharsons are not the only ones. In the change that is coming, we will all lose our estates.

The Sphinx is sometimes called the closest thing that Britain has to a glacier. There is something rather pathetic in that; a hint of desperation. Not remotely massive enough to move under its own weight, a glacier's defining characteristic, the patch is a stranded oddity that bears no resemblance to those ancient bodies of ice that grind over epochs through the landscape, terraforming the earth below, remaking the world in their image. There have been no glaciers in Britain for at least eleven thousand years.

Or have there? In 2014 a geomorphologist at Dundee University made headlines with a startling claim that the

Cairngorms may have been home to one as late as the eighteenth century. At Coire an Lochain, another corrie several miles north of the Sphinx's lair, Martin Kirkbride claimed to have identified a moraine – the distinctive rubble of rocks deposited by the retreat of ice – that suggested that a lone survivor might have lasted into the 1700s: the period known as the Little Ice Age, when rivers froze every winter even in the south of England and average temperatures were 1.5 degrees colder than today. If true, this would dramatically upend scientific orthodoxy, dragging Britain's glacial age eleven millennia forward. His paper was backed by a parallel study by researchers at the Universities of Exeter and Aberystwyth, who developed a model of historical climate conditions. They concluded: 'Our findings show that the Cairngorm mountains were probably home to a number of small glaciers during the last few hundred years – around 11,000 years later than previous evidence has suggested.'

These claims at once provoked a fierce, if arcane, debate. A stern rebuttal came from Adam Watson, the ecologist, mountaineer and writer whose lifelong study of the range earned him the sobriquet 'Mr Cairngorms', a name it's hard to argue with. The so-called moraine, he said, was nothing more than a 'protalus rampart' created by rockfall and avalanche debris building up over the years. 'Both papers are uncritical in dismissing the possibility of protalus ramparts on the basis of the authors' personal opinions on the unlikelihood of boulders and other debris travelling so far in avalanches. This signifies that they have never witnessed avalanches in these corries or their aftermath'. In pointing out that the soil horizons had entirely the wrong profile, he could not resist a scathing jibe at geomorphologists 'who fail to dig a single soil pit and ignore fundamental principles of soil science'.

Kirkbride defended his paper, including the soil horizon part. He argued that the boulder ridge in question might indicate both a moraine *and* the effect of avalanches – the avalanches, in fact, were destroying the glacial evidence – but Watson was having none of it. Not only was the science incorrect, but there was a damning lack of historical corroboration. *Cool Britannia*, his comprehensive study of climatic observations from the Little Ice Age – co-written with Iain Cameron, the country's leading snow patcher – compiles hundreds of accounts of the locations of ice and snow made by contemporary travellers. '[Y]ou must understand,' wrote one of them in 1618, 'that the oldest man alive never saw but the snow was on top of divers of these hilles, both in Summer, as well as in Winter.' Another reported in 1771 that the people of Glen Awain (another spelling of Avon) had assured him that 'neither they nor their Fathers ever remembered to have seen Ben Awin, or the hills West from it, free from snow'. Other intrepid mountaineers describe peaks 'never wholly divested of snow' and slopes where 'the snow lies perpetually'. The 'immense unmelted mass of snow' at Garbh Choire Mòr, where the Sphinx lurks today, is mentioned numerous times, as is the 'Snow-house' at Ciste Mhearad, near the summit of Cairn Gorm, which 'never yields its frigid contents to the power of the sun'. But nowhere in these travellers' tales, from the seventeenth to the nineteenth centuries, is there mention of a glacier at Coire an Lochain.

Most glaciologists sided with Watson, and the case was closed. That eleven-millennia gulf was restored, and Britain's glacial period was safely relegated to where it belonged, into a past more distant than anyone can imagine.

The difference between a protalus rampart and a bona fide moraine, to someone unversed in the science, is about as obscure as the difference between a geologist and a geomorphologist. But when I think of that eighteenth-century glacier, disproved though it is, I feel something fall away. Gravity gets stronger.

The simple thought experiment of a glacier existing here, surviving into modern times, only a dozen generations back, produces a sense of vertigo, as if my stomach has dropped. I have stepped on to the fragile cornice on the edge of Garbh Choire Mòr and felt it collapse under me, sending me plunging into space.

Geronimo!

Like the boulder field below, deep time rushes up. What seemed impossibly far away is suddenly much closer.

As with the desert of Dungeness – the disproven status of which did not stop it transporting me to a desert of the mind – Kirkbride's non-glacier is a portal to a frozen age. The possibility of it being here, even if it was not here, pulls the ancient past up close: this scarred land of absences with its corries and glacial breaches brutally fills back in again, its negative spaces flipped. The world is familiar but transformed. The moraines are levitated; house-sized erratics, encased in ice two or three miles thick, hang suspended in the sky like a crystallised meteor shower. From where I stand, the ice stretches for hundreds of miles in every direction. Scotland becomes, once again, an extension of Scandinavia, where Ymir's body, bones and blood gave substance to the world.

Is it possible to feel solastalgia – that existential ache caused by environmental change – for an ice age that no one ever knew, that lies unimaginably distant? The novelist Gregory Norminton has coined an alternative word, *archaiostalgia*, 'a painful longing for the long-ago', or even *ante-anthropostalgia*, 'a longing for the time before humans existed'. Climate researcher Mark Goldthorpe suggests *telestalgia*, 'yearning for the far-off in time and space', as well as *terrancholia*, 'earth-melancholy'. The Dictionary of Obscure Sorrows, an online compendium of 'newly invented words for strangely powerful emotions', contains the word *anemoia*: 'nostalgia for a time you've never known'. Meanwhile the German word *Fernweh* means a painful yearning for the far away, while *Sehnsucht* fills the space between yearning, craving and pining. The Romantic poet Friedrich Schiller wrote a poem of that name, describing an unbearable longing to be transported to distant hills from which he is separated by a raging river. Replace the hills with glaciers and the river is time, unfrozen . . .

But language is inadequate. Words can only be the map and never the territory.

My own encounter with a glacier – albeit a dying one – happened about a decade ago, not in the Arctic north but in the Himalayas. I was in Indian-occupied Kashmir, near the border with Pakistan, so close to the Line of Control, with its militancy and terrorism, that it had been off-limits to scientists for decades. Having gone there as a journalist, I had somehow managed to get myself invited on an expedition led by an eminent Indian glaciologist. During the two-day walk up the valley, past regular Indian Army checkpoints, our Kashmiri guides pointed to places where the glacier used to be, when they were younger men; its shrinking had left a grubby tidemark on the valley walls, like the dirt on the sides of a drained bathtub.

Its name was – still is? – Kolahoi. When we reached its base, it was not the white immensity I had pictured but a brown, collapsing thing that resembled a hunk of rotting meat. The glaciologists used terms that made it sound like an animal: it had a 'snout', a 'tongue' and a 'toe' (and when ice breaks apart the process is called 'calving'). It was cornered: only a stump was left, with rivers bleeding out of it. Tentatively we set foot on the mushy flank – the scientists wished to walk over it – but were called back. It was too unstable. The surface was Slush Puppy-soft. They did their measurements and observations from the edge, sombre doctors prodding at the flesh of a terminal patient.

About fifteen years left, they said. Twenty if it was lucky.

Judging by temperatures over the last decade, it has not been lucky.

Soon afterwards I joined a three-day pilgrimage to the Amarnath Cave, where half a million Hindus trek through the Himalayas every year – in saris, flip-flops, bobble hats – to worship at the shrine of the Shiva-lingam. This is a six-foot phallus of ice that grows and melts annually in a cave 3,888 metres high, where Shiva revealed the secret of eternity to his consort Parvati. In recent years the lingam had melted early due to warmer temperatures, and this year it had not formed at all. The cave was empty but pilgrims went there all the same, some standing vigil through the night. What conclusions did they draw from the non-appearance of their god? 'He is god,' someone said, 'he'll come back when he wants to.'

On the descent the slopes were covered with plastic bags, foil wrappers and glittering empty packets of *paan*, despoiled like the slopes of Everest. There was sewage in the streams, washing down to the villages of Kashmiri Muslims in the valley. 'God doesn't care about that,' I was told. 'You think such things matter to him?'

Shiva's vanishing might be local but the story of ice-melt is global. The health of a glacier is measured by its net balance of accumulation (from fresh snowfall) and ablation (from melting or sublimation, when ice evaporates before becoming liquid). Across the Himalayas, the Roof of the World, this balance has been wildly tipped; eight billion tonnes of ice are ablating every year, too fast to be replaced by snow. In some regions glaciers are shrinking by five metres annually. In Europe, the Alps are forecast to lose ninety per cent of their glaciers by the end of this century, with fifty per cent disappearing within the next thirty years regardless of future emissions reductions; the process is already in motion, the carbon already in the atmosphere from historical industry.

The World Glacier Monitoring Service, which has kept observations for over a century across nine mountain ranges, reports that the average rate of loss has more than doubled since the year 2000: 'The latest figures are part of what appears to be an accelerating trend with no apparent end in sight.'

In Greenland, meanwhile, glaciers are vanishing seven times faster than in the 1990s. The oldest and thickest ice in the Arctic has declined by ninety-five per cent. The vast Antarctic ice sheet – by far the largest frozen body on earth – is calving and sliding into the sea at an even more precipitous rate, shedding, according to recent studies, an incomprehensible two hundred billion tonnes of ice per year. This leads to a feedback loop known as the albedo effect: as brightly reflective ice-cover declines, the surface of the world becomes darker, causing more heat to be absorbed, causing more ice to melt.

In the last half century the loss has amounted to 9,625 gigatonnes. A gigatonne is a billion tonnes.

But these statistics are even less of a territory than words.

Back on the edge of the Lairig Ghru, with the snow-shelf precarious under me, this is the vertigo I feel, a tumbling inside my gut: in fifty or a hundred years people will look at parts of the world that are currently frozen white and see what I am seeing now. An absence, an empty hole. The post-glacial landscape below, in all its damaged majesty, is not a vision of the distant past but of the future.

Something is emerging here, like a Brocken spectre in the mist. Am Fear Liath Mòr, the Bodach Glas, the Dark Grey Man portending death. As the ice drips away he steps into the light.

~

But for now, on this arctic crossing, I have found my permanence – the eternal snows, the tundra of my childhood imaginings – and it is impossible to believe that it could ever vanish. The snowfield stretches on immensely, so dazzling I have to squint. The white does strange things to my eyes, wonking my vision and turning it green. Time is measured in the crunching of our footsteps. My eyelashes and my beard are frozen – the clichéd accoutrement of hoary Arctic maleness – and the muscles of my face are slow, which makes speaking sluggish. Words emerge part-thawed, still icy at the core. When I move my mouth I hear the chink of ice.

Dougie is far ahead of me, a distant flake against the sky, the Grey Man of the Snow. I am following the long line of his footsteps. They seem to stretch infinitely, growing only slightly smaller between here and the horizon, constantly renewing themselves. Distances could be in metres or thousands of miles. Halfway through the afternoon appears one final miracle: from the edge of the cornice rise a dozen smoking plumes, brightly illuminated threads of icy spindrift spiralling on thermals from the powder slopes below. They dance, collapse and dance again to their own hissing song, and each collapse drives a wave of whipping, stinging ice-dust. I watch them for a long time, until Dougie is out of sight, spirits of the mountain made visible by the cold. They will continue dancing after we are gone.

We are coming down at last. The mild brown world awaits. Descending an uneven hillside clumsily, we want to stop – for broken oatcakes, frosty cheese – but the cold wind will not let us. The snow is only in patches now, draped across dark foliage. In the middle of the hill a lone sapling struggles up, a pioneering Scots pine hundreds of metres above its range. Dougie drops to his knees and bows to it.

And then we are back in the Lairig Ghru, following the river called the Allt Druidh to the north, leaving the arctic-alpine tundra to its winter. We have walked through the afternoon and the evening and into the night. We are halfway through Rothiemurchus Forest, where the reindeer started out, and the underbrush and wood-ant nests are covered with a layer of snow that holds the last light of the sky. The moon beams like a spotlight. The trees are ancient Scots pines with red, contorted bark, and their warm colour glows after so much whiteness. The Gaelic name for the Cairngorms is Am Monadh Ruadh, the Red Hills, after their reddish rock. Dougie, with his fox-like gleam, has something of the *ruadh* about him too.

The snow, the pines, the sandy soil, the white moon caught in the trees: it feels like a journey that could last for days of winter night, tired but with a bouncing step, accompanied by the yipping of herders and the jangle of reindeer bells. But now we have reached the road. The tarmac is strange to walk on. We have only been away three days but it has been more than three days.

My feet are numb. My body hurts. My skin feels thicker.

The car is there by the side of the road, with the note still in the windscreen: *Tuesday 15th Jan. Off to Ryvoan, then Hutchison, then Corrour. Back on Friday 18th.*

We have to wipe the snow away with our hands to read it.

POLAND'S JUNGLE

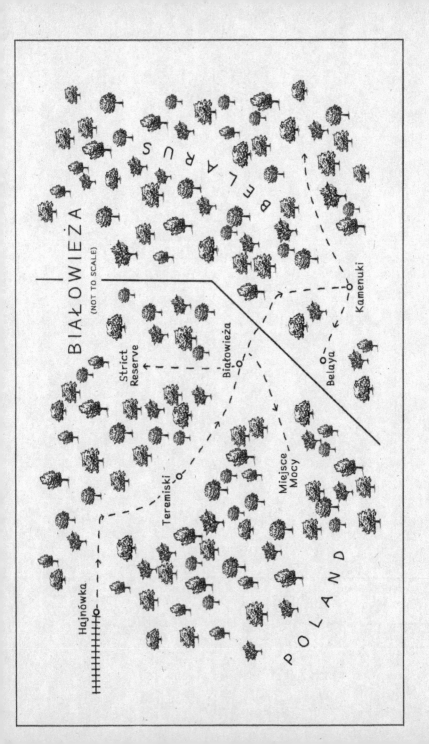

To my left and right, ahead and behind, are only trees and trees. The trunks are uniformly straight, shooting up almost branchless to a leafless canopy in which a few early buds are scattered like green stars. Though tall, the trees do not look old – by 'primeval' I had imagined gnarled limbs and twisted bark – but perhaps they're not supposed to be. An old-growth forest does not mean that the trees themselves are old, as an ancient civilisation does not mean ancient people.

I have been walking for an hour and there are hours more to go. A narrow track runs eastwards for as far as I can see. The trees slide smoothly past and the repetition is hypnotic, a scene that alters constantly yet is constantly identical. Apart from the occasional half-fallen trunk, diagonally propped, which interrupts the monotony of the vertical and the horizontal, it could be the same hundred metres caught in a loop. I recognise spruce, oak and lime, but before I have walked far the distinctions merge into a blur. My eyes are not yet attuned to the intricate relationships, the permutations of the groves in their different neighbourhoods. I can't see the trees for the wood. I am blinded by the shade, unable to draw focus.

Some miles into the forest, in a clearing south of the path, stands a small wooden chapel with a blue roof and onion domes. Its three-barred cross indicates that it is not Catholic but Orthodox, founded, according to an information board, by thirteenth-century Kievan monks fleeing an invasion of Tatars. In a smaller structure behind, under icons of gaunt-faced saints with squared beards and narrow eyes, is a covered well and a bucket on a rope. It is miraculous water, apparently, blessed with healing properties.

I fill a chipped china cup and drink. The water tastes of wood.

Some miles further on, I come upon a patch of ravaged earth. A tuft of brown matted wool is snagged on a twig nearby. As I lean down for a closer look, the stink of it kicks me in the gut. I do not know what it is, but it smells wild.

~

Forests of wind turbines covered the North European Plain. Branching railway tracks led through Belgium and the Low Countries, across the grey Rhine at Cologne and into northern Germany. In Berlin I stayed the night with friends and left soon after dawn, past the Soviet futurism of the telecommunications tower at Aleksanderplatz, chewing on a pretzel that was almost inedibly salty. The air was cold, clammy with the damp from buried marshes. Fifty miles from Warsaw the train escaped the lid of cloud that had shadowed the land since the Low Countries and passed into the golden sunlight of a spring day. Deer stood alert in a field. There were hunting towers everywhere. Two large white birds, storks or cranes, were landing on a barn roof. In my mind, Warsaw was entrenched as a city of vertical planes under gritty, neon night – an image derived entirely from David Bowie's synthesised 'Warszawa' on the album *Low* – but looked bustling and bright. I changed trains there once again. East of the Vistula River we entered Poland B.

'Poland A' and 'Poland B' correspond to the country's west and east, one facing Germany, the other facing Russia.

The two sides had diverging histories of annexation and occupation: the west experienced industrialisation under Prussian and Austrian rule, its intellectuals drawing on the ideas of the Enlightenment, while the east was a feudal backwater and tsarist hunting ground. I spotted occasional eastern hints – silhouetted onion domes and a sign to a Tatar cemetery – but otherwise A and B looked the same through the rushing window. At Siedlce my final train, which had only two carriages, filled up with chattering families, and I closed my eyes in an attempt to absorb some of their language. It sounded doughy, soft-hearted, henlike, mothering, which seemed completely at odds with how it looked written down: the entangling barbs of *ł*s and *ę*s, the impenetrable thickets of *szczy*s, consonants as dense as an uncut grove.

On the page the Polish language looks like a forest.

Twenty-one hours after leaving London I was in a room in Hajnówka, a lumber town fifteen miles from the border of Belarus. The man who had driven me there from the station was much amused by my attempt to get in the wrong side of the car, chuckling '*Angielski!*', 'English!', as if I had made his day. The room was furnished in bilious lilac with a wallpaper design of tessellating 3D cubes, a stopped plastic clock on the wall. My brain had not yet told my body it was no longer on a train.

There is a certain line in Europe, corresponding more or less with the border of the former Eastern Bloc, beyond which dogs bark all night in towns and villages. Not as individual dogs but as a baying chorus. A charm to guard against wolves, or perhaps to welcome them, it is like nothing you would hear in Belgium, France or Germany. As I stepped outside before bed, I heard that I had crossed it.

The next morning I woke up to a crippling sense of dread. I didn't know where it had come from but I couldn't get out of bed; the idea of going outside felt impossible. I lay there for an hour, two hours, staring at the lilac cubes, thumbing through the internet, avoiding looking at the map of what lay ahead. There are times when I am overcome by a kind of traveller's shyness. I don't want to be seen or heard, my foreignness made obvious, but to disappear from sight, to merge unnoticed into my surroundings. There was no possibility of that here, where I struggled even to pronounce the name of the forest I had come to find: Białowieża. The 'ł' is pronounced as a 'w' and the 'w' as a 'v', while the 'ż' is a slurring sound unknown to English phonetics. The closest I could get to it was 'Bee-ow-ov-ezh-a'. I concentrated on learning the name, one syllable at a time, until I could say it back to myself. As many fantasy novels will tell you, the act of learning something's name is to gain power over it.

At last I rang my partner, Caroline, back home in England. Her advice was simple and direct: get out of bed, pack your bag and walk out of the door. It helped. I did these things in the order she suggested. Now I was walking down a suburban street on a glaring-bright spring day, past communist-era apartment blocks in faded pink and yellow shades. The forest was not far away, just a mile down the road. Signs on chain-link fences said '*Uwaga!*', which means 'Attention!' The blocks came to an end and on my left was a modern church with a monument outside, draped in flowers and Polish flags. In my strangely fearful state this wasn't what I hoped to see: two soldiers in berets and camouflage loitering with automatic weapons and fixed bayonets. My nervous smile was met with blank faces, stony stares. The monument bore the word 'Katyn', the name of the massacre of Polish officers and intellectuals by the Soviet Union in 1940; twenty-two thousand of them, buried in a Russian forest.

The tarmac petered out and tree cover lay ahead. This was the no-man's-land between the town and the trees, an uneasy meeting ground, prowled by passing joggers. A track of sandy soil led eastwards past shack-like cottages with freshly painted clapboard walls, behind which lay the rotting hulks of older dwellings and disused barns, like embarrassing relatives. Dumped TVs, tyres and fridges littered the forest fringes.

When I reached the shade of birch and pine it felt like going under water.

The dappled dark slid over me. My breath came slower and deeper, the twinges of panic diminishing. The glare of exposure vanished. No one could see me here.

For the past two days, for a thousand miles, I had travelled through a clearing; across the ghostly footprint of a vanished forest.

~

Its story begins at least ten thousand years ago, in the vacuum left by the vanishing of the ice.

With the end of the Last Glacial Maximum, the mammoth-grazed arctic tundra that had covered the North European Plain – stretching from what is now the Netherlands and northern Germany to Russia – underwent a process of rapid recolonisation. Species that had fled the ice thousands of years before came back, creeping across thawing permafrost in the warming climate. The first pioneers to arrive were the tiny seeds of birch trees, which, carried by the wind, can travel great distances to populate open ground; their pale trunks were like the blueprints of the future forest. Behind them came alder, poplar, willow and Scots pine. Oak came later, fanning in a slow explosion from the south, where it had waited out the ice age sheltered by the protective wall of the Alps and Carpathians; then, in staggered waves as the climate warmed, cooled and warmed, came hazel, elm, ash, beech, maple, lime, holly and hornbeam. By the early

Neolithic the forest was general over northern Europe, reaching from the Atlantic Ocean to the Baltic Sea.

It was as if a great roof had been woven across the continent, blocking out the light of the sky. Europe was reinhabited not only by trees but shadow.

What about the people who lived through that great shadowing? For thousands of years they had hunted here, following the great herds across the wide-open plain, and now, in the space of a few generations, their horizons were filled in. Saplings shot up everywhere, too fast to be grazed back; in an altered landscape where predators might be hiding behind every fallen bough, ruminant herds could not linger long and quickly moved away. Some people surely kept following them, to lands beyond the range of trees; some, or so I would like to think, migrated with the reindeer all the way to Scotland and the receding glacier that once carved the Lairig Ghru. But others stayed and adapted to life beneath the leaves.

Perhaps those forest-adapted folk, remote and unknowable to us, did not see it as one forest but as many different ones, continuous nations of tree communities days or weeks apart from each other, territories of dark pine or lighter realms of oak and lime. With the exception of scattered patches cleared by slash-and-burn farming, as in the Amazon today, people must have passed their lives without leaving tree cover.

The story of the forest's disappearance is the story of agriculture, that great, world-changing shift from foraging to farming. Starting in the Fertile Crescent around 8000 BC, the practice reached southern Europe five thousand years later. It spread slowly northwards as the forest had once done, colonising the same terrain.

As the shadows left the ground, light flooded in again.

Trees were cleared by axe and fire for cropland and pastureland, to provide materials and fuel for iron smelting. As the new culture spread, these clearings ran together. Whether hunter-gatherers adopted agricultural ways of life or were victims of a conquest is one of history's great debates – it was probably elements of both – but some forest people and their way of life clung on in the deeper groves. It was not so much a disappearance as a fragmentation. Again I think of the Amazon: those satellite pictures that depict the forest's unravelling year by year, a threadbare green carpet nibbled from all sides by moths, are a fast-forward replay of what occurred in Europe.

Analysis of pollen samples shows forest cover declining gradually until two thousand years ago and then plunging rapidly as a tipping point was reached. Civilisation followed the axe. By Roman times the south and west of Europe was largely deforested and only the unconquered forests of Germania held out, beyond the Danube and the Rhine. That mysterious, densely wooded realm, which the Romans called Hercynia – the refuge of Wodin-worshipping, warlike Teutonic tribes who were said to hang the bodies of sacrificed victims in oak trees – was the frontier between light and shade, the civilised and the barbaric.

Białowieża is the largest surviving stump of that original forest that once stretched from sea to sea across the continent. First protected by Polish-Lithuanian kings and later by Russian tsars for use as a hunting reserve, this exclave of primeval woodland is now a national park, UNESCO World Heritage Site and Natura 2000 Special Area of Protection. Straddling the border of modern-day Poland and Belarus (with two-thirds in Europe's last communist state), it covers over a thousand square miles of oak, lime and hornbeam groves, along with tracts of alder and spruce, divided into zones of greater and lesser protection. While its outskirts have been logged and euphemistically 'managed', whether by medieval foresters or modern governments, its protected, tangled heart has remained inviolate for at least eight hundred years.

The Amazon rainforest is the image I keep reaching for simply because I cannot conceive of a greater expanse of trees. Spreading for over two million square miles – despite the logging, the mining, the burning, the road-building, the construction of dams and the other ecocidal incursions that are reducing its area, and its integrity, by football-pitch-sized swathes every day – it is the largest forest on earth, the closest thing I can imagine to Europe's primeval wildwood. The trees, of course, are not the same, being tropical rather than temperate. But the denseness, the otherness, the inconceivable sense of scale: these, I think, come close to evoking a continent-sized forest.

As the word 'arctic' has come to mean something other than simply the polar north, 'Amazon' is a kind of shorthand for authentic wilderness (along with 'virgin forest', with everything that term reveals about the kind of people – the kind of men – who set store by conquering it). While the Amazon may be the world's largest single forest, the vast semi-contiguous belt of coniferous trees that enwraps the Northern Hemisphere – known in Russia as the taiga and in North America as boreal forest – is the planet's largest forested biome. Köppen classifies it as Dfc, 'continental, no dry season, cold summer'. To the north lies the tundra and to the south lies the temperate zone, where Białowieża can be found, the closest thing that Europe has to a true jungle.

'Jungle': the word derives from Sanskrit and originally meant 'wasteland' or 'desert', a place considered beyond the pale of human habitation. Over time its meaning changed; became overgrown with trees. 'Forest': from the Latin *foris*, which simply means 'outside'. In Britain, swathes of treeless land that were 'afforested' by the Normans – including the open fields of Essex and the bleak upland of Dartmoor – are technically forests in this sense.

Weirdly, the word 'forest' has nothing to do with trees.

The Polish word for forest is *las*, but Białowieża is more commonly referred to by another term, *puszcza*, which is not quite translatable: something between 'ancient forest', 'wilderness' and 'wildwood'.

I am entering this *puszcza* now. Out of the light of the modern day and back into Europe's shadow.

'Entries by car break the low' say signs at regular intervals. The hours go by and the endless trees strobe past identically. Occasionally there are signs that warn against straying from the path, indicating the jurisdictions of various forestry agencies, and at one point comes a notice for the Dębowy Grąd Reserve – an area of protected oak-lime-hornbeam forest along the Dubitka River – on which some detractor has scrawled, in chalk, 'REZERWAT IDIOTY'. I don't need to know much Polish to guess the meaning of that. Not everyone is delighted with the forest's protected status.

My destination for the day is a village called Teremiski, where, thanks to the internet, my arrival is expected. At last the monotonous track meets the right angle of a road. The road leads through a broad clearing where the forest has been pushed back to make space for meadowland, now fringed with pioneer birch. From a distance the treeline is a dark and menacing wall. Ramshackle houses are dotted about, some dovetail-jointed and shingle-roofed, others newer and concrete, though no less shabby, each with its stack of firewood and its covered well. Rows of painted beehives stand in small fenced gardens. An old woman in heavy boots, planted solidly in the street, rotates like a heliotrope to monitor me as I pass, and further on a car reverses to investigate a man who is lying on his back with his legs stuck in the road. After a prod from the driver's foot he grunts, clambers to his feet and shakes himself like a bear. The stench of alcohol flaps off him in waves.

A soft-eyed dog waits for me outside the building I am looking for: a large wooden house with yellow walls and a faded 'Information' sign. The dog escorts me dutifully from the gate to the front door. I can't see a bell so push my way into a dark anteroom full of camouflage jackets and boots, binoculars, posters of boars and deer, a smell of woodsmoke, sweat and rain. Another door opens into a room flooded with afternoon light. An enormous dining table takes up one side of it; elsewhere there are bookshelves and maps, a rumbling wood-burning stove, pickled things in murky jars, a hammock slung between two posts. '*Dobry dzień!*' a voice says, and that's how I meet Augustyn.

He is in his late twenties, perhaps, and speaks near-perfect English. With a tufty blond beard and intensely blue eyes, dressed entirely in green, he walks with an energetic lope as if he were crossing a wide terrain; the kind of person who makes more sense outside than inside. He gives me a lightning tour of the house, an induction performed many times – no alcohol or drugs, no meat, donations for communal meals, and I am welcome to any empty bed in the dorm rooms upstairs – then takes the kettle off the boil and pours me a mug of coffee. I have only just sat down when he says, 'We are going to the forest. Want to come?'

'We' is him and Marianka, a young woman with thick-framed glasses and a low, anarchistic fringe. They cross the road and I follow them through the pale meadow. Next to some slumped hayricks they pause to point something out: a camera trap strapped to a tree, facing a patch of flattened grass and a chewed lump of plastic. 'Wolves,' says Augustyn. 'Our neighbour keeps seeing them here. They like to play with this plastic thing.'

Marianka seems annoyed. 'Why would he want to watch them playing with some shitty plastic?'

Wolves! A kind of slow electric pulse goes through my

body. We are just outside the village; I am amazed they come so close.

'Right up to the garden gate,' says Augustyn when I mention this. 'They are getting into conversations with the dogs.'

We pass through stands of silver birch like X-ray trees, photographic negatives, and into the green-grey shadow that lies beyond. Once under cover the two of them veer seemingly randomly through the trunks, heading vaguely south. They haven't said what they're doing here and I'm glad I do not ask. It soon becomes apparent that they're not *doing* anything. Their intention is simply to be with the forest, with no purpose or direction, for the same reason that Nan Shepherd went to the mountain 'as one visits a friend with no intention but to be with him'.

The trees I saw from this afternoon's track were anonymous strangers. Now, Białowieża and I are being introduced.

It doesn't happen in words, because once in the forest no one speaks. It happens in small illuminations as the spotlight of their attention swings from one point to the next, picking out details that delight them or make them curious. All I have to do is follow that wandering beam. One moment they are examining a patch of lichen or a beard of moss, and the next they are looking at a leaning trunk that is seemingly suspended in the air, caught in a web of twigs so fine that it looks like levitation. Here a hornbeam and a spruce have wrapped around one another, merging in a grafted kiss, and there the body of a two-foot fungus is rippled like candle wax, powdering the earth below with a snowfall of white spores. Although the leaves are not yet out in the canopy above, the forest floor seeps with green. Spongy moss glows so brightly it appears to burn. In one place Augustyn stops and traces something on the ground: wood anemones have grown in the absence of a fallen trunk that has completely rotted away, thriving off its nutrients, highlighting its vanished shape like police chalk lines around a corpse. Wherever I look there is something living growing on something dead.

Earlier the forest appeared as a replicating mass, one theme repeated a million times. Now, by slow degrees, my eyes start zooming in.

After we have walked for an hour or so – *looked* for an hour or so – they abruptly sink to the ground in a strip of golden sunlight. Thousands of wood anemones are sprinkled like stars on a church ceiling, each one radiating a six-bladed blaze of white. We sit here until the sunlight has narrowed, a closing door, and when we get to our feet we blink as if waking from sleep. 'Dark soon,' says Marianka.

Back at the border of the forest we pass a patch of churned black earth, like the one I saw earlier as I walked from Hajnówka. 'Boar,' I say with confidence.

'Bison,' corrects Augustyn.

I look closer: deep, wide hoofprints have been pressed into the mud.

Another slow electric pulse. But bison are a tale for later.

~

At dawn the next morning Augustyn and I go looking for wolves.

It is 4.45 a.m. and the air is astonishingly cold, a dry, burning-freezing wave that sizzles on the skin. Exactly half a white moon hangs in a sky that is weak and clear, as if it has been stretched too thin. The topmost branches of the forest are molten with the sun.

We walk in silence down the road, skirting the pale meadow. At the edge of the village, between two trees, stands a pair of wooden crosses next to a concrete pole topped with a circular platform built to support a heavy nest, the symbols of three local cults: Catholic, Orthodox and Stork. Candles burn behind red glass and I wonder who lit them.

Not far away from the crosses, a banner is strung between two posts:

PSEUDOEKOLODZY
BRUDNE RĘCE PRECZ OD PUSZCZY
MIESZKAŃCY

Augustyn translates with a smile: 'Pseudo-ecologists, dirty hands off our forest. The residents.'

But it is far too early in the morning for politics.

We go south into the meadow, walking on frost-hardened ground, and then along the fringe of the forest, stopping often to watch and listen. Even with gloves it is too cold to hold the binoculars for long; I scan the horizon in slow sweeps, following Augustyn's lead, not quite sure what it is I am supposed to be looking for. The thought of wolves feels abstract and far away from what I know. I am not even sure whether or not I believe in them.

By the time we have beaten the bounds the sun is up above the trees. 'We started too late,' says Augustyn. 'Earlier tomorrow.'

Back in the house we chew some bread and I fall asleep in an armchair, waking to find a black cat purring and dribbling on my chest. Not seeing wolves this morning might have been a dream.

This is the start of almost a week in the house of the dirty-handed pseudo-ecologists. I have a whole dorm room to myself, and chip in towards vegan meals: potato soup, pasta, lentils, salads, toasted nuts and seeds, pickles, fruit compotes and preserves. Sometimes a visitor smuggles in cheese, which is eaten furtively. On one occasion the cat steals a cured sausage from my rucksack and runs around the house with it, with me in discreet pursuit, attempting to herd it back into my room. At any given dinnertime it is hard to know if there will be five people, or fifteen, gathered around the gleaming table, sharing donations and offerings. The population of the house fluctuates on a regular basis, from half a dozen permanent residents to a shifting composition of activists, ecologists, biologists, scholars and journalists who might stay for days or weeks, making this their base for excursions into the *puszcza*. For this is a house of 'forest defenders' and many of the people here – Augustyn and Marianka included – are veterans of the 2017 Białowieża uprising.

During the course of my stay I hear the story many times. It started with an infestation of spruce bark beetles.

Yesterday, in the forest, Augustyn peeled back a strip of bark to show me the invaders' work: a labyrinth of boreholes riddling the inner bark, along with sticky shelves of sap where the tree had attempted to flush them out. Such outbreaks weaken and kill spruce trees, leaving behind bleached skeletons; they have always been part of the life and death cycle of the forest. But in 2016, in response to a larger-than-usual infestation, the Polish government announced the commencement of a logging campaign that went far beyond anything that had been seen before. Limited felling was already permitted in many parts of Białowieża if justified by public safety – trees that might fall on a road, for example – but this proposal involved the removal of 180,000 cubic metres of wood, or tens of thousands of trees. Ecologists warned that the 'cure' risked doing irreparable harm to the ecosystem and might even have the effect of spreading the infestation further. The government ignored the warnings. They needed to kill the trees, they said, to stop the beetles killing the trees, an argument reminiscent of the line from the Vietnam War: 'We had to destroy the village in order to save it.'

Logging started the following year, to an international outcry.

It was initially promised that no old-growth groves would be cut, but almost immediately trees came down in supposedly protected areas. The work was done by harvesters, twelve-tonne armoured tractors with hydraulic claws that grip the tree firmly at its base. Once the chainsaw has severed the trunk, feed rollers force it through a gauntlet of delimbing knives that neatly strip the branches off; the whole thing takes two minutes. They weren't simply taking diseased spruces, surgically removing one tree at a time, but clear-cutting swathes of forest and trucking out the lumber.

The forest defenders started out as a loose coalition of civic groups attempting to limit the destruction. Before they were given the use of this house – donated by the environmental journalist who lives next door, the man who films wolves playing with plastic – they lived in tents and trees. They organised 'disobedience walks', breaking down cordons and trespassing in areas that had been sealed off, attached themselves to logging equipment and blocked roads with their bodies. A friendly resident called Asia – who looks more like a primary school teacher than a hardened activist – shows me photographs of people chained to the arms of harvesters; men, women and children lying, as if they have been felled themselves, on stacks of severed trunks to stop them from being removed. Columns of Forestry Guards clad in camouflaged body armour escort a convoy of giant logs like soldiers escorting a missile in a military parade. 'They were drafted from all over Poland,' she says, 'effectively deputised to use violence by the state. It was a paramilitary force.' Other pictures show activists being dragged along or pinned to the ground, handcuffed, their faces pressed into the loam. There were many claims of assault. I remember my paranoia at the sight of those soldiers in Hajnówka; a shadow, perhaps, of the violence lurking in these trees.

In the end what stopped the logging was less direct action

than documentation. Patrols of volunteer observers collected data to send to the European Commission; based largely on this evidence, the European Court of Justice ordered the programme to be suspended until the case could be reviewed. The Polish government continued, citing 'public safety'. It was only after the threat of fines of hundreds of thousands of euros a day that the government backed down and the harvesters withdrew. In April 2018 – by chance, a year ago this week – the final verdict was handed down: the government's actions had been illegal and further logging was suspended.

Satellite images confirmed the scale of what had taken place: quadrants of shattered timber punched into the green. I think of the Amazon once again; the images are identical. In a single year Białowieża had lost between 10,000 and 180,000 trees, many of which were centuries old, which would be an impressive target for any spruce bark beetle.

For now there is a ceasefire, but the forest defenders have not stopped patrolling. 'These people have not gone away,' says Asia. 'We do not trust them.'

From the banner strung outside, there are clearly those who do not trust the forest defenders either. While many Poles were appalled by the logging, there were others who believed that the programme was necessary. It fed the sawmills of Hajnówka, a lumber town that had lost its purpose, and restored a sense of industry to this economically depressed and neglected corner of Poland B. Ecologists and writers might see beauty in the *puszcza*'s tangled rot, but in the view of many locals, forests need management. Leaving acres of valuable timber to be eaten by worms and slugs was seen as a waste of natural resources, not to mention a fire hazard. A story even did the rounds that the forest is man-made. Jan Szyszko, the much vilified environment minister during the logging – a former forester himself – claimed that, far from being primeval, large parts of this wilderness were created by the 'enterprising hand of man' on land that was farmed in ancient times. Asia finds another photograph: a pro-logging demonstration organised by the government, at which an old man holds up a neatly printed sign that reads: 'This forest was made by my grand-mother'. This refers to a peculiar local arboreal conspiracy theory: in Hajnówka's cemetery is the gravestone of a woman who claimed to have single-handedly planted Białowieża.

This belief is apparently fairly widespread. Asia tells me of her confrontation with a red-faced Forestry Guard: 'Why are you people doing this? Don't you know this forest isn't natural?'

'It's twelve thousand years old.'

'What are you saying? Forests like this just grow by themselves?'

In this staunchly religious country, governed by conser-vative Catholics and currently undergoing an upsurge of nationalist traditionalism, it is easy to see why a notion like this has traction. A forest twelve thousand years old is older than biblical time; it is directly threatening to Christian theology. An unproductive wilderness being left to its own devices is an affront to mankind's role, divinely appointed, as stewards of the earth, with dominion over all living things. I think of those gripping steel claws: the enterprising hand of man. And what the hand of man (or woman) gives, it can take away.

The science-fiction images of brute machines attacking nature, and of paramilitary troops dragging people out of trees, are accurate representations of what happened in these woods. But the conflict is less black and white and more dappled grey. What strikes me over the time I am here is how everyone in the fight – forest defenders and Forestry Guards, ecologists and logging crews, anarchists and conser-vative Catholics – claims not to be destroying the forest but rather acting in its defence, as guardians of the trees and even of Poland's identity. Each side is shouting at the other: 'Dirty hands off our forest.'

~

Augustyn takes me on a tour of the conflict's aftermath. He has the restless evangelism of someone who understands that things might not be permanent, that time – or beauty, or life itself – is finite, that nothing is guaranteed. We go north from the village into an area that was only partially logged in 2017, not clear-cut but decimated, with just the spruces taken out. Halfway down a rutted track, where greenery is growing back over tyre-ruptured earth, he stops and indicates left and right. 'You can see the difference here. This part was logged, and this was not. This is how it is, and this is how it was.'

The forest to the left is spacious and simplified, with gaps in the canopy where the sunlight pours through. Once the spruces had been stripped out many of the ancient oaks, deprived of the windbreaks provided by their protective neighbours, came crashing down in storms, the muddy tombstones of their roots thrust up here and there. The rare pygmy owls and three-toed woodpeckers that nested here have gone, retreated to the deeper woods. The forest to the right is darker. Two worlds: light and shadow.

Later still – a slow acclimatisation to annihilation – we progress from this partly ruined grove to a nearby clear-cut. Another resident of the house, a PhD student called Adam, is studying the ways in which plants are recolonising the space, with an emphasis on invasives; the theory is that alien species now have an opening, thriving in shattered environments, like disaster capitalists. Adam is a heavy-set, inscrutable and pensive man with a face that never quite smiles, high cheekbones and narrow eyes. There is a shyness and a toughness to him. 'I am going to do some research on the clear-cut,' he says by way of introduction. 'Better to have company. Some people don't like us here. My car was destroyed several times.' Driving through a village on the way, we overtake a family with a little boy in camouflage holding a realistic toy gun – or perhaps simply a gun – which he aims at the car's back window, drawing a bead as we go by. His mouth moves in the Polish equivalent of 'Bang'.

Adam does not seem to notice this. He is talking about spruce bark beetles and what underlies the infestation, which is the same inescapable reality that underlies everything. Białowieża exists at the intersection of two of Europe's great climate zones – the boreal coniferous biome of the north, and the drier steppe zone of the south – which makes it especially vulnerable to change. Global warming effectively means an expansion of that southern zone; as hotter, drier conditions push north, spruces, which prefer cold and damp, become less resilient, their defence systems weakening. Spruce bark beetles exploit this weakness. They are not the cause but the effect of a larger breakdown.

According to the recent Red List published by the International Union for Conservation of Nature, over half of Europe's endemic trees are at risk of extinction, including species as common as rowan and horse chestnut. The most immediately visible causes are climate change and habitat destruction, but infestations – from invasive beetles, moths and fungal diseases such as *Hymenoscyphus fraxineus*, the ash dieback currently ravaging Britain – are more insidious. Against the backdrop of global heating, these localised declines are not isolated events but connected to a grander pattern in which human intervention can be seen as part of a feedback loop: climate change leads to weaker trees, which lead to more infestations, which lead to more logging, which leads to more climate change.

Perhaps, on some metaphysical level, humans are not fighting the beetles but somehow working with them.

After half an hour's drive we come to the aftermath of this cryptic human–beetle alliance: a neat square of devastation punched into the wilderness. Between the road and the border of the uncut forest only one tree remains standing: a single spruce twenty metres tall, a lone survivor in a field of smashed dead wood. Why did the loggers leave it there? There is something sinister in that, like a killer's calling card, as if it has been left as a warning to other trees. Its upper branches spring back and forth like rubber in the wind as I follow Adam and Augustyn through a wreckage of splintered limbs, breaking sticks with every step. It reminds me of following those sombre Indian scientists on to the Kolahoi Glacier all those years ago; there is a similar trepidation of unstable ground.

Their destination is an area marked by little twists of wool – infused, I learn, with wolf pheromones to discourage grazing deer – where Adam is making a study of the rate of regrowth. While they crouch with a book, absorbed in the minute identification of plants, I retreat to the edge of the clearing and beneath tree cover. The feeling, as with yesterday, is one of instant relief: back into concealing shade, out of merciless exposure. Before I have gone far, however, I am hit by a stench. Something dead. Something large and dead. The seething whine of flies. A few more steps and the forest reveals a hunk of dark purple meat the size of a concrete breeze block, boiling with maggots. A shoulder? A slab of leg? Further on lies a heap of bones that are grotesquely oversized: vertebrae the size of fists, a leg bone that resembles a cartoon Stone Age war club. Propped against an oak stump is the broad chest plate, clumped with curly brownish fur. The skull is nowhere to be seen, nor the upward-thrusting horns.

With mental paleontology I can reconstruct the rest, for

images, fully fleshed, are on display everywhere. It is Białowieża's iconic beast and the national animal of both Poland and Belarus: the *żubr*, the wisent or the European bison.

Bison – forest-dwelling cousins of American buffalo, which they closely resemble – are Europe's largest and heaviest land mammal. Once, like mammoths, they roamed the extent of the North European Plain, but few would now recognise them as a European animal; they are more easily pictured thundering over Midwestern prairies, pursued by Apaches on piebald horses or gunned down by white men from trains. But bison are survivors of another, more ancient frontier. Descended from aurochs, the ancestors of modern domestic cattle, they were driven from Europe's own wild west as the forest was pushed back and clear-cuts, like the one behind me, opened space for settlement. 'Even in the first century', writes the historian Simon Schama in *Landscape and Memory*, 'Pliny had noted that the bison had retreated in the face of colonization to the depths of the great Hercynian forest that marked the eastern border between ancient "Germania" and the unknown and unconquered barbarian wilderness of Scythia.' By the Middle Ages bison survived only here and in a few isolated spots like the Carpathian Mountains, relics of a bygone age. Like the primeval forest itself they endured beyond the edges of agricultural civilisation.

The stories of bison and Białowieża are inextricably linked. They are mutually dependent, almost symbiotic, like the algae and the fungus that comprise a lichen. Without the protection of the forest the bison would never have survived, yet without the bison – and their status as a prized hunting animal – it is likely that the forest would have been cut down long ago. The *puszcza* was first protected in the early fifteenth century by Władysław II Jagiełło, who started his reign as the last pagan Grand Duke of Lithuania and, after converting to

Catholicism in 1386, went on to lay the foundations of the Polish-Lithuanian Commonwealth, which would become the largest and most powerful state in Europe. The name Białowieża derives from 'White Tower', after a royal hunting lodge; for centuries the forest was the preserve of nobility, and prowess in the bison hunt was, as Schama writes, 'as important to the Lithuanian-Polish cult of knighthood as the bull was for the Spanish warrior caste at the other end of Christianity's frontiers'. As Poland's fortunes waned and its borders collapsed – disastrously sandwiched between Germans on one side and Russians on the other – 'bison became a talisman of survival. For as long as the beast and its succouring forest habitat endured, it was implied, so would the nation's martial vigour.'

When the east of the country was taken by Russia in the eighteenth century, Białowieża's special status remained unchanged. The tsars enthusiastically continued the sport of Polish kings, displaying their mastery of the forest in a bounty of horns and mounted heads. Trainloads of moustached, fur-hatted officers came from St Petersburg and Moscow for a chance to bag a living, breathing symbol of Polishness. This atavistic assertion of dominance was even more grossly displayed during the Nazi occupation, when Hermann Göring – who Schama calls 'the monstrous, jewel-encrusted hippopotamus of the Third Reich' – personally took control of forest management. Primordial and uncorrupted, the *puszcza* represented to him a vision of Germany's mythical past, with the bison being a perfect 'symbol of hairy Teutonic bullishness'. Obsessed with hunting, he drew up plans to enlarge Białowieża – once purged of inferior Slavs and Jews – into the largest game reserve in the future Greater Germany. He even invented for himself the title of *Reichsjägermeister*, Master Hunter of the Reich.

Like the reindeer of the Cairngorms, Białowieża's bison

were also hunted to extinction, though their absence lasted only years and not centuries. In the winter of 1918 occupying German troops, starving and on the verge of defeat, butchered hundreds of them for meat, reducing the herds so drastically that by the end of the decade only four individuals were left. The last died, of natural causes, in the early 1920s. Today's population – the population that Göring idolised – is descended from captive breeding stock reintroduced in 1929 by Jan Stolczman, a Polish biologist. The animals came from zoos in Germany and Scandinavia, and their names were suitably durable: Kobold, Borusse, Stolce, Faworyta, Gatczyna, Biserta, Hagen. They merged back into the forest as if they had never been gone. Now there are around nine hundred of them split between Poland and Belarus, partly in enclosed reserves but mostly in free-living herds.

Over the coming days and weeks I will see evidence of their presence everywhere. I will learn to recognise the areas of churned black earth, the deep imprints of their hooves, the wisps of snagged, pungent hair and the cowpats – bison-pats – caked around water holes. I will often think I see the shapes of their jutting heads, only to discover that I am looking at a boulder or a log. I will dream about them. But, as someone explains at the house, I have come at an unlucky time. In leaner months they often graze in the meadows near the villages, but in spring there is so much greenery ('bison salad') on the forest floor they contentedly stay in the under-growth, where they are much harder to see. Also, an outbreak of African swine fever has killed off many wild boar, leading to a glut of acorns, which bison love to eat. They are gorging themselves in the deep woods. Apparently the herds have grown extremely fat this year.

For now the closest I can get is this lump of maggoty flesh, the bones that look like fossils. I pick up a curved rib bone almost as long as my arm and wonder what killed this individual. Wolves? Old age? A child with a gun? The mal-evolent ghost of a Russian tsar? There is no way of knowing.

Far away, Augustyn is calling from the clear-cut. They have finished their study. It is time to go. Adam's car has not been destroyed. I leave the insects to continue turning flesh to loam.

~

The next morning we get up to look for wolves again. It is earlier: 4.15 a.m. The sky is half in darkness. The dawn chorus from the forest, a full circle around the house, is intense almost to the point of violence, less an awakening than an eruption, with the airhorn honks of a crane blasting out a rhythm. We complete our circuit of the village, walking the other way this time, letting the binoculars do the looking. It is the same as yesterday: the dream-clear light, the freezing air. Again we see no wolves.

'I'm just going to the forest' is one of the phrases I hear most in the house at Teremiski. People go to the forest all the time, sometimes for specific reasons – to look for bison or wolves, to check the footage on camera traps, to show people around or on patrol – but mostly just for the sake of it. Everyone here, like Augustyn, is a biophiliac, someone who loves wild nature and feels at home beneath the trees. It often feels that the forest is the reality, and the house, for all its convivial meals and its easy comradeship, is little more than a waiting room for the woods outside.

I lose myself in monotonous hours of walking the long, straight tracks. It feels a bit incongruous: the *puszcza* is divided into a grid system of regular quadrants running east to west, north to south, the axes as regimented as the street plan of Manhattan. Each division is marked with a numbered concrete plinth that corresponds to the map, so that, keeping to the paths, it is almost impossible to get lost. Tramping the woods is not allowed. I understand the reasons for this, but it feels unsatisfying. Lost is what I *want* to be. On occasion I break the rules and follow prohibited paths into zones of higher protection, marked by signs showing human silhouettes struck out by crossed red bars, and at once the oaks and the horn-beams are altogether huger. There is a sense of deepening, of submergence in a different level; despite the alarm calls of the birds there is a greater stillness. Instantly guarded, I am aware of my noise and my lack of subtlety. My brain is alert for Forestry Guards – those images of body-armoured men are often in my mind – but also generally *alert*, in a wider sense. Forbidden ground has that effect. I am not just flouting Polish law but trespassing in another world, a world that does not belong to me. It is the same realisation I had seeing the miniature reefs of ice high on the Cairngorm plateau: there are things happening here that have nothing to do with people.

Halfway down one of these tracks I find fresh wolf scat on a rock. I have been told what to look for: the shit is clogged with dark hair. Its smell – musky, rank and sharp, weirdly intimate – makes me physically recoil, a reaction so visceral that it must be instinct. As I straighten up there is crashing in the undergrowth and I see three, then four, then five red deer leap away in graceful, frightened bounds, startled by a predator that is startled by a predator. A phrase comes to mind: 'landscape of fear'. The presence of apex hunters like wolves keeps grazing herds constantly on the move, preventing them from stripping back any one area. Thicker underbrush, in turn, provides more cover for predators, allowing them to hunt more effectively and cull the ruminant population to levels the forest can sustain. To the forest, fear means health.

It keeps me moving too.

The moment I step off these regimented pathways I am

lost. I can vaguely navigate by the sun's position through the trees, if the sun is visible, but twice when I think I have been walking straight, carefully aiming north or south, I find that the woods have turned me a full 180 degrees and brought me back to my starting point. The trick makes me laugh in disbelief; it almost feels deliberate. Meandering trails, snags of bog and the obstacles of fallen trunks combine to make straight lines impossible. On another occasion I try to navigate by the roar of the road that runs eastwards from Hajnówka, only to realise that the noise is the crashing of the wind in the trees; not the breaking of waves against a coastline but the roaring of an open sea. It gives me the impression that the forest has no edges.

Gradually, remembering the lesson of Augustyn and Marianka's attentiveness, I am learning to distinguish between arboreal neighbourhoods that are as different from each other as the postcode zones in a city. In spruce-dominated areas, where the ground lies thick with cones, sunlight falls in lancing shafts that look solid enough to grasp. Under pines no sunlight penetrates; dank and lurid moss carpets the forest floor and enwraps the lower trunks, glistening with fungus. There are boggy alder groves that resemble tropical swamps, seemingly continents away from the spacious stands of oak and lime, or the clusters of silver birch that shine like polished metal.

Much of Białowieża is characterised as oak-lime-hornbeam forest, and this is the first time I have really encountered hornbeams. They are trees I am not familiar with, perhaps because their lumpish wood is not considered economically useful, and so they are rarely to be found in managed forests. But here they are everywhere, sprouting among the oaks and limes, their rippled, undulating trunks smooth and softly gleaming. They are dense, hard, irregular, with a quality like candle wax that has melted and reformed. When knocked they give a ceramic ring a bit like bone or even horn – perhaps this explains the name – unlike the depth of oak or the softness of pine. I walk through the forest tapping trees, as if asking to come in.

Half an hour's walk from Teremiski is a tourist-frequented grove known as Stara ('Old') Białowieża. For the price of an entrance ticket – which I don't pay for, discovering the place unexpectedly from the forest rather than from the road – you can follow a boardwalk trail leading around the 'century oaks' that are venerated as icons of Białowieża. This isn't only for their age – many are half a millennium old – but for the history they embody: each one bears the name of Polish-Lithuanian royalty. The Jagiełło Oak is named for the forest's first protector and defeater of the Teutonic Order in the Battle of Grunwald ('Greenwood') in 1410, a landmark in Polish nationhood. The tree fell in a 1970s storm but still lies as a noble ruin. On a signboard it says: 'King Władysław Jagiello initiated the tradition of royal huntings in Białowieża Forest in 1409', and then – in what is either a typo or a claim of immortality – 'Władysław came here in 1926, protecting himself from the plague.' By the Old Zygmunt Oak it says: 'King Zygmunt constituted the law, that a death meets the one, who would kill an animal in the Royal Forest.' By the Helena Oak, named for the wife of King Aleksander Jagiellończyk: 'This lady of hot blood was so unrestrained in her hunting spirit, that only the most tenacious could keep up with her.'

If I did not know what they were I might not even recognise these giants, on first encounter, as oaks. The ancient oaks I am used to seeing – English oaks lining the driveways of grand country estates – are short and squat, knobbled with galls, often lightning-struck or dying from the inside out. These oaks, deprived of the roominess in which to spread out wide, launch themselves directly up to heights of thirty or forty metres, practically branchless for most of the trunk and then crowning at canopy level into mazes of enormous limbs. Their girth is formidable, machines pulling water from the earth. Touching the bark of an English oak is like touching noble but corrupted flesh; this, by contrast, feels like laying my hands on living power.

Craning my neck to see their tops produces an inverse vertigo, as if I am not looking up but down through time. It is easy to understand why such trees were once worshipped, the ancient forest-dwelling tribes placing sacrifices in their branches. These oaks, with their official designation as 'national monuments' – afforded the same status as statues or war memorials – are symbolic reincarnations of the figures they represent, the royal heroes of the past still living in the form of trees.

This patriotic overlay has roots deeper than the nation state. How else to describe this place but as a sacred grove?

Augustyn takes me to a place outside Stara Białowieża where another century oak grows. No boardwalk leads to it, only wandering bison trails. It was christened more recently, not after a king or a queen but in honour of the activists: the Oak of the Defenders of the Forest. Perhaps it's an effect of the name but it has a much greater impact on me; six metres wide at the trunk, thirty metres tall, with fissures in its grey bark deep enough to fit my arm into, it stuns me in a way the royal oaks did not. The experience is not quite awe. Respect would be a better term. I feel small, not in physical size but in history.

In this disjointing state I feel a sense of enormous peace.

Peace, too, is the wrong word. Perhaps what I feel is relief.

At the end of the day, just after midnight, I leave the tea and the conversation around the wood-burning stove – they are about to watch *Game of Thrones* – and walk to the edge of the property to stand in the white moonlight. Dogs are in a state of disturbance, an emergency chorus of outraged barks booming around the village. From the trees beyond the meadow – from the direction of the Oak of the Defenders of the Forest – comes a series of answering cries that are not dogs and are not birds.

One long, ecstatic howl.

That electric pulse again.

~

I leave the forest defenders' house for now and follow the road to Białowieża village, the forest's main settlement, which lies in another clearing near the entrance to the national park. My plan is to hire a guide to take me into the Strict Reserve – the only way to gain access there – and then, in a couple of days, to cross the border to the greater two-thirds of the forest in Belarus, the last hardline communist state in Europe.

The village is cheerfully touristy, with a couple of upmarket hotels (they style themselves as 'lodges') and wooden sculptures of bison, boar and other forest mammals everywhere. Its greatest delight are the stork nests integrated with the infrastructure – one is on top of a telephone pole with cables snaking from its base – complete with resident pairs of storks. The huge, awkwardly jointed birds sit unruffled by the cars, bicycles and beer-drinking teenagers passing under them, glancing down occasionally as if on lesser beings. Their throaty grackles sound like heavy stones turning in a stream, filling the air with a clattering that is startlingly loud. When I first hear it I think it's a car backfiring.

I go from a house of teetotal vegans to its opposite: a guest-house at the edge of the woods whose walls are thick with animal pelts, antlers and mounted skulls, all shot by its stocky, blue-eyed, shaven-headed owner. No sooner have I settled in than Marcin comes bounding up the stairs with a plate of his home-made sausage and four different brands of beer ('So you can see which one is best'), plus a bottle of Belarusian kvass, an alcoholic beverage made of fermented rye bread, the colour of swamp water. 'Polish kvass is shit,' he says, 'the communist one is better.' Outside, an old man with an axe, whom I take to be his father, is hacking his way through a pile of logs that stands twice as tall as him; both of them used to work as lumberjacks, Marcin says. I do not say who I've just been staying with, guessing what the reaction might be. He slaps me powerfully on the back and welcomes me to his home.

I cannot decide which beer is best, least of all three bottles in. The kvass is surprisingly good. The sausage is like a sliced-up truncheon or a missile of meat, mined with nuggets of chewy fat, and I only manage a piece of it. It may come in useful later as wolf-bait.

Tonight I dream of trees growing into and out of one another, as if my consciousness is becoming entangled in their roots. In the morning I remember another dream from several nights before that I had forgotten about: great beasts beneath an orange sky, things that are bison yet not quite bison, with strange, flat, inhuman faces, rising with groans to greet me.

Early the next morning I dress warmly and cross the sleeping village to meet my guide.

She is waiting outside the park headquarters. Her name is Joanna and she is tiny, barely reaching up to my shoulders, which makes the impressive pair of binoculars around her neck look even bigger. At first I think she has mossy green hair, like some kind of forest sprite, then see that she is wearing an oversized woollen hat stuck with twigs and leaves, its tassels hanging almost to her waist. She gives me a curious, critical look, as if appraising my motivations.

The Strict Reserve lies between the Hwoźna and Narewka rivers, bordering Belarus to the east. To reach it we walk through the Palace Park that was laid out by the tsars. The magnificent palace that was once here, built by Alexander III, was spitefully torched by the Germans as they retreated in 1944, and has been replaced by a hotel clearly intended to suggest a hunting lodge in its architecture, but which more resembles a conference centre in Basingstoke. The only remnants of tsarist style reside in a few outbuildings of chalky blue with embellishments of carved white wood, like lace, around their windows and doors, and the red-brick Tsar's Gate with its tin roof. 'Look,' Joanna says. A greater spotted woodpecker is drumming its beak on the hollow metal, having discovered its acoustic properties. 'It is sending out messages.' About what, she doesn't say. She produces a telephoto lens almost as long as one of her legs and takes a few rapid snaps.

On the far side of a spacious meadow – fringed, as always, by silver birch – the Strict Reserve stands darkly. The yellow grass has been cut for hay, trimmed to a stubble. The forest is fenced, and the entrance is through a strange, imposing gateway with a wood-shingled roof, bearing the words PARK NARODOWY in jerky, rustic letters. The style is a traditional one from Kraków, Joanna says, but it looks vaguely familiar to me for another reason. As the local story goes, the director Steven Spielberg used it as an inspiration for the gateway to Jurassic Park, the entrance to another primordial world that has vanished from the rest of the earth, filled with ancient life and antediluvian monsters.

Passing across that threshold and into the gloom of shade, we are stepping into a similar sanctuary. Out of modern Europe and into Eurassic Park.

～

As with other protected parts of the forest that I've wandered into, my first impression is that everything has been subtly scaled up. It's not a dramatic difference, yet, but the oaks, limes and hornbeams seem weightier, taller, thicker. The more immediately obvious change lies in the amount of dead wood. Everywhere lie the hulks of trunks like hagfish-nibbled whale carcasses, oaks long dead but still standing, upright skeletons. Sometimes a tree strains upwards on triffid-like root legs with clear space underneath, from where it grew around a fallen body that has since rotted away. There are double-trunked oaks and hornbeams, one trunk bleached and bare while the other sprouts with fresh green, stuck to – and living on – its deceased conjoined twin. Here, not so much as a twig is removed from the crowded forest floor but left to quietly decompose, or – judging by the eruptions of growth that cover everything – to *noisily* decompose. Funguses in great racks and bergs. Lichen ranging from cool grey-green to fluorescent orange. Rashes of tiny puffballs spurting spores at the slightest touch. Slimy oozings of strange life that I cannot name.

Białowieża is said to contain, by mass, more dead than living wood.

As fear means health to the forest, death means life.

'Golden saxifrage,' says Joanna, pointing to a yellow flower with waxy, rounded leaves. 'Red-banded polypore,' an orange-crimson fungus. 'Toothwort,' a parasite with leaves like sickly purple hands. 'Dead man's fingers,' black fungus that pokes through damp moss as if it is searching for something. Each of these species is here, in the precise place we find it in, to perform a specific role, part of a chaotic order whose complexities I do not have the knowledge to understand; Joanna, trained as a biologist, does not only notice more but sees things more deeply, past their surface appearance and down to their inner function. The polypore, for example, she describes as a 'disturbance agent' whose role it is, like other funguses, to break down nutrients, releasing them to be recycled into other forms of life. The dead man's fingers, morbid though they seem, are misnamed.

Once, to look closer at one of these growths — a cascade of fungal forms spilling from some riven flank — I take a few steps off the path and am instantly reprimanded. Not even a footstep is permitted. I have the sense of breaking a religious prohibition.

Almost immediately Joanna spots something rare: a three-toed woodpecker rattling against a tree, raining splinters to the ground. Her camera aims and clicks. Soon afterwards she points out another, this one a white-backed woodpecker, and then a black woodpecker minutes after that. Over the next few hours I will almost stop noticing them, for woodpeckers are everywhere; the trees are pocked with their holes and the forest echoes with their insistent, manic hammering. Joanna can tell each species apart by its particular rhythm, as she can distinguish the warning call a blackbird makes when it sees a human from the warning call it makes when it sees a pine marten. She doesn't refer to bird noises as 'calls' but 'voices'.

I have booked the longest tour, which leads off the wider track with its lengths of boardwalk and along the 'wild path', for which we need special permission. At once our progress becomes slower and more awkward. We push through dense sapling growth and go carefully through spiked obstacle courses; where fallen trunks have blocked the path she goes under and I go over. The oak, lime and hornbeam darken into alder swamps, and here, more than anywhere else, I feel the forest's age. New trees are sprouting from islets formed from ancient stumps, land masses of leaf decay, a rich, creative rot. The surface of the water is marbled with sludgy bands that look like slicks of chemicals, but are, Joanna says, the drifted pollen of lime trees. In all but the coolness of the air it might be a tropical jungle.

Again and again my attention is drawn less to the living

trees than to the decomposing wrecks that moulder all around them. The textures and consistencies of rotting wood are wildly varied, from chitinous walls of gleaming black, webbed with residues of slime, to spongy flakes and dry crumbs indistinguishable from soil. Later I will look up the process by which one becomes the other. Funguses with ghoulish names like wet rot fungus and jelly rot fungus feed off the lignin and cellulose of which wood is comprised; as their webs of hyphae spread, they create honeycombed labyrinths that provide further access to moisture, bacteria and insects. The hatching larvae of burrowing beetles create layered galleries, allowing more species in: woodlice, millipedes, slugs, snails, wood wasps, springtails and earthworms that mine the rotten seams, dying and decomposing in turn, adding sediment to sediment.

Depending on the type of tree, a fallen trunk can take anything from several decades to several hundred years to be broken down, during which time it is home, and food, to multiple generations. Eventually, when its physical mass has entirely disappeared, it can be said to no longer exist; but its components do, in innumerable other lifeforms.

The forest does subversive things to conceptions of life and death. We tell ourselves that these states are opposites and absolutes, separated by a line that there is no crossing back from. But here that line is indistinct. The living support the dead, suspending them above the ground and prolonging their decomposition by holding them clear from microbes and bacteria in the soil. The dead support the living, as their nutrients, released, allow new life to grow. Elements are dispersed from one species to the other, a process of redistribution that might as well be called reincarnation. The claim that over fifty per cent of the forest's wood is dead – 'a vast botanical charnel house', to use Schama's phrase – appears somewhat meaningless, as much of what we're walking through is dead and alive at the same time. The dead and the living are constantly in the process of becoming each other.

Civilisation's ancient fear of what the forest represents – the dark, mysterious, tangled woods beyond the village in a fairy tale – surely has its roots in this. As well as being a refuge for the stubbornly uncivilised, a forest is a reminder of death, a living *memento mori*.

'This is a house of many species,' Joanna says as she examines one riddled, teeming bough.

There are more microbes in a handful of forest soil than there are people on the planet.

The tour is over halfway through. On the reedy banks of the Narewka River, the point from which we will loop back, we catch the iridescent dart of a diving kingfisher and the struggling silver fish caught in its beak. Joanna's camera whirrs. She offers to send me the photographs but they don't feel important. More than individual sights – the focused images of birds that she has been collecting, beautiful though they are – what I want is something else, a feeling that I can't quite name. We leave the river behind and too quickly the wild path merges back with the main track. I feel a twinge of frustration, even of desperation. I have only seen – can only see – the smallest portion of this verdant, dying mass, which stretches on, unknowable, to the north and the east; and further back, into the ultimate outland of the distant past.

We stop to eat some lunch near a hornbeam covered with epiphytes, the mosses, ferns and lichens that grow directly from its bark, making me think of the oak limbs of Wistman's Wood on Dartmoor, another – infinitely smaller – scrap of temperate jungle. On the ground lies the ghost-shape of a lime that rotted and disappeared forty or fifty years ago, in the acidic shadow of which wild garlic still doesn't grow.

Joanna identifies the acrid, pungent scat of wolves. 'Three days old,' she says.

We are almost back at the entrance gate. Another guide passes with another paying customer. They are laughing about something and give us cheerful waves. Before we reach the gate, however, is a monument to another kind of death: two wooden crosses that mark the site of a massacre. In the Second World War, German soldiers brought two hundred local people here, gunned them down and shovelled their bodies into a mass grave. Such collective punishment for the actions of partisans, who used the forest as a hiding place, was a common terror strategy; there are reckoned to be thousands of such corpses in Białowieża.

A human body, unembalmed, rots much faster than a tree. Depending on the temperature and the environment in which it is laid, most of it will disappear within a decade. It passes through five main stages – fresh, bloat, active decay, advanced decay and skeletonised – during which it is assailed first by its own bacteria, which start digesting its soft tissues within a couple of days of death, and then by staggered waves of other organisms. Blowflies lay their eggs, maggots hatch and start to feed, rapidly consuming the greater part of the body's mass – and being consumed themselves by predatory beetles, wasps and ants – opening holes in the flesh that provide ingress to other insects, fungus and protozoa, and allowing fluids to seep out. The body stiffens and relaxes, bloats and evacuates, turns from green to purple to black, putrefies and liquefies until only the dense matter of cartilage and bone is left. Eventually this is eaten too. The microbes, maggots, beetles and funguses have done their work, disturbance agents recycling their nutrients into new life, to be distributed through cell-thick networks of mycelium. Those bodies are part of the forest now, encoded in its pattern.

The nitrogen, phosphorus, magnesium and potassium that

are released alter the chemistry of the surrounding soil for years. I think of the death-shadow of that lime, where the wild garlic doesn't grow.

The granite memorial at this site, with its graven Polish words, will endure for a couple of centuries, perhaps. But the crosses are simple sticks with the mossy bark still on them. It seems appropriate that they will also rot, in time, becoming one – becoming many – with this living dead wood.

~

The following morning I am poised to cross a different border.

In my hand is a visa-free document with two antithetical coats of arms: one is pure feudalism and the other pure communism. The former depicts a stag and a bison standing on their hind legs ('rampant' in heraldic terminology) on either side of a spreading oak tree and a shield that bears a crown, two pairs of crossed hunting horns and the profile of another bison ('passant'). The latter shows a red star and garlands of wheat around a globe, the rays of a rising sun proclaiming a bright socialist dawn. This unlikely pairing combines the symbols of Belovezhskaya Pushcha National Park – the Belarusian part of the forest – alongside the crest of the Republic of Belarus.

The crossing point ahead of me, at Pererov, is one of the few places where the country can be entered without a visa, and only by walkers and cyclists ('Entries by car break the low'). It is forbidden to cross the border with more than three litres of alcohol or two hundred units of 'smokables', cultural valuables, or books or newspapers intended for sale. Also prohibited at the checkpoint are photography, videography, making phone calls and, revealingly, 'Leaving money in the documents presented for checking'. If anything goes wrong, the tourist office that handled my paperwork has provided the address of the British Embassy on Karl Marx Street, Minsk.

Last night in Marcin's guest-house, another bottle of kvass at hand, I did some disconcerting internet research. The country I am entering is a relic of Stalinism where the KGB never changed its name, and has the lowest Democracy Index rating on the continent. Ruled since 1994 by Alexander Lukashenko, a strongman in the old mould – propped up by the usual cult of personality – the state tolerates no opposition and is the last place in Europe with the death penalty; executions are carried out by a bullet to the back of the head. Looking for information on attitudes towards forestry, I learned that in 2012, angered by delays to upgrades and reforms, Lukashenko banned employees of state-managed conifer plantations from resigning, or retiring, until their targets had been met. Thousands of workers, though salaried, were effectively enslaved, forbidden from quitting or changing their jobs without governmental permission.

What is equally disconcerting is that, for primeval Białowieża, totalitarian rule has proven kinder than democracy. The forest on 'the other side', as I have heard it called, is wilder, freer, more biodiverse, much of it an effective extension of the Polish side's Strict Reserve. No doubt this is more to do with its function as a buffer against the capitalist west than any special regard for ecology, but geopolitics – the forest's chance position wedged between empires and rival spheres of influence – has always been a factor in Białowieża's preservation. As in the Korean Demilitarised Zone or the border between north and south Cyprus, some of the world's richest ecosystems survive between closed borders.

The origins of the country's name are more apparent in its older form, Byelorussia: *Byelo* means 'white'. Historically, White Russia referred to the parts of this region colonised by Christianised Slavs, as opposed to Black Ruthenia, populated by pagan Balts. At the height of their power the tsars in Moscow styled themselves as the Tsars of All the Russias: Great (what we now call Russia), Little (Ukraine) and White (Belarus).

A few days ago, I borrowed a bicycle from the forest defenders' house to get some rubles from the bank at Hajnówka. It wasn't possible, I discovered; I could only change my zlotys to euros, and euros to rubles once I had crossed over. The bank teller, a cynical woman with one eyebrow archly raised, brushed aside my attempts at Polish. 'So you go to Russia?'

'Belarus.'

'Same thing.'

'Have you been?'

'I have been.'

'What's it like?'

Her response was what I recognised as a very Polish expression: a look of unimpressed amusement, the equivalent of a facial shrug. 'Nothing special. Same, like here.'

It is not the same like here.

On the Polish side a relaxed young man in a green shirt casually waves me through. I walk towards the barrier, assuming that's where I'm meant to go – the green and red Belarusian flag, with its white-patterned border, is visible there – and a soldier who looks like a teenager runs forward in alarm. With a look of shocked astonishment he motions me back towards Poland again. Behind another window I find the Belarusian counterpart of the laid-back man in green: a grave, unsmiling officer in an olive uniform with hard blue eyes and stars of rank on his epaulettes. After checking my documents with exaggerated disapproval, he disappears from behind the glass and comes round to search my bag. For this procedure he has donned an impressively large hat, and – leaving nothing to chance – handcuffs, a baton and a leather-holstered handgun. He takes my rucksack apart methodically, spreading its items across the floor, unwrapping, unfolding and unzipping, and spends the longest time staring at the cover of my Olga Tokarczuk novel, finally handing it back to me with obvious reluctance. Then comes a full body scan with a metal detector. He checks my documents once again, as if they might have somehow changed, and only then does he gesture me back to the barrier.

There is plenty of space to walk around but the barrier is formally raised, its slowness adding an air of improbable gravitas. Between two barbed-wire fences lies a stretch of no-man's-land. It is not just no man's land but no tree's land, no animal's land; a devastated corridor has been clear-cut through the woods, a boulevard-wide strip shorn of foliage. Aware of the armed boy watching me, I glance left and right as casually as I can; it runs in both directions for as far as I can see. The forest has been sliced in two. This free-fire zone was carved by the Soviets, for whom – Schama's words once again – 'forestry was a branch of state security'.

The detail I find sinister is the fact that the strip is covered in neatly raked sand, as on a hotel's private beach, so that it is impossible to cross without leaving footprints.

Once past the second barbed-wire fence I am summoned to a hut that sells souvenirs: carved wooden bison, bisongrass vodka, fridge magnets with bison on them. Here, a woman whose position of authority is unclear to me rifles through my documents once again, spending even longer at it than the uniformed officer. She stamps various bits of paper and requires my signature here and there. Is there a place to change money? I mime. 'Niet.' She shakes her head. The nearest bank is twenty kilometres away in Kamenuki.

That will take me about four hours at a steady walking pace. The first place I pass is a military base that looks like an underfunded school. As I enter the forest down an unmarked road a khaki truck overtakes, from under the canvas hood of which stare the faces of young soldiers in blue and white striped vests, guns resting on their knees. Over the next hour others follow in the same direction with similar faces gazing out, interspersed with the smaller blue vans of the border police. There is no civilian traffic. Whenever I hear an engine coming I put away my notebook.

It takes me a moment to work out why the forest seems altogether blacker: there is a denser concentration of spruce, Scots pine and other evergreen trees, which haven't been cut back from the road – no 'public safety' felling here – but crowd right to the edge of the tarmac, glooming it with their shade. Between the trunks is a needled floor and the gleam of fly agaric. Did the spruce bark beetles, those subversives, not get past the border checks? Or is the forest playing up to its Russian associations?

Some miles east of here, as unlikely as it seems, lies the grotto of Ded Moroz, the East Slavic Father Christmas. His name means Grandfather Frost, and in his long embroidered furs, travelling not by reindeer sleigh but by horse-drawn troika, he is accompanied by his granddaughter Snegurochka, Snow Maiden. Both of these characters can be met, year-round, for the price of an entrance ticket, but it would add hours to my walk; plus, I have no money. Instead I continue south past the unexpected Lake Liadskoe – a dazzling widening of space, fringed by beds of reeds as yellow as the wheat on the communist coat of arms – and back into dark woods through a hamlet called Laskie.

Beneath an observation tower taller than the canopy (what are they looking for, exactly? Polish troops? Americans? NATO or the EU?) is a street of pleasant dachas, wood-framed country bungalows. Each has its shaded stoop and its rows of vegetables. At last I see people who are not military personnel, old women in headscarves and old men in baseball caps, stooping at their plots of land. A smile, a raised hand.

The road leads past alder trees with their roots sunk in pollen-clogged pools. The faces of frogs arise and submerge through the sediment and mating balls of brown toads grapple under dank leaves, two or three males clutching at a larger female. The calls of unseen birds are muted, deadened by the pines. The *puszcza* – or *pushcha* – on this side of the border feels like a door that has been softly but firmly closed, impenetrable in a way the other side was not.

I find myself taking care to walk more quietly, my footsteps placed deliberately, as if across a carpet.

Kamenuki is preceded by an open-air reserve whose perimeter I skirt, glancing into the nearest enclosures. If I chose to I could see bison and wolves here, but the sight of two brown bears makes me turn away. The cages are concrete-floored, covered in shit and flies, each with a shredded tyre hanging from a length of chain. Their inmates, shuffling in circles, are traumatised and insane. There have been no wild bears in Białowieża since the late 1800s, and keeping them here – inside the forest, yet utterly apart from it – seems worse than simply shooting them. I walk on, upset, into further incongruities.

There is a resort hotel and signs for tourist walking trails next to a statue of a stern, unsmiling worker, all chiselled cheekbones and piercing eyes, doing something heroic with what I take to be a bullet-making machine. Utilitarian tenement blocks sit next to cottages. Sleek, expensive-looking cars share the road with horse-drawn carts driven by men in rubber boots and women in shawls, loaded with sacks of grain. Schoolchildren with hoes and spades are returning from a work expedition, laughing and squabbling, past the multiple cupolas of an Orthodox church that sprout as profusely as mushrooms from a rotten log. The sunlight seems much hotter here, its glare befuddling. I turn in circles like the bears. At last I find the bank. I remember '*dengi*', the Russian for 'money', which turns out to be unnecessary – why else would anyone come to a bank? – and the blonde woman at the desk counts out the banknotes carefully, performing the operation twice, like the big-hatted customs official.

But I do not stay in Kamenuki long; after days in the woods the immersion is too much. With a pocket full of rubles, culture-shocked, exhilarated, I follow the nearest walking trail back into the forest. There are nods towards tourism – signs for the lair of Grandfather Frost, a carved, smiling wooden bear in the hollow of a riven oak – but they disappear as I gain distance from the road. A meadow abuts an alder swamp, and here a berm of raised earth leads past wetlands into pines, and offers a view of meadows from the concealment of the trees. It looks like the kind of open space where bison might come at dawn. Two great oaks have fallen here, one on top of the other, forming a protective chevron enclosing a hollow space that is hidden on three sides, a bed of leaves and loam. Tentatively I lie down and spend some minutes listening, trying to gain a sense of whether I am welcome here. Nothing tells me I am not. The birdsong, which stilled as my appearance punched a hole in it, has filled back in again, a pattern recompleting. The border, with its shaved strip and its trucks of conscript soldiers, feels comfortably far away.

By sleeping here perhaps I am hoping to cross another border.

After clearing sticks and debris I prepare my nest – a sleeping mat inside a sleeping bag inside a bivvy bag – and lay branches overhead to make a flimsy ceiling. The ceiling is psychological; it would do nothing against the rain. But tonight there is more chance, I think, of wolves than rain. I am not exactly scared of them, as I am not exactly scared of the soldiers, but the knowledge that both are out there, prowling on their separate beats, sharpens the edges of everything, makes the sunlight lighter and the darkness darker.

Tonight will be a pink moon and already the clear sky is growing gently luminous, a tide before full swell.

At dusk the birdsong lulls, as if the forest and everything in it is taking a steadying breath, before a final upsurge as the last of the daylight leaks away: a cascading architecture of indescribably complex sound that assembles, deconstructs and then abruptly stops. The weird bubble of the moon is bulging up between the trees – not quite pink and not quite white, the colour of a tired eye – and the birds seem overcome. It gains height so rapidly I can see the shadows move.

In the absence of the birds another register begins: the exploratory padding of small beasts in the undergrowth, an origami rustling among the dry leaves. The pattering is everywhere and nowhere, as generalised as rain. By concentrating my attention on one movement at a time I attempt to peel back the dark, to bring forth an image of the creature behind each noise, but the pictures do not form. My ears are out of focus. Faraway things sound close and small things sound extremely large; beetles trundling in the leaves take on the imaginary proportions of wildwood monsters. As I go to hang my food a respectable distance from my camp, my boot lands on a brittle branch that cracks like a gunshot. At once there is an answering *crack* from somewhere not far away. I hold my breath, listening; my silence feels mirrored. Whatever it was that made that noise is standing stock-still, as I am, waiting for me to move again. I know that it is watching me but I cannot watch it back.

I take another step. Nothing. Then another step. *Crash*: the thing is galloping in a wide circumference around me, bounding in the dark, horribly loud and then distant and then gone. In my hand is a lump of wood, brandished uselessly. That phrase again: landscape of fear. Slowly I breathe out.

In my rucksack is a small bottle of expensive whisky, bought as a gift for the activists before I knew the house was dry. I offer some now to the forest, glugging it on rotten wood, and then I offer some to myself. I walk to the end of a fallen oak and hang my food high in its roots. There is crashing everywhere, at different increments of scale. Wired and totally awake, I watch the progress of the moon. Then I raise my head from the ground and it is morning.

I have no memory of sleep, or even of settling down. The pink moon has departed, the wolves and the bison did not come. The secret border of the night did not let me in.

~

Back in Kamenuki, opposite the statue of the hero of socialist labour, is a diner catering to visitors to the national park. Its decor surely has not changed in forty years – heavy browns, plastic tables, lace curtains in the windows – and the menu gives the weight of everything in grams. Having walked out of the woods I order cold pickled mushrooms, fried potatoes, eggs, fruit soup and a glass of cool fruit compote. Then, with these cheap and nourishing grams of food inside me, I take the road that leads west from the Orthodox church.

My visa-free document gives me a total of three days here, which must be spent within this sylvan border zone; I am forbidden from leaving tree cover, as if the primeval forest does not count as Belarus but rather a kind of make-believe realm where foreigners are harmless. For the next two nights I am booked at a guest-house in a smaller village – Belaya, another name suggesting 'white' – tucked close to the border four or five miles away. The walk there leads past sagging dachas painted yellow, blue and green, three-barred crosses draped with traditional scarves and gaudy plastic flowers, gardens of foaming pink and white cherry blossom. A path away from the road leads through acres of Scots pines that are clearly deeply old, the trees twisted, with red flaking limbs, the ground between them buried in moss. For a moment I am back in Rothiemurchus Forest. Then there is a little river and a sign: БЕЛАЯ. The village seems deserted apart from the place where I am staying, a ramshackle smallholding in which every resident creature stands out with the totemic clarity of a dream: the black puppy, the honey-coloured dog, the ginger cat, the ginger and white cat, the white geese with their orange beaks, the creamy brown clucking hens, the pair of white storks in their absurd, cartoonish nest. And Natalya with her pale blue eyes, chapped red face and straw-coloured hair, in a green headscarf and red shoes, carrying eggs in a bucket.

She seems delighted, if slightly confused, to have me here as a guest. Few people come, I gather, and even fewer foreigners. Miming our way through the introductions and the elaborate paperwork – a byzantine bureaucracy of forms, stamps and signatures – we spend an hour at the kitchen table drinking tea brewed from forest leaves; occasionally she departs and reappears with another plate of blini, tiny pancakes smothered with sour cream and jam. She speaks no English, so at first we are mutually tongue-tied. But something is happening that I did not anticipate. Asking where something is, the Russian word *gde*, 'where', speaks itself from my mouth without my having told it to. Asking what something costs, *skolko?*, 'how much?' appears. The blini are *ochen vkusno*, 'very tasty'; the garden is *krasivyy*, 'beautiful'; and the *sobaka*, 'dog', is whimpering outside the door. The Russian that I learned in school – choosing it over French or German largely due to a teenage fixation with communism – is miraculously springing back, a language that I have not spoken, or even thought about, for twenty years. The process is spontaneous; I remember each word and phrase in the act of saying it. Buried by subsequent sediment, the language has only needed the right conditions to sprout again, like a spruce cone in damp soil or a birch seed on cleared land. Of course the grammar has rotted away but the nouns and adjectives are lying there intact, just waiting for me to pick them up. The words with their rounded corners, hard angles and blunted edges are things that I can touch and hold, familiar ergonomic forms. The act of recollection is more muscular than mental.

In my room – walled in wood, furnished in wood and smelling of wood – I sit with a view of green-budded trees and spend the afternoon making lists of everything I can remember. Each word seeds the next. It feels miraculous. I can hardly string a sentence together, let alone have a conversation, but Russian feels primally familiar in the same way the forest does.

'Primally familiar' is the expression of the journalist Alan Weisman, who used Białowieża as a test case in *The World Without Us*. The book is a series of thought experiments, based on studies of biology, archaeology and physical science, that chart what might happen to the planet's natural and built environments a week, a year, ten years, a hundred years, a thousand years, a million years, a billion years after humans disappear (it is not important how or why), leaving our infrastructure behind. What is most striking – or most reassuring – is how rapidly nature returns to fill the spaces that humans vacate: mere weeks for weeds to sprout, months for roads to become rivers, years for prising roots to break apart concrete. Five hundred years without humans would be enough to return northern Europe to its original wilderness, the expanded *puszcza* burying most traces of cities and industry as the jungles of Guatemala, Belize and the Yucatan have tracelessly absorbed the civilisation of the Mayans.

In Białowieża, Weisman saw a vision not just of the past but of a post-human future in which the forest reclaims its range, like a returning memory:

It is startling to think that all Europe once looked like this Puszcza. Seeing elders with trunks seven feet wide, or walking through stands of the tallest trees here – gigantic Norway spruce, shaggy as Methuselah – should seem as exotic as the Amazon or Antarctica to someone raised among the comparatively puny, second-growth woodlands found throughout the Northern Hemisphere. Instead, what's astonishing is how primally familiar it feels. And, on some cellular level, how complete.

That unexpected sense of completion marks the forest and the language both. In this cabin in the woods in a Stalinist state, I start to have the strangest feeling of returning home.

'*Severu niet*,' says Natalya the next morning, shaking her head emphatically. I have asked where I can walk and her answer is clear: 'Not north.' The border runs close behind the village and approaching it is forbidden. '*Soldaty*,' 'soldiers', she says, making a gun with her fingers. Standing in this garden with its fruit trees and its covered well, the puppy fooling around my feet, the prohibition gives the place the malevolence of a fairy tale: danger lurks beyond the trees; do not take the northern track. Instead I should travel east, where Ded Moroz and Snegurochka wait in a permanent Christmas.

But I can't resist it: I go north, ready to turn back at any time. The road has a sense of abandonment, its tyre-tracks filled with moss, blocked by fallen trees that no one has bothered removing. A young deer strolls ahead of me, glancing back occasionally, before dematerialising in the verticals of shade. The woods have a silent, watchful feel. I place each footstep gently. It is like a scene from Weisman's book – the border abandoned, the road overgrown, the barbed wire rusted away or absorbed into the boles of trees – but after a mile the route ends at a fence and a locked gate, beyond which lies the aesthetic shock of that raked, denuded strip.

The EU lies on the other side, close but impossibly far away. For the first time it occurs to me that forest species are divided by this border as much as humans are. Bison, being larger than anything else, are the worst affected. 'An iron curtain bisects this paradise', writes Weisman of the barricade. 'Although wolves dig under it, and roe deer and elk are believed to leap it, the herd of these largest of Europe's mammals remains divided, and with it, its gene pool – divided and mortally diminished, some biologists fear.' Having survived centuries of hunting, poachers and starving German troops, the greatest long-term threat to the bison is a frozen conflict that ended everywhere else in Europe with the fall of the Berlin Wall.

There are no *soldaty* in sight. I spend some time considering the different barbed-wire fencing styles of the Belarusian and Polish states – on this side the posts have crosspieces, like the extra bars on an Orthodox crucifix – before spotting the security camera, like a trap for wolves. I step back into the shade and vanish like the deer.

Two hours later I am east again, back where I am supposed to be, following signs towards Tsarskoe Polyana, the Tsar's Glade. The road is less militarised on the other side of Kamenuki; occasional battered Ladas pass, along with flashier cars, and once a group of cycling girls who look like they're on holiday, singing something very tender in Belarusian or Russian. The glade is a clearing in the oaks that is rumoured to be the feasting place of the last Polish-Lithuanian monarch Stanisław II Augustus – excoriated by many Poles for failing to stand against Russian invasion – and later where triumphant tsars came to celebrate their hunts. A display of black and white photographs shows officers in fur hats and greatcoats, and a few stiff noblewomen in matronly attire, posing with that day's kill: the soggy pelts of wolves and deer, carpets of slaughtered boar, antlers heaped in untidy stacks like kindling.

In one picture stand no fewer than forty-six men, lavishly moustached and grave, around the corpse of a single dead bison, like observers at a traffic accident.

How many of these gentlemen, so solemn in their power, were to be mown down themselves on the Eastern Front a few years later? When they saw the bodies piling up, did they think back to the carefree slaughters of this glade?

Trudging home towards Belaya, I come upon another place where history insinuates itself: a place of alders and standing water called Tatarskoe Bagno, Tatars' Marsh. Gently infringing Belarusian law for the second time this day, I step off the road and into the morass. Between pollen-scudded pools, rotten wood gives beneath my boots with a soft, collapsing crunch, as if I were stepping on old bone. I walk an archipelago of matted, spongy humps. Forms grow indistinct and hard lines soften and blur together, composting into the mass. Borders lose their integrity, one thing moulds into another. There is a permanent twilight here, in this patch of temperate jungle.

This is where, in the thirteenth century, when the marsh was much larger than it is today, the Tatars are said to have watered their horses during campaigns into the west. Nomads from the expanse of the Eurasian Steppe, picking their way through a tangled forest that must have been totally alien to them, emerging on the other side – into the cleared land beyond – to fall upon the villages of settled Germans, Slavs and Balts; I can picture them here in their felts and furs, mounted on sturdy ponies. The folk memory of the terror of their swift, deadly raids permeated Christendom, a clear sign of God's displeasure, the last in a series of nomad invasions that stretched back many centuries. An indefinable sense of sadness lingers in this gloomy place. The Tatars have gone from these trees and only the marsh remains.

A similar sense of sadness arrives when I say goodbye to

Natalya. It is the following morning, and my right to be in Belarus expires at the end of the day. The animals gather around my feet – the black puppy, the honey-coloured dog, the ginger cat, the ginger and white cat, the white geese, the brown hens, though not the condescending storks – as I muster my last Russian words: *Do svidaniya*, 'goodbye'; *spasibo bolshoye*, 'thank you'. Natalya gives me hardboiled eggs and small, sour apples for the walk and waves me off from the gate. As I go I feel that I am leaving someone else's past.

Halfway back to the border, some sixth sense makes me turn my head. A few seconds later there is a crack, and I watch the top two-thirds of a spruce detach and plummet, in what seems like slow motion, to the earth not far away. The aftershock spreads through the woods; a silence, then an uproar of birds. The top of the trunk is a splintered spike. There is not a breath of wind, no clue as to why this has occurred; perhaps an early warning sign that the bark beetles have breached the frontier? Immediately afterwards a khaki truck rolls past, the visage of a pink-tongued Alsatian framed between conscripts' shaven heads. The two events feel obscurely connected. Nothing else happens for miles.

On the final, foot-weary stretch I follow the old Tsar's Road, marked intermittently with stanchions displaying the double-headed eagle of the Romanovs and the letter A, presumably for Alexander. More remnants of a feudal past as vanished as the Tatars. The barrier appears; the sandy strip; another nervous teenager. A different officer in a different hat takes my belongings apart, performing a minute dissection on the customs office floor, and leaves me to put it back together again after – more cheerfully than the first – waving me through the gate. I pass from the land of blinis back to the land of pierogis.

The forest seems gentler, less watchful on the Polish side. It occurs to me that, in the last few days, the trees have burst into leaf. The canopy pulses with chlorophyll green from east to west.

~

I walk for a long time parallel to the borderline. I walk until the greenness fades and everything shades to grey. At dusk, a little way off the path, comes a clearing with a hunting hide – a wooden shed on stilt legs with a ladder leading up – and from its slatted window I watch the forest sink into night. Roe deer graze below, glancing up misgivingly. After dark a large black something paws noisily at the ground, raking through dry sticks and leaves, and my torch-flash reveals only startled amber eyes before it sprints away. Later there are piercing shrieks. I lie on the wooden floor through the cold, clear night, my deep sleep interspersed with wide-eyed wakefulness. Morning reveals a large hole scratched in the earth below.

I walk west again, then north. Green-gold sunlight fills the leaves, what is termed in German *Maienschein*, the 'May-shine' of early spring, almost sweet enough to taste. The flickering barcode of the trees endlessly scanning past, some thicker, some thinner, some nearer, some further, is an unreadable algorithm. I am lost inside its pattern. At midday I stop for crumbled bread, cucumber and cheese, a few swallows of Belarusian kvass, and continue walking.

The forest opens to reveal fragments and suggestions. Here, between two brooding oaks, is a wooden cross with a plaque in Cyrillic letters, which I laboriously translate: 'Here lie unknown village people of Belavecha that died in 1710 from the terrible disease.' Nothing else, no other clue. And there, ahead of me on the path, miles from any house or village, appears a cat that looks domestic until I get close to it and see its matted hair and expression of spitting malevolence; no longer domestic, not quite wild, but feral, self-rewilded. It bounds into the undergrowth with a look of pure hatred for me.

Following a subtle path no more than a footstep wide, I come suddenly upon the ghost of a railway line. Narrow gauge, long disused: the remains, I presume, of the track laid down by the Germans in the First World War, during which time they sent trainloads of timber west to the Fatherland, reducing the forest by five per cent of its former area (the Polish government seemingly tried to emulate the occupiers by doing much the same exactly a century later). Then, further down the track, is something lounging in the shade: the elemental wedge of a head, a massive body at rest. Bison. I am seeing a bison. Holding my breath, I approach. The bison becomes a rock and then becomes a bison again. With every step I change my mind. Bison. Rock. Bison. Rock. Another step. Rock. Rock. The transubstantiation stops.

But, as if in compensation, something is approaching me: a chocolate-brown flowing shape, the lithe body of a pine marten, so absorbed in its private business that it pours itself right up to me. Again I hold my breath. It almost bumps into my boot. Then it looks up, leaps in shock and vanishes in seconds. Tree. Human. Tree. Human. *Human! Human!*

By the end of the day I am standing in another sacred grove.

Unlike Stara Białowieża, with its iconic oaks-as-kings, Miejsce Mocy appears on few maps and requires no entrance fee. A dirt path snakes off the road, past bins and picnic tables. At first glance the site is underwhelming, a patch of bare earth dominated by an oversized wooden observation deck, a kind of New Age hunting hide for spiritual energy. Here and there moss-covered boulders give the vague impression of a stone circle, if I squint at them hard enough, and in another place people have pushed coins into the cracks of a carved oaken post as good luck charms or offerings. Signs in

Polish and English – sponsored by Żubr (Bison) beer – give some background information: it is believed that this was once a place of worship for the ancient Slavs, where initiates gathered to 'fend off foes and evil powers'. Positive radiation apparently rises from the earth in the form of 'subtle vibration' that is supposed to restore vigour and reinforce intuition. 'Responsive people who stand at a proper spot may feel a whole gamut of subtle vibrations, from those purifying the mind and fully relaxing to those shaking one's balance and causing some dizziness. The arrangement of the stones itself can prevent particularly responsive people from entering inside.'

The circle of stones, disappointingly, admits me without the least resistance. I stand inside, attempting to feel something, but all I feel is warmth from the sunlight, tiredness from the long walk. I close my eyes and wait. Nothing. Not even the subtlest vibration.

But when I open them again, my eyes have refocused.

There is something unusual about the trees beyond the boundary of the stones. The nearest oak has four – no, five – separate trunks shooting up from a single massive bole. Its neighbour has three or four. Turning inside the circle I see another, then another, which at first seem to be the result of very ancient coppicing; but the bifurcations and trifurcations appear to occur naturally, not man-made but mutated, as if the vigour of their growth cannot help but overspill. Narrow paths criss-cross the grove, and leaving the circle to follow them I come across increasingly bizarre and multifarious forms. These trunks, rather than the stones, are suggestive of strange energies; has positive radiation caused these thrusts and forkings?

Around one towering double-trunked spruce, two whole trees growing out of one, I discover seven china plates arranged in a circle. Each plate holds an offering: moss, bark, an oak leaf, a spruce cone, a handful of soil, a single boiled sweet and a guttered candle.

Miejsce Mocy means 'Place of Power'. But its former name, according to the sign, is Devil's Swamp.

The ancient Slavic universe was conceived of as an enormous oak whose branches stretched to heaven and whose roots reached into the underworld, with the mortal realm as its bole; like ants, humans lived their lives in the fissures of its bark. At its top sat Perun, god of the sky, fertility, thunderstorms, metal and war, associated with the axe, whose body took the form of an eagle perched in its uppermost branches. Around its roots was twined Veles, whose body took the form of a snake, god of the underworld. The two were always fighting.

Veles crept up from the earth to steal the cattle of Perun, slipping in and out of shadows, friendly with the darkness. Perun chased him away with dazzling bolts of lightning that made the world as bright as day, but he could never catch him. Dry weather was the victory of Veles, rain the victory of Perun, and thunderstorms were battles in the eternal war between them. If lightning hit the earth near you it was probably good luck.

As oak was sacred to Perun, willow was sacred to Veles, and in many ways the trees and their gods acted as opposites. Perhaps it was not so much a war as a cosmic balancing. The cool, damp-loving willow contrasted with the dryness of oak, the earth with the sky, down with up, night with day, dark with light; and, ultimately, death with life.

It takes all of these elements to make a forest.

As Europe's wildwood was cut back, that balance became skewed. Christianity, a desert religion centred on the worship of light, flourished in the cleared land while the tree gods of the pagan Slavs – along with their Germanic, Baltic and Scandinavian counterparts – retreated, in the way of the bison, into the shadowed darkness. The ancient deities of the trees were turned into folk-tale imps and sprites. The forest became sinister, its Places of Power now Devil's Swamps.

Axe and fire: their destructive qualities had been associated with Perun, god of metal and lightning. Now they were used, ironically, to fell the groves that embodied him. There is something more complex, though, about the shift from dark to light. Like the dappling of sunlight and shade on the forest floor, or the layered interplay between the living and the dead, the process was less a clean slate than an entanglement.

Although in many places the pagan gods were simply destroyed – in the Principality of Kiev, the wooden idol of Perun was dragged behind horses, thrashed with sticks and then tossed into the Dnieper River – there was inevitable overlap between the new faith and the old. Post-Christian depictions of Perun showed him as a figure on horseback killing a serpent with a lance, an image almost identical to that of St George and the dragon, or the Archangel Michael impaling a snakelike Satan. As with the Norse god Thor, the Greek Zeus, the Roman Jupiter and other Indo-European sky-father deities, the Christian myth was overlaid on the pre-existing heathen one; the sky god did not so much replace Perun as grow into him, as the limbs of different trees meet and graft together. Veles, meanwhile – the underworld deity recast in Satanic form – was crudely trampled underfoot and pierced through with metal. Unlike in the old dispensation, he did not creep back again as part of a cosmic balancing. Light had triumphed over darkness, the sky over the earth.

But outside the figure of Christ-Perun, the old gods endured much longer on this wooded fringe of Europe than they did elsewhere. Forest-dwelling tribes of Balts, Finns and West Slavs clung to their ways so obstinately that in 1195 Pope Celestine III launched the first of the Northern Crusades to force them to convert. This series of genocidal invasions was carried out by the Teutonic Order, which – having failed to rout the Muslims from the Holy Land – slaughtered its way northwards through the Livonians, Latgalians, Selonians, Estonians, Curonians, Old Prussians and other tribes who attempted to resist the coming of the light. The last Lithuanians and Poles were converted two centuries later by Władysław II Jagiełło, the king now embodied, Perun-like, in the form of a century oak – deity of metal, war and vigorous fertility – in the other sacred grove I visited in this forest.

But evidently the old beliefs were never uprooted, only cut back. Pagan superstition has proved resilient. A hundred miles north of here is a village called Święta Lipka, Holy Lime, the name of which bears testament to the special reverence for lime trees, which were associated with femininity, protection and rebirth; lime wood is traditionally used for Orthodox icon painting, and shrines to the Virgin Mary are often found in the hollows of limes. As Schama notes, in the nineteenth century pious Christian peasants were still invoking the name of Perkūnas, the Baltic variant of Perun – 'the lord of the thunderclap and the lightning bolt' – for protection during storms. (Hercynia, the Roman name for northern Europe's forest, comes from the same root as Perkūnas: both derive from 'oak'.)

Another survivor of the woodland gods is the figure of the Leszy. This guardian spirit of the forest – his name translates as something like 'Woody' – humanoid, hairy, sometimes horned, often surrounded by wolves and bears, is morally ambiguous, neither evil nor good; he can either lead travellers astray to become hopelessly lost or else guide them safely home. He is an arboreal Fear Liath Mòr, a Big Green Man. The enduring popularity of this small god of place, along with a quiet pantheon of other folk-spirits, has caused religious authorities to bemoan the semi-heathen ways still practised by the forest people into modern times.

Some of them, in this staunchly Catholic country, are still practised today. There may not be sacrificial corpses hung from Miejsce Mocy's oaks, but, as evidenced by the seven china plates beneath that spruce, pilgrims are still coming here – to this quiet Place of Power – to leave offerings to trees.

I decide to spend the night here and hope the Leszy comes.

Further away from the circle of stones is a cluster of wild pear trees. I make my camp between them, in my layers of waterproof bags, and eat the rest of my food and drink the last of my kvass. Once more the forest slides by grey degrees into night. Light fades; birds sing; anonymous rustling begins. Positive radiation, perhaps, seeps from the earth.

With twilight settling I walk back to the stones. In a certain place someone has made a circle within the circle – from moss, bark, leaves and sticks – and I step inside. Is it my imagination or does my skin feel slightly charged? Is there a creaminess to my limbs, like the onset of a high? Or is it only an after-effect of walking, walking, walking? I take off my boots and socks and press my feet against the cool earth. I stand in the darkness with my eyes closed, listening.

~

Augustyn has left the forest defenders' house when I return; he spends the other half of his life working as a tour guide in Kraków. There is no sign of Marianka or Adam, and a man I have not seen before is sitting at the long table working on a laptop and listening to hardcore Polish punk at blistering volume.

In the evening Asia appears, dealing with one of the intermittent crises of the cold war between activists and foresters, the struggle for hearts and minds. The army has just issued a statement claiming that unsafe explosives are stored at a military base within the boundaries of the forest, and the lack of management — the dead wood on the forest floor — has increased the risk of fire; an accidental explosion, they say, could start a conflagration that spreads to Hajnówka. Asia is attempting to compose a response but can barely conceal her scorn. 'Why don't they move the fucking explosives? Always the forest is to blame! The solution? Cut the forest! Get rid of it, it'll be easier. Get rid of the mountains, get rid of the seas, we'll all be safer then . . .'

It is even earlier when I force myself up the next morning, just before 4 a.m. My body attempts resistance. The dawn chorus is an urgent broadcast that I am incapable of understanding, blaring and hollering in praise or imprecation. The air is slightly warmer now; it no longer hurts to breathe it. First I walk to the meadow on the south side of the house and drag binoculars around its hem, seeing nothing but blurry grain. I am not expecting anything so this does not surprise me. Then I cross the garden to the north side of the house and enter the meadow there, following the muddy path that leads towards the Oak of the Defenders of the Forest. I am not really looking any more, just following my feet.

In the middle of the clearing is a brake of rough scrub where white mist pools above a pond. It would be cinematically appropriate, I think, to see a wolf emerging from that mist. Then one does. Scanning the meadow, I suddenly become aware that my vision is flowing at the same speed as a pale shape — white and grey, bounding low, prick-eared, archetypal — as if it has been poured into my consciousness. My whole body becomes alert, somehow fluid, but at the same time the sensation is immensely calm. It does not last long; the shape is almost at the trees. In the space of twenty seconds everything is transformed: 'I have never seen a wolf. I am seeing a wolf. I have seen a wolf.'

Perhaps each of us gets only one, and when it's gone, it's gone.

The meadow, this swathe of open ground, stands as a kind of no-man's-land between the daytime and the night, a border as stark as the sterile strip dividing Poland from Belarus. With that after-image of wolf in mind, I understand the contrast as one of the oldest in human consciousness: the forest our species started in and the plains it adapted to; entanglement and openness; darkness and light. It is only when I am back in the house, gazing at a map, half asleep, that I notice the Polish word for 'clearing' is *polana*. Struck by the similarity of this word to 'Poland', I check the etymology of the country's name.

The mnemonic is hiding in plain sight, a clue to the epic deforestation that changed the face of the continent. 'Poland' derives from an eighth-century Slavic tribe called the Polans, who in turn took their name from *pole*, 'field' or 'cleared land'.

I think of my journey here by train, two days and a thousand miles across the agricultural swathes of the North European Plain. From west to east I have travelled through the Clearing, a name that might as well be applied to the continent itself.

This afternoon, my last in Białowieża, I see bison. Unlike this morning's wolf they are not wild or free. Not without reluctance I have come to the Bison Show Reserve, an hour's walk from Teremiski, a series of large enclosures set within the forest. This is the site from where the herds were re-introduced in the 1930s, where their gene pool is preserved.

Conditions are incomparably better than on the Belarusian side, with spacious, partly wooded enclosures rather than iron cages. There are grazing deer – reds and roes – dozing elk with their oddly amphibious-looking faces, wild boar and wolves, which I glance at once but not again. The wolves are not bounding in the mist but loitering with doggy grins; I am not sure a captive wolf can even be called a wolf. Then there are the rarer breeds, other throwbacks to the past: koniks, semi-feral horses related to the extinct tarpan; and zubron, which are hybrids of bison and domestic cattle. Again I think of Eurassic Park, a sanctuary to populate a lost world. But here the landscape of fear has been replaced by a landscape of boredom.

In the central enclosure stands a bison.

At first I see parts of him rather than the whole. The massive haunch. The matted wool. The upward-curving horns. The chest, absurdly forward-heavy, a sledgehammer of muscle enveloping the squat front legs. The longer, daintier back legs. The earth-churning hooves. He is huffing at the ground, raising dust with his hot breath, a walking anvil of meat. The profile he presents to me is eminently dignified: the patriarch beard, the sloping face, halfway between a thug and an aristocrat.

Behind him, grazing, is a herd of ten or twenty others. My eyes cannot help but see buffalo, which puts me not in a European forest but on American plains, jolted out of place. Then, abruptly, I am jolted out of time as well. It occurs to me in what other context I have seen these thrusting lines: in images of prehistoric cave art from the other side of Europe, most strikingly from Lascaux in the south of France. In ochre red and charcoal black, hematite and manganese, almost six thousand figures crowd the walls of limestone caverns deep beneath the Dordogne: stags, bears, ibex, aurochs, tarpan-like wild horses, lions, birds, rhinoceroses. And bison, exactly like the bison that stand before me now. They were painted in the Upper Paleolithic, twenty thousand years ago. The glaciers had not melted then. This forest had not grown.

These bison are deeply of this continent, deeper even than the trees. That Alan Weisman quote again: *primally familiar.*

Perhaps the archaic English name – wisent – suits them better. A bit like 'wizened', a bit like 'wise', a bit like 'ent', the tree-people inhabiting J.R.R. Tolkien's Middle Earth. Matted root-balls hummocked with moss, their horns a sharp and deadly wood, they are shaggy fragments of the forest come to life.

They are living, breathing Leszys, guardians of the *puszcza*.

An ice-cream-eating family approaches the wire fence. Two little boys in urban camo have brought their plastic guns to pretend to shoot the animals.

The wisents endure.

~

During my time in Białowieża the temperature has jumped ten degrees and dampness has come to the air. New leaves flicker like green flames along every branch. As I walk back towards Hajnówka the hard, clear light has gone and everything is softened and blurred. When I make my last bed in the woods it feels almost tropical; for the first time I have to slap away mosquitoes.

In the morning, pushing through foliage, I almost step on a grey snake that flows like water beneath my boot and slides away into the earth. A farewell from Veles, going back to the underworld.

I am reluctant to face the light but my train is leaving soon. I walk out of the woods and back into the Clearing.

SPAIN'S DESERT

High summer in the south of Spain and the countryside is baked raw, but there are still snow patches on the Sierra Nevada. Up on the unshaded slopes, beneath a sky as hot and blue as a gas flame, they look impossible. Do they have names? I think of the Sphinx in Garbh Choire Mòr, at the other end of the continent, similarly hanging on. In this skewed summer, northern Scotland is almost as hot as Spain.

South, from the window of this train, is less a direction than a colour. The purple lavender fields of Provence and the green of the Pyrenees wore themselves out hours ago, leaving only yellow. Everything looks threadbare, stunned, pounded stupid by the heat, from the fields of wheat and the scabrous hills to the sharp and brittle mountains always somewhere on the horizon. If you ran your finger along that skyline it might draw blood.

A bit deranged from lack of sleep, nursing a very small, very good coffee in a paper cup, I have the disconcerting idea that I am not sliding across the world horizontally but plunging vertically, as if on a rollercoaster in freefall down the side of the globe. South equals down. Down equals heat. All I can do is keep facing forward and clinging on. The trajectory feels out of control. Where will it end? Mad temperatures are on the way, according to the news, and weather warnings are in place across much of the continent. It is the hottest summer since last summer, which was the hottest since the one before; the record statistics come too fast to mean anything these days. But this one has lodged in my mind: the European Satellite Agency has reported that June, as a global average, was the hottest month in recorded history.

July is set to be even hotter.

It doesn't seem like a sensible time to walk into a desert.

I am approaching Almería, in the far south-east of Andalucía, the driest and yellowest corner of this dry and yellow peninsula that lies on the Mediterranean like a discarded piece of toast. 'Andalucía' comes from al-Andalus, the Moorish name for the land they ruled, in ever shrinking and more beleaguered parts, for almost eight hundred years, but a more fanciful theory says it derives from *anda en luz*, 'walk in light'. As I step from the train it is the light, more than the temperature, that shocks me the most, like being caught in a camera flash that does not end. South equals down. Down equals heat. Heat equals light. Stunned by the glare, I armour my eyes in UV lenses and make for the shade.

~

Half an hour later I'm being driven through a sea.

At the wheel is a white-goateed Englishman in a bright tropical shirt. He has a gentle, attentive face and a look of benign curiosity. 'I'm interested in everything,' he tells me early on. His name is Kevin Borman and he is a travel writer – 'The Bill Bryson of Almería', it says on the jacket of one of his books – and he has invited me to spend a few days at his home. He points out arid-loving shrubs and trees whose names I did not know, birds I would never have noticed, and the debris of collapsed and abandoned human infrastructure: ruined farms and irrigation systems, the rubble of a nineteenth-century pigeon loft by the side of the road. He indicates a gap between hills: 'There are hundreds of garnets lying around up there.' But the most impressive sight is the synthetic sprawl through which we pass for minutes on end, a vista of reflective whiteness stretching on and on.

They call it the Mar de Plástico, the Plastic Sea.

The *plásticos* are polytunnels constructed by agribusinesses that range from family-run concerns to multinationals such as Monsanto. They cover – literally cover – around 150 square miles of this coastal plain, an area so large that it can be seen, like the Great Wall of China, from outer space. Despite their total dominance of the land as far as we can see, they are not considered permanent structures, so their growth is unrestricted. Under that level polythene ceiling there is no soil; the produce is grown in bags and drip-fed with fertilisers, pesticides and herbicides, the distribution of which is controlled by computers. The temperature can reach as high as forty-five degrees Celsius, which allows multiple harvests a year. Together they produce over two million tonnes of fruit and vegetables annually, over half of the produce that is sold in Europe.

The outer layers appear to be abandoned or unprofitable; glimpses through shredded plastic walls reveal heaps of desiccated plant matter, fibrous and grey, that wilted as soon as some manager's hand switched off an unseen tap. What we can't see from the road are the people who work further in: a precarious labour force of 100,000 migrant workers, mostly North and Sub-Saharan Africans, who sweat for thirty-five euros a day in conditions like a sauna so that people in colder climates can eat strawberries in December. Accommodation is in slums on the outskirts of nearby towns, or in shacks they have built themselves, and many workers suffer from health problems caused by exposure to chemicals. The supply chain that ends in the freshly picked, luxurious aisles of supermarkets starts here, far from the eyes of consumers. The *plásticos* have a dual function: to heat and to hide.

Further along the coast, says Kevin, is the Central Térmica, one of the worst-polluting coal-fired power stations in Europe. This baked periphery is a place of dirty secrets.

We reach the end of the Plastic Sea and wind upward into hills. The landscape is bare and bright, polarised by the glare. A steep road brings us to La Rondeña, the hamlet of scattered houses in which Kevin and his wife Troy have built their home. The car's engine splutters out and again I step into the light, which shocks me less this time.

The house is on a hill with a cliff rising up behind it almost to roof level on one side, so that it feels concealed and exposed at the same time. It has a small square tower with a terracotta-tiled roof, which gives it a faintly Roman look, white rendered walls and a shaded terrace. The wind blows right through it. When they arrived, there was only a four-roomed house on a gritty, treeless mound. Over the last fourteen years they have coaxed a paradise from the barren ground.

Troy – perspicacious, bright, in a colourful flowing dress – shows me around the garden later that afternoon. Its fruitfulness is the opposite to that of the Plastic Sea, not force-grown in intensive conditions but planted sympathetically so that every element complements what is next to it: the fruit trees, the vegetable plot, the desert flowers, the false pepper tree, the grapevine, the eucalyptus, the silvery olives, the cascades of succulents. In the orchard grow oranges, lemons, limes, figs, quinces, pomegranates and a fruit I have never heard of before called *níspero*, the stones of which can be used to make an amaretto-like liqueur. Troy was a gardener before she came here, but in this harsh climate she had to learn everything again. Years of trial and error lie behind this plenty. Around the border plastic bottles have been stuck on poles, the local way of asking goatherds not to let their goats ravage the crops; a traditional form of pesticide that requires no chemicals.

Beyond the garden desert plants are scattered across the hills, alien things I cannot name. On the journey here, Kevin pointed out the most noticeable ones: the pink flowering oleander that brings an ice-cream-like sweetness to the land ('All parts of the plant are poisonous'); the pale, feathery fronds of retama that flow like horse's tails; the clusters of bamboo-like *caña* shooting up along dry riverbeds. And the cactuses everywhere, but that is a sorry story. In an echo of Białowieża, magnificent outcrops of agave have been devastated by weevils, and the thickets of prickly pear by a plague of cochineal beetles. On the hillside below the house lies a ruined kingdom of their fleshy, fibrous leaves mined hollow from within, revealing the desiccated husks of their internal structure. Although they seem to belong so well, neither of these species is native – both were introduced from Mexico, a blowback from Spain's empire – so the local government has done little to stop the decline. Stranded immigrants, they have been left to their fate.

Back at the house, Troy puts me to work cracking a bucket of almonds on a table-mounted nutcracker, each explosion sending shrapnel skittering over the tiles. 'Listen,' says Kevin in the silence of a pause. A bee-eater is whooping softly down the hill. Later we hear the fluting call of a golden oriole.

Why did they choose to come here, so far inland from the coast, with its glittering sea and its easy community of Brits? Initially, they say over dinner, out of simple curiosity, having heard of this desert-like landscape and wondering what it was like. They stayed because they fell in love with the arid zone's surprising, often startling, beauty. Because of the starkness and the light.

Everyone talks about the light.

After dinner I go for a test-walk in this new environment, following a winding path further into the hills. Even this late in the day the brightness is all-consuming and each stone-chip, pebble and stem stands out individually, casting a shadow so perfect it looks as if it has been inked. As the sun lowers I walk through intermittent gloom and glare, strobed by blinding flashes, making it hard to see my way. From the top of the hill the Plastic Sea, somewhere to the west, and the real sea, somewhere to the south, have been merged into one by a pall of brownish haze.

Walking back I see how the sparseness brings each object into focus, as if it has been magnified. The shrubs and trees exist separately, not entangled in a mass but spaced apart from one another as individual specimens. It also highlights the sheer mess of humanity's presence. Pylons, abandoned construction projects, dumped rubbish and the scars of roads are littered in plain sight, with nothing to hide them.

There is no hiding anything here, in this place of high exposure.

~

Kevin has a library of travel books and an impressive collection of maps. In the morning we sit down to study my route ahead. East of Almería the *plásticos* are marked like a geological formation – which they might be one day, a millimetre-thick white layer folded into the sediment – but I will start further north, at the village of Níjar. From there a mountain road leads into the Sierra Alhamilla, which runs parallel to the coast: the northern wall of the Plastic Sea and a smaller cousin of the higher, snow-patched Sierra Nevada to the west. I will spend the night up there and, the following afternoon, drop down on the far side of the range into what the map depicts as a contoured orange stain.

That is Tabernas, our continent's only desert.

Of the many desert-like or semi-desert places in Europe, whether natural or man-made, only Tabernas fulfils the criteria to be climatologically 'true', putting it in the same league as the Gobi, the Kalahari, the Arabian or the Sonoran; or, indeed, the frozen deserts of the Arctic or the Antarctic. A desert is an arid region with scarce plant coverage that receives under 250 millimetres of precipitation a year. Twenty-five centimetres: the length of my elbow to my wrist. It is the lack of precipitation, rather than the temperature, that is the deciding factor, and the Köppen classification distinguishes four general types: BWh, 'hot desert'; BSh, 'hot semi-arid'; BWk, 'cold desert'; and BSk, 'cold semi-arid'.

Tabernas has patches of all of these. It is four deserts in one.

As deserts go, admittedly, it is rather small. Bounded by the Sierra Alhamilla to the south, the Sierra de los Filabres to the north and the Sierra Nevada to the west, it is not much more than a hundred square miles, which gives it an area smaller than that of the Plastic Sea. This is no Empty Quarter that can swallow an army without trace, although, as in anywhere this dry, a person getting lost without water could easily die. Nor is it a desert of shifting sands, sculpted by the wind into crescent-shaped dunes, like the iconic *ergs*, the sand seas, of the Sahara. Tabernas is a desert of rock, a contusion of limestone and gypsum hills divided by *ramblas* – in the Middle East they would be called *wadis* – sheer-sided canyons or ravines prone to flash floods when it rains. The sun shines for 325 days a year, so that doesn't happen often.

I've packed a lightweight hiking shirt woven from some miracle fibre that claims to decrease body temperature, a hat with the widest brim I could find – it is actually absurdly wide – and suncream so protective it spreads on more like paint. I've also brought rehydration salts (technically for diarrhoea) and a plastic bladder that fits in my rucksack and holds three litres of water, suckable through a rubber tube, which I test on Kevin and Troy's porch later. It feels like carrying an extra organ, the outsourcing of a bodily function, or like an item of medical gear, which in a way it is. Walkers in deserts are advised to drink five litres of water a day. Thirst is what worries me most. My body deals with cold much better than it does with heat.

'This whole region used to be a lot wetter,' says Kevin. 'In the hills you'll see old threshing circles from where they used to grow cereal crops. They don't grow them any more. Up above Níjar there used to be the biggest concentration of watermills anywhere in the ancient Mediterranean world. Our old neighbour Paco is in his seventies and he can remember the *ramblas* running for seven or eight months of the year. They were always full in December and February. That pattern has broken down now.'

Lots of things have broken down on this semi-desert fringe. Standing on the roof that evening, watching swallows cut the air, Troy points out the delicate rubble of old drystone terraces angled flush against the hill on the far side of the valley, abandoned half a century ago. There are also ruined houses up there, entire villages slumping and collapsing back into the land, a sign that the area once supported a much larger population. 'Franco punished this region severely after the Civil War, because it was very Republican,' she says. 'There was a lot of starvation. In the 1950s and 1960s people moved to Germany, England, America. Much of this area was depopulated.'

Depopulation is an affliction older than the twentieth century. After the final victories of the centuries-long Reconquista of Spain – Christian forces retook Almería from the Moors in 1489, and the last Islamic kingdom of Granada in 1492 – Muslims who refused to abandon their faith were expelled, along with Jews. Those who converted and stayed were never fully trusted. In 1571, after a rebellion erupted in the Alpujarra Mountains, even these converted *moriscos* were exiled over the sea as well, and with them went hundreds of years of knowledge of hydrology. The Catholic monarchs tried to encourage Christian resettlement, but, once emptied out, the land was hard to fill again. Farmers from the greener north saw bare soil and unrelenting heat, wild mountains full of bandits, and a poorly defended coast that was notorious for piracy.

'Many of the Moors who had been expelled had gone to North Africa and, knowing the . . . area well, acted as guides for incursions by pirates, who seized the people they found and sold them at slave markets in Algeria', I read in one of Kevin's books. The Barbary Coast – named after the Berbers, the indigenous people of North Africa – became a base for corsairs such as El Joraique and Sayyida al Hurra, Andalucian Muslims who had been exiled after the conquest. El Joraique, after taking part in a failed anti-Christian uprising, took refuge in the Sierra Alhamilla before escaping to Morocco and assuming command of a pirate fleet, returning in 1573 to attack Sorbas and Tahal, towns almost forty miles inland, leading to the panicked depopulation of fifteen villages. Sayyida al Hurra's story is even more remarkable. A noble-woman from Granada, she became governor of Tétouan after her husband's death and took her revenge on the Spanish by turning herself into a pirate queen, terrorising the Andalucian coast and controlling, at the height of her power, much of the western Mediterranean as the Ottoman corsair Barbarossa controlled the east. These continuing Muslim attacks were less pirate raids than guerrilla resistance, a sign that the wars of the Reconquista had never gone away.

The slave-raids and incursions continued, though with decreasing frequency, into the seventeenth century, and piracy was a major threat into the early nineteenth. It is estimated that anywhere from 100,000 to a million people were kidnapped from the Iberian coast and sold into slavery in

North Africa and the Middle East. Coupled with the harsh conditions, the poverty, the frequent droughts and the chronic lack of development, no wonder it was difficult to encourage people to settle the south. Andalucía remains sparsely populated to this day.

Another definition of a desert is a place that has been deserted.

'The question is,' Kevin says, 'we know the meanings of a semi-desert and a desert. But when does one become the other? At what point do you enter the actual desert? Here, some years, it's rained less than 250 millimetres, which technically means we've been living in a desert. Other years it's 250 to 500, which means we've been living in a semi-desert. But some years it rains torrentially. So where are we living then?'

Before I go to sleep that night I have the image of the desert fluctuating year by year, sometimes expanding to fill the space around it and sometimes shrinking back, as if it were testing its boundaries, seeing how far it can go.

In a sense it has gone as far as the Channel Tunnel. Emerging into the grey light of France two – or is it three? – days ago, the first thing that greeted my eyes was row upon row of metal fences topped with razor wire, mounted with security cameras, electrified, patrolled by vehicles, the stark face of the militarisation of Europe's northern border. These anti-human barricades are designed, overwhelmingly, to stop the flow of migrants from the desert countries of the south: refugees not only from wars but from famine, water shortage and ecological collapse. Surrounding villages and farms, these fortifications impose a shadow on Picardy's dull countryside. Geopolitically they are the deserts' northernmost frontier.

~

Níjar is a hillside village of narrow, shaded streets, built to shield its inhabitants from the sun. Its shops sell cheap, colourful pottery and *jarapes*, rag rugs. Leathery old men are drinking glasses of red morning liqueur, smoking their way determinedly into another scalding day. After Kevin drops me off I order coffee.

'*No hay lluvia!*' 'There's no rain!' yells a loitering policeman pointlessly, gesturing at the cloudless sky. He is addressing a young woman holding an umbrella instead of a parasol and he clearly finds the sight amusing. *Para-sol*, 'for the sun', as opposed to *para-agua*, 'for the water'; the same lack-of-nonsense directness as in the word *sombrero*, which simply means 'shader'. This is what I like about Spanish, its bluntness and simplicity. It is the only foreign language I speak with any degree of proficiency, having previously lived in Madrid and before that in Mexico, but the Andalucian dialect sounds like another language altogether, as rubble-strewn, rough and unrefined as the landscape that gave it shape.

As suggested by all these *al*s – Almería, Alhamilla – Spanish is also strongly influenced by its long contact with Arabic. It has even been described as a form of Arabised Latin. Arabic lends it my favourite word, *ojalá*, which is roughly translatable as something like 'would that it were'. It is an echo of *inshallah*, 'if God wills it'.

Ojalá that I don't get sunstroke. *Ojalá* that I find some shade. *Ojalá* that I don't die of thirst. I finish my coffee and make my way to the Museum of the Memory of Water.

The melancholy of the name has drawn me more than the exhibits. In a high-ceilinged hall stand half a dozen information panels, along with some forgettable models, that tell the story of how the various civilisations that came to these lands – Phoenicians, Greeks, Carthaginians, Romans, Moors and Christians – all struggled with the same concern: irrigation, irrigation, irrigation. The Romans built their aqueducts and the Moors – for whom cleanliness was central to their religion, and who mocked the Spanish for their dirty ways – developed fountains, bathhouses and water cisterns known as *aljibes*, which are still dotted everywhere. After the Reconquista the valley above Níjar became known for its many watermills, which the first part of my walk will trace.

Leaving the village I follow a lane of shade on the road's eastern side, which narrows with every step until it is only my body's width. I cleave to it so closely that my shoulder scrapes the wall. Then I'm in the patchy, dappled shadow of olive trees, and after that all shade is gone.

I climb the hillside in the memory of water.

The barnacle of the next village, Huebro, lies above, white against the stark brown mountain.

On my left an abandoned car has bullet holes in its passenger door. 'There's a story there,' as Dougie might say.

Barely five minutes in and my whole body is dripping.

Above Níjar a ruined Moorish watchtower looks out towards the sea. They built it facing in exactly the wrong direction: their enemies came from the north. Now its only vantage is over the *plásticos*.

From here I can see the artificial plain in its entirety. Browned by the morning haze, the merged-together polythene looks more mineral than synthetic, a wobbling salt desert. The whiteness bends the air above it, creating a strange distortion. The coverage is so large, I read back at Kevin and Troy's, that it produces its own albedo effect, reflecting back the sun's rays and minutely cooling the atmosphere. While in other parts of Spain the average temperature has climbed by one, two or three degrees over the last forty years, this area has actually become one degree cooler. Despite the infernal heat inside, the Plastic Sea has the same effect as an ice cap or a glacier; a giant Sphinx, not ablating but spreading, a snow patch for the Anthropocene.

And out of sight the descendants of the Moors, who brought fountains to this land, work in a sweltering hammam of pesticides.

The walk up the valley towards Huebro leads past stone-walled canals, ruined irrigation systems overgrown by succulents and scrub. Abandoned terraces are bare but for yellow grass, utilised as rubbish dumps for the village I've just left. But there are still noisy streams flowing from the mountain above, channelled along an aqueduct to cascade into the footprint of a vanished water wheel; oleander blooms on the banks and my arrival is heralded by a panicked plopping of frogs. I splash my face, neck and arms, knowing this might be my last chance.

The weevils have reached this valley too, judging from the withered husks of agave on the slopes. Their offspring shoot up next to them – the miraculous unfolding of those heavy, spear-tipped leaves, each one imprinting a spiked outline on the younger leaf below, like a blueprint for the next design – but they will soon be weevilled too, clones waiting for their turn. Through the dead and moribund plants descends an elderly man from the village, his face creased against the sun. He has a long-extinguished cigar clutched between two thick fingers and a walking stick that resembles a club.

'*Buenas*,' he says resentfully, but does not look as if he means it.

After forty minutes I reach Huebro, wading up into grapevine, figs and a paddock of smiling goats in the shade of a walnut tree. There are millstones propped outside the doors as ornamental features. On an island of scum in a stagnant cistern, a golden lizard as long as my arm, its back flecked lapis lazuli blue, lugubriously watches me as if trying to calculate exactly how stupid I am. Through an open window comes the hoarse shrieking of an old woman who is either raining down curses on someone or just making conversation.

In the plaza is a tiled icon of the Virgin, bearing a haloed child.

These flat-roofed houses are so nearly Arabic, and one day they might be again.

The flower-filled valley is gone; from Huebro the track switches into the mountain, its slopes as dry as biscuit crumbs. The road grinds beneath my boots. Sweat rolls into my eyes. The morning bakes towards midday and there is not a hint of wind. When I stop, my heaving breath is syncopated with cicadas, a rhythm of heat and thirst.

My rucksack is far too heavy. It always is.

How much of my water-bladder have I sucked down already? Half a litre? A litre and a half? How much have I sweated out? A fly keeps settling on my lip and lifting off again, stealing sips of moisture that I am not aware of. I find myself resenting it, needing all that I can get. If it is this hot in the hills how will the desert feel?

A respite presents itself: down the road is a ruined *cortijo*, a hacienda-like farmhouse with a weed-choked threshing circle and an enormous pine, by far the largest tree in sight, densely clustered with cones, casting a lake of shadow. After squeezing through the padlocked gate I wander through rubble-filled rooms – cracked blue paint on window frames, a smashed tile floor that holds a hint of Islamic geometry – before returning outside. Water is crashing from a pipe into an echoing stone cistern, an invitation too good to turn down. I fill my stomach, empty my flask, and approach for a refill.

This involves a negotiation with a lazy swarm of bees who have claimed the cistern, and the bubbling pipe, as their own. I have to extend my arm deep into the buzzing cloud, leaning into empty space to catch the flowing water. Bees settle on my arm, my neck. I keep still and ask their permission: 'Please, bees.' Activity intensifies. Bees clamber in my hair. The flask fills slowly until clear water washes over the lip and I withdraw, gratefully. The bees allow me to retreat and I feel that I have asked for, and received, a blessing.

By 1 p.m. it is too hot to walk. Another *cortijo* offers shade and a hollow in the grass suggests space for a siesta. I wake up covered in insects and ruffled by a warm wind, eat some almonds, bread and cheese, and carry on up the track.

Heat drives me to a standstill again on top of the Loma del Perro, the Hill of the Dog. From here I can see over the mountains to the northern side of the range, a muddy yellow blur, but the desert lies further west, a prospect for tomorrow. For the rest of the afternoon I trace the top of the sierra, skirting the summit of Pico Colativí, and towards evening the path leads through tinder-dry montane forest. Holm oaks and pines give shade for the first time today, and as the sun loses height a sense of enormous relief spreads through me, or perhaps through the trees, or perhaps through everything. I'm looking for a place to sleep but the terrain on both sides of the road is marked by inhospitable signs: it's a choice between trespassing on land claimed by the Sociedad de Cazadores Virgen del Mar – the Virgin of the Sea Hunting Society, a curiously feminine name for macho slayers of wild boar – and the Ministerio de Defensa. Which men with guns would I rather avoid? I take my chances with the hunters.

The stars turn through the night and the thumps of a distant rave carry up to where I sleep, the sound waves travelling for miles in the moistureless air. I am lying in the overhang of a pitted limestone cliff, a hollow underneath the rock, and I wonder dreamily if the Muslim rebel El Joraique hid here, or in some similar place, before turning corsair. In the early hours I leap awake to the crack of a hunter's gun.

Morning brings a simple lesson in physical geography: the coastal plain to my left is swaddled in creamy cloud while the valley to my right – Tabernas – is crystal clear. The barrier of the mountain range stops moisture spreading inland, hemming it against the sea; this sierra is the cause of the desert's dryness. Now my eyes can start to guess at the shapes of shadowed hills, purplish brown and faint, the spreading and the seeping of a wide expanse of barren land. As I stop to study it three skinny dogs lope across the road, turn their heads to look at me and vanish into the scrub. Long-nosed, with high pointed ears, they do not appear to be owned; they look like dingos, wild dogs, on the hunt for morning rabbits. Around the corner is the torn-off leg of some hoofed animal, bent at the elbow like an arrow pointing down.

Obediently I follow in the direction indicated.

A reptilian line of hills, the Serrata del Marchante, drags itself from the east like fossilised vertebrae. Beyond it lie the windings of a bleached and twisted labyrinth. Through the haze I have an impression of ravines and riven rock, but if I stare at them too long the lines detach and lose their form, dissolving into pale glare. My eyes cannot get a grip; it is too hot to see.

Downward now on a slope of dust, past shattered canyons of grey and kidney-purple rock. The sun is high overhead. Trees are an extinct species. My boots crunch on gypsum shards which I mistake, at first glance, for broken windscreen glass. The ground is white, baked hard, interspersed with flaking plant life. I am now level with the serrata. Then it is above me. The transition from the relative greenness of the range is startling and I feel unprepared, already far out of my depth. The heat bounces from the road. Overhead power lines buzz. This is still the semi-desert fringe, not the true desert yet. But, as Kevin said, where is the line?

~

The woman who serves me eggs and potatoes has, I *think*, leprosy; her fingers and her thumbs end in blunt, shining stubs. She clumps the plate in front of me with cheerful informality and starts stacking plastic chairs. It is almost siesta time.

The town that shares the desert's name lies on the other side of the Serrata del Marchante. Having reached the flyover of the N-340a highway – the Puente Moreno, Brown Bridge, which is, as far as I can tell, the official boundary of the Desierto de Tabernas Natural Area – I did not continue west but slunk instead towards this last outpost of civilisation; food, a shower and a clean bed in the nearest one-star hotel were too tempting to turn down. I am not ready for the wilderness yet. As with much else in Andalucía, it can wait until *mañana*.

Tabernas is a drowsy town of peeling two-storey buildings painted in yellows, whites and pinks. The shade of palm trees stripes the road. All the cactuses are dead. There is a public swimming pool, a bull-ring and a ruined Moorish castle on a rocky hill. The benches on the main street are shaped like film director's chairs.

By the middle of the afternoon it is too hot to sit outside, even in the shade, so I hide under the ceiling fan in my tiny bedroom. When I emerge the streets are gently humming with the sociable sound of families taking their evening promenade and swallows are soaring in the sky above the castle. Climbing the steep hill to get a sense of where I am, I look down on an irregular jumble of rooftops and angled walls, which, with the arid slopes behind – if it wasn't for the Romanesque church – could be a view of anywhere from Morocco to the Middle East. Of the castle itself not much is left, only a few fallen arches and the remains of battlements; the site is littered with plastic bags and the corpses of prickly pears.

This is where, the story goes, the second-to-last Nasrid sultan Muhammad XIII, whom the Spanish called El Zagal, surrendered the keys of Almería to the Catholics.

But the view, in more ways than one, is of the west.

In 1964 an Italian film director was scouting for a location. The popularity of the 'sword and sandal' genre of historical epics, in which he had started his career, was on the decline, and his curiosity had turned to American Westerns. Up until then the market was dominated by clean-shaven cowboy heroes chivalrously righting wrongs, with no moral ambiguity – the good guys literally wore white hats and the bad guys wore black hats – but this Italian newcomer had ideas for something different. He had recently seen Akira Kurosawa's masterpiece *Yojimbo*, the story of a rogue samurai freeing a town from evil gangs, and transposed its violent plot from Edo-period Japan to the Wild West. The *rōnin* became a gunslinger. Six-shooters replaced samurai swords. And the backdrop of Tabernas – empty, arid and above all cheap – became the rugged borderland between Mexico and the United States.

His name was Sergio Leone and the film, starring a handsome TV actor called Clint Eastwood, was *Per un pugno di dollari*, or *A Fistful of Dollars*.

It was a critical success and Eastwood became a star. His character, the Man With No Name – glowering, mysterious, dirty, violent, enigmatic, unshaven, with a cheroot stuck in his mouth and wearing his signature dust-caked poncho – was a new kind of antihero, a break from the boyish do-gooders who had come before. The fact that Leone spoke no English and had never been to North America was no obstacle; on set he mimed moves for the actors to follow and communicated through a translator. The lawsuit he faced for what was, in effect, an unauthorised remake of Kurosawa's film was eventually settled out of court. He went on to make more films in Tabernas and Cabo de Gata, the rocky headland to the south, pioneering a gritty new genre that became known as the 'Spaghetti Western'.

For a Few Dollars More came out in 1965 and *The Good, the Bad and the Ugly* in 1966, completing the Man With No Name's blood-soaked trilogy. *Once Upon a Time in the West*, a sprawling frontier epic, was released two years after that. But Leone wasn't the only director attracted to the desert. Since the 1960s those dry ravines, rugged escarpments and cracked hills, lit by a reliable forty-five weeks of sunshine a year, have comprised the scenery of a thousand films. A large number have been Westerns with tough-guy titles so generic they become comical – *Bullets Don't Argue*, *Blood at Sundown*, *Ten Thousand Dollars for a Massacre*, *A Coffin for the Sheriff*, *A Town Called Bastard*, *Kill Them All and Come Back Alone* – but Tabernas has also doubled as other landscapes, both real and imagined: the deserts of the Middle East in *Lawrence of Arabia* and *Indiana Jones and the Last Crusade*, the Hyborian wilderness in *Conan the Barbarian*, and the Dothraki Sea in *Game of Thrones*.

From this Moorish castle, a directional pointer indicates nearby locations. To the north, a sandstone butte named Cabeza del Águila, Eagle's Head, was the backdrop for escaping convicts in *Lucky Luke and the Daltons*. The bleached plain further south was where they filmed the tank battle scene in the Second World War movie *Patton*, and near there, on a rocky rise, I can dimly make out a cluster of unlikely structures: the walls of a stockade fort and a scattering of tepees. That is Texas Hollywood, otherwise known as Fort Bravo, which – along with Oasys Mini Hollywood and Western Leone – is one of the surviving sets where hundreds of these films were made.

Scenes are still shot there on occasion, but the sets exist largely as theme parks now. For a small entrance fee you can see daily cowboy shows complete with gunfights, stunts on horseback, saloon brawls and bordello girls. That is not Spain over there but a projection of the Old West.

I am not just walking into a desert but into a fantasy.

The sun goes down in the west and I go back down the hill. Later, as I'm picking the five dying flies out of my beer, an old man in the street utters a loud 'Yee-ha!' He gets no response and does it again, longer and louder: 'YEEE-HAAA!' A few moments pass, and he is answered by a slightly more muted 'Yee-ha!' from further down the road. Into view comes a purple-skinned foreigner with a grey handlebar moustache, a black leather cowboy hat, a black leather vest and, unwisely, a pair of very small black leather shorts. He looks as if he gets yee-ha'd on a regular basis and has grown accustomed to it. The old man cackles as he goes by, pleased to have provoked a reaction. The leather cowboy is accompanied by a younger woman with dyed black hair, and as they pass I catch a few English words in an affected rock and roll drawl.

They seem to be walking in a fantasy too, but I'm not quite sure what of.

In the morning the drenching golden light in the streets is cinematic. Outside my hotel a sign informs me that *The Valley of Gwangi* was filmed here, a 1969 'Western fantasy' in which cowboys battle dinosaurs in a lost world. Sitting with coffee in the shade outside another café, I see the different populations of this small town on display, each one separate and distinct: the old *señors* and *señoras* at their gender-divided tables; the Roma women in their bright, clashing colours; the local drunk shuffling past the church in his shabby suit; the Muslim mothers in their hijabs; the Africans who sit apart, at the edges of things, watching. They are like stock characters in a film. Last night's English cowboy was also in his costume.

I feel a twinge of panic at the thought of leaving this town, in which everyone knows their place. It feels like walking off the map. First, though, I have an appointment with Standing Eagle.

'There are three types of people drawn to the desert. Aces, jokers and wild cards.'

He is tall and very thin, with shoulder-length black hair. The word 'aquiline' was coined for a face exactly like his. He has high cheekbones, deep folds beneath his clear brown eyes and a delicate webbing of wrinkles, crow's feet, frown lines and laughter lines that recalibrate themselves into different arrangements when he smiles, which he does often. Long legs folded under the table, he is sitting opposite me rolling a cigarette.

Aces, Jokers and Wild Cards: it would make a good title for a Western. 'Aces are the people you want around when things go wrong,' he explains. 'Jokers are the ones you don't. Wild cards are the ones who could turn out to be either.'

'Which one are you?' I ask.

'Probably all three at different times.'

He is talking about the community he founded with his wife, Bri, at a place called Agüilla Salada (Salt-water Valley) on fifty-two hectares of land at the edge of the sierra. They bought it with a dozen other people twenty years ago and have been there ever since, in a house constructed – according to Kevin, who put the two of us in contact – largely from scrap materials scavenged from skips, abandoned buildings and the desert itself.

On his T-shirt are a tepee, a rainbow and a snake. Flies feed at a small graze on his arm; he doesn't seem to mind. I later find out he is seventy-five but he looks fifteen years younger than that. His face is somehow careworn and carefree at the same time.

Standing Eagle, it turns out, is not his original name. His name is Laurence Burton and he comes from Tottenham. In the festival scene back home he was known as Big Eagle and was renamed Standing Eagle – 'as I was master of my own space' – by a shamanic teacher when he first came to Spain. He calls himself a guardian, not an owner, of the land.

The story of his life is told in interweaving threads. He grew up in London, trained as a chef and later became a carpenter. The houseboat he was living in sank with all his possessions on board, his artwork and his record collection, leaving him with nothing but his tools, which were in his car. He drove the car to a festival where it was stolen, along with the tools, by a hitchhiker he picked up on the way. 'The best thing that could have happened to me. I was free!' With nothing to burden him any more he went travelling. He ended up in the Sinai Peninsula with a group of Bedouin undergoing an eleven-day shamanic initiation on jimsonweed, during which he travelled to other dimensions, saw visions of UFOs and was given insights into the secrets of gyroscopic propulsion. 'I hadn't even smoked dope until then. I made up for lost time.' Later he lived in Amsterdam, where he developed designs for gyroscopically powered aircraft; a principle explained in his sci-fi novel *The Astral Twins*, about an Atlantian space nomad trapped in a human body.

It wasn't until he was thirty-five that his mother told him that the man he thought was his father wasn't his father. His real father was a Blackfoot Indian stationed in England during the war, who had taken part in the D-Day landings. It explained the aquiline face, the powerfully Native American features that had always set him apart. It explained, he says, the close connection he feels to Mother Earth. Perhaps it also explains the deserts. During the course of his life he has been drawn to live in Egypt's Sinai, Israel's Negev and the Thar Desert in Rajasthan. Now he feels at home here, on the outskirts of Tabernas.

It occurs to me that his name is a compound of two famous desert explorers: T.E. Lawrence (of Arabia) and Sir Richard Burton. He finishes his orange juice and I finish my coffee. 'Would you like to see our place?' he asks, stubbing out his cigarette.

He drives me there in his battered white van – won in a bet, apparently – on a dirt road up the same *rambla* I followed down from the mountain. With the red rock walls on either side it feels like ambush territory; I almost expect the silhouettes of horsemen aiming weapons. Standing as a sentinel is what Laurence calls the 'god-rock', pitted, alcoved and eroded, in which, he says, he sometimes sees the figure of Ganesh after Bri once set candles there, casting the shadows of elephants. The *rambla* narrows and opens out, and ahead is Agüilla Salada.

I actually glimpsed their home from above as I passed two days ago, but didn't know what I was looking at. I still don't quite know. Surrounded by derelict caravans, yurts, rusted vehicle parts, the skeletal rigging of geodesic domes and half-built experimental structures, is a dwelling that defies architectural categorisation. It is something between a permanent building and a nomad's tent. We enter through a door or a wall – I am not sure exactly which – into a room that seems dim and light, dusty and airy, closed and open at the same time. There is a cluttered table and a motley assortment of armchairs. Wooden beams support a ceiling that is partly made up of panels, partly of fabric and partly of glass; some of the walls are solid and some are made of canvas. Past the wood-burning stove is a library that turns out to be the back end of the Bedford van in which they first arrived from England, now absorbed into the house. The books are coated in heavy brown dust. When the wind blows hard the whole structure lifts and settles like a ship at sea.

Laurence puts coffee on the boil and goes to find Bri, who is resting in a yurt they use as a bedroom. It takes her some time to emerge; it turns out that she is in recovery from anaemia. 'You have to be a toughie,' is one of the first things she says. Living here off-grid, on the edge of the desert, is hard – infernally hot in the summer, bitterly cold in the winter, and on the rare occasions it rains flash floods can turn the *rambla* into a raging river that can sweep away a car (and once swept Laurence away too) – and both of them have suffered from ill health in recent years. But they have stuck it out, along with seven other members of the original community – scattered up and down this valley in similar self-built habitations – while less tenacious pioneers have burned out, packed up and moved on. The aces and the toughies survive, the jokers come and go.

Bri is red-haired with bright blue eyes and amazingly pale skin for such a harsh environment; her laugh is gravelly and deep, as if it comes from far away. 'You can only come to the desert to learn,' she says at one point, fixing me with a heavy stare. 'The desert is the teacher.'

'The desert drives people crazy,' says Laurence. They both laugh at this.

· Later I help with the water run, driving with Laurence to the public cistern a little way outside town. Filling scores of eight-litre jugs with snowmelt from the Sierra Nevada and wheelbarrowing them back to the van is sweaty, exhausting work, and gives me trepidation about my own water needs. My plan is to spend a week in the desert but I can't possibly carry enough liquid to last that long; once I have found a place to camp I will have to make trips back and forth from town to build up my supplies, in the early morning before it gets too hot to walk. Laurence invites me to spend the night here so I can start at dawn. It feels like an appropriate way to lower myself in, a gradual acclimatisation, descending from the mountain to the town to the tented settlement – and before the mountain, the fertile garden – and ahead the wilderness.

The heat builds through the afternoon, steeping between the *rambla* walls, and by evening the air in the house is as warm as bath water. Listless dogs, some owned, some stray, groan occasionally from the shade. I go out walking for a while and get back to find that Laurence – amazingly, in this heat – has prepared a full roast chicken dinner with all the trimmings, even gravy from a gravy boat. 'You can take the Englishman out of England . . .' he says as he serves. The wine he pours has to be sieved to filter out the vinegar flies. Bri smiles as she shows me the label: Pata Negra. Black Foot.

After we eat he shows me a selection of his designs and diagrams. A series of mandalas represents the Twelve Steps to Harmonic Healing, a meditation guide towards higher consciousness. Sacred geometry also underlies his designs for refugee shelters, symmetrical multi-storeyed structures that sprout from the earth like beautiful flowers, and his blueprint for a robot, of whom I have only a brief glimpse ('Forget about him,' he says dismissively, flipping the page). His main engineering focus is on designing flying machines powered by gyroscopic propulsion, which harnesses centrifugal force to generate lift and thrust. Beyond the pale of mainstream physics, the principle is a holy grail for alternative energy theorists, promising almost limitless non-polluting energy that would transform society, and perhaps even consciousness. The designs look like classic flying saucers. He first gained insights into the technology on his Sinai vision quest. From Moses and Mohammed to the skies above Area 51, deserts have always been places where revelations are received.

I go to bed with my mind full of patterns, not sleeping in their home but rolling out my inflatable mat in a stand of eucalyptus trees on the other side of a low hill elsewhere on their land. Above the floodline, Laurence said, though there is no hint of cloud. Bats dip close, almost skimming my face, and I realise that I am the bait for mosquitoes, a mutually beneficial partnership. In the night there is distant howling and a short, sharp scream. I am on my feet before the sun. There is no dawn chorus.

~

Six hours later I've burrowed my way into the shade of a slot canyon as deep into the desert as I can get before midday. The sun is directly overhead but the canyon twists and turns, shadowing the sandy floor between layers of standing rock. I am almost naked, pumping out sweat like some kind of malfunctioning drain, dazedly watching the slow drips pool inside my belly button, where they brim and overspill each time I take a breath. I raise a flask to my lips and take a sip, but not too much. In the collection of bottles around me are twenty-two litres of water.

Getting them to this canyon has been a hard morning's work. In the grainy light of dawn I lugged the first eight litres – three in the bladder, two in my rucksack and a three-litre jug in my arms – underneath the threshold of the N-340a flyover, empty of cars at that hour, and followed the Rambla de Tabernas westwards into the desert. The sun had not yet cleared the hills and so my first glimpse of the land was variegated greys receding into silhouettes, the features cooled and simplified, planed into two dimensions. Little by little the rocks took on a radiant, ominous glow.

Every hundred metres came a red, black and yellow sign: 'Cinema Studios Fort Bravo 500 mts', 'Cinema Studios Fort Bravo 400 mts', 'Cinema Studios Fort Bravo 300 mts' . . . a countdown to unreality. Then, around another bend:

TEXAS HOLLYWOOD

in familiar white letters on a sagebrushy hill, a knock-off of the rather more famous sign five thousand miles further west. There was a fork in the road: right led into fantasy, left into the real desert. I took the left-hand path. Fantasy will come later.

Hardened clay shattered with a porcelain tinkle under my boots, a reminder that the *rambla* was a long-dry riverbed. On each side mounted cliffs of sandstone and mud. The geology was complicated: in some places the valley walls resembled poured concrete – gothic, sludgy dribblings – while in others they collapsed into heaps of brittle shale. Then came walls of harder rock ribbed with intricate striations, twisted and folded back on themselves, as if the cliffs had been extruded from the crust.

After an hour's slog south-west I found what I was looking for: at the base of the cliff was a ruined *cortijo* – no more than four ill-balanced walls, a failed attempt at settlement – in a clump of eucalyptus, beyond which winked the dark eyehole of a cave. The cave was man-made, gouged by picks, perhaps a place for storing food or for sheltering hardy goats. I dumped my supplies there and sat breathing for a while. It was 8 a.m.

Unburdened, I retraced my own footprints – the hackneyed trope of every desert explorer – reaching Tabernas town to the sound of a clanging bell. The community was slowly waking up with coffee, cigarettes and first-drink-of-the-morning beers; the local drunk leaned near the church, eyes closed, with a dreamy smile. In the little *supermercado* I bought an eight-litre jug and four 1.5-litre bottles: the jug for my empty rucksack, two of the bottles for the rucksack pockets and one for each of my hands. Staggering under this liquid weight I got halfway back through town.

By that point I was dripping wet, my shirt a sodden, clinging flap. At the last café terrace I collapsed for coffee. As my sweat evaporated and my shirt turned crisp again – a reversal that seemed to take mere seconds – I checked the news on my phone.

A mistake.

'Hell is coming!'

The headline was a quote from a Spanish meteorologist warning of extreme temperatures rolling through Europe, a heatwave unprecedented in severity and scale. From the south of Spain to Switzerland, the Sierra Nevada to the Alps, the heat over the next few days would reach or exceed forty degrees Celsius; humidity would make it feel more like forty-seven. Authorities were warning of dehydration, heatstroke, death. Children and the elderly were advised to stay indoors. In France emergency 'cool rooms' were being set up in municipal buildings and school exams had been postponed. The Italian government was calling it the most intense heat-wave in a decade. Germany, Poland and the Czech Republic were preparing for record highs, and Switzerland – normally vigilant for temperatures at the other extreme – had issued a 'severe danger' alert for much of the country. Even in Scandinavia it would reach into the mid-thirties. Berlin would be as hot as Rome. The temperature in the south of France was comparable with Death Valley.

My phone buzzed with concerned messages. One of them was from Dougie. 'Extreme, dangerous heat coming your way,' wrote the man I had last seen crunching through northern snow. Another message included a link to a weather map.

The map looked like a medical photograph of a terribly injured body or a microscopic image of a ravaging disease. A crimson, puce and purple stain lay across Europe's nation states, pale pink at its centre and blotched yellow at its edges, virulent, malignant, the colours of infection. It was as if the Köppen-Geiger map – those defined and seemingly stable bands organising the world into colour-zones – had mutated, burst its bounds, the south exploded northwards.

Climatologically this was much what had happened: the cause of the heatwave was hot air sucked up from North Africa by a combination of high pressure and a storm over the Atlantic. While I'd come south to find Europe's desert – this tiny scrap of fake Sahara – the real Sahara had reached up to engulf the continent.

I sat there for a long time, checking weather report after weather report, returning again and again to the livid trauma of the map. Dehydration, heatstroke, death: these were real possibilities. What did I hope to learn by putting myself at risk? That heat feels hot? That deserts are dry? I scrolled the news again. Other customers came and went, ordering drinks and greeting friends. Time was heat: every minute I wasted the hotter the morning became.

I ordered another *café cortado* that I didn't want to drink, and returned to the doom-roll of apocalyptic temperatures. My body was frozen in the heat, unable to tear itself away. It was like that morning in Hajnówka, on the edge of the unknown forest, fearing the exposure that lay between me and the trees; only here the exposure might be life-threatening. The thought occurred to me that I could simply not venture back, or not today, at any rate; the hotel was three minutes' walk away, with its cool sheets and its ceiling fan, and several floors of vacancies. No one would blame me for doing this. There was a fine enough view of the desert from the Moorish castle.

But then I thought of what Bri had said: 'The desert is the teacher.' The teacher of what? If I stayed in town, I would never know.

Leaving the infrastructure of Tabernas felt like unplugging myself from a life-support system. Aware of the rapidly climbing sun I walked as quickly as I could, re-retracing my steps underneath the flyover. The countdown to Texas Hollywood seemed faintly ominous now. I would be all right, I thought, if I found a sheltered place before noon, an hour that felt almost superstitiously significant, a kind of desert witching hour. It was coming up to eleven now; I had wasted far too much time. The weight of water on my back drained me and increased my thirst, but drinking it felt, illogically, like my effort was being wasted. It was a water paradox: the more you carry the more you need. The weight and the necessity worked against each other.

When I finally reached the cave I considered sheltering there, but the air was sweltering. In its mouth I sat and dripped, turning the dust to mud. On the far side of the valley, birds – the first I'd seen all day – were wheeling in the air, twittering from alcoves in a wall of honeycombed rock: a colony of sand martins, shoaling like fish around a reef. They swooped in complicated arcs, almost skimming the cliff with the tips of their wings as they banked and doubled back, parting the air like tiny scythes. It was a relief to see them. Studying the rockface that housed their metropolis I noticed a narrow cleft and a promising strip of dark. Shade. An opening.

The slot canyon, a dry tributary of this dry riverbed, did not run straight but twisted back and forth into the rock. Sunlight did not reach its depths. Each bend drew me inwards. Water had left its mark in deep grooves in the sandstone walls, rills and runnels sculpted by the passage of flash floods. Slowly I went deeper, upstream without the stream, ferrying my water bottles in stages as I climbed. Pink oleander and *caña* somehow grew along here, and in one place I even brushed the leaves of a young fig tree. Climbing a ten-foot lip of rock – the plunge pool and the undercut of a vanished waterfall – brought me to a gallery of eroded stone formations: sprouting mushrooms, pancakes and bulbous domes of gritty rock whose bases had been gouged away, a miniature Cappadocia. Another non-waterfall lay beyond that, and another beyond that, so I tossed my bottles up and climbed them hand over foot, using their striations like the rungs of a ladder. I wasn't sure how to get back down but there was no point stopping now: the deeper I could penetrate the safer I would be. At last I reached an upper level with a yellow sandy floor, an overhang of smooth stone, and stopped to catch my breath.

A sharp *crack*: a fist-sized rock ricocheted off the wall, narrowly missing my head. I looked up to see a hairy back leg in retreat. Debris cascaded down the cliff and when I looked up again I saw, against the blinding sky, the silhouette of an ibex with the sun caught in its horns, perfectly composed. We stared at each other. More stones rattled down. The beast dissolved into the light.

I peeled off my sodden clothes and lay down in the shade of the overhang. As if on cue, cicadas whirred.

It was five minutes until noon.

~

The heat of the afternoon flattens me, even in the shade. I cannot move or think, can only sit and breathe. The air is heavy, as warm as blood, windless, stultifying. I top up my internal reserves of sweat with sips of water.

The itchy rhythm of the cicadas switches on and off, an electric circuit being interrupted and reconnected. Impossible to locate, seeming to have no origin point but to be present everywhere, even in the rocks and the air, the manic drill – produced by tymbals, rib-like structures in the abdomen – stops abruptly whenever any creature gets within close range, like a reverse intruder alarm. Never laying eyes on one, I find myself thinking of their noise as a manifestation of the heat itself, as if the temperature has been converted into waveform.

Occasionally the sound is broken by the swish of sand martins cutting across the narrow band of sky above; against the light, their wings look as transparent as dragonflies'. Sometimes I hear the bubbling, urgent voices of rock doves. I doze off and come awake to a distant conversation – a person chattering busily somewhere in the canyon's depth – before realising it is the droning of a small black bee. Apart from these interjections and the cicadas' frequency – so constant I cease hearing it, and am startled when it stops – nothing else occurs. There is only heat and waiting.

Now, and over the coming days, I discover that I can spend long periods of time doing nothing, simply looking at the rocks and the changing shadowscapes. It is too hot to do anything else. There are gradual transformations. After an hour of staying still the tips of my feet start to burn; when I look, they're glowing white. My shade is not secure. A glaring floodline is flowing unstoppably along the rock, seeping down the sheer walls, filling the hollows and the cracks. Now it is at my knees. I retreat to higher ground but the spillage catches up. Now it is at my waist, my chest. Stones become thermometers as they turn from grey to white. The light is up to my neck, drowning me in temperature, and I imagine – 'Hell is coming!' – that the same is happening the length and breadth of Europe.

At last it drives me from this place, a climate refugee; and from the place after that, and the place after that. The canyon forks, narrows, widens, narrows and forks again. Sometimes the sky feels further away and sometimes closer. It would be easy to get lost; I make a map as I go, sketching out the zigs and zags, a thread leading back through the labyrinth. The *ramblas* are the desert's internal secret avenues, a ghostly circulatory system, subdividing and connecting in baffling configurations. I can move around unseen, buried within the land. I am not *in* the desert but somehow underneath it.

A narrow corridor goes upward through a rubble of fallen rocks, the sky looming close again. The sun is past its zenith now and the heat is less severe. At last I find myself emerging on to the desert's surface level: a moonscape – a Marscape

– of shattered, shining stone piled into bell-shaped hills that roll into the distance. After being concealed all day the exposure is unnerving. The light is like another world's, as if the spectrum has been nudged towards infrared. A waste of naked minerals stretches to the north and west, while to the south the hills appear to throw themselves against the sierra, piling up on one another as if trying to overwhelm it.

There exists, to my surprise, a rocky road up here, winding rather pointlessly around the gypsum-covered humps, looping back almost to meet itself before perishing in a stony field. Some of the stones leap up and sprint away: small, brush-coloured rabbits. Attempts have been made at agriculture – half a dozen olive trees are crookedly suffering and there is even a patch where some Sisyphean masochist appears to have raked the rocks into furrowed lines – but the site has the feel of terminal neglect. On my map the Tabernas Desert is marked with numerous *cortijos*, but, from what I've seen so far, few of them remain intact. What were they farming? Stones? I follow the direction of the rabbits up the slope.

Here the ground plunges steeply into the cleft of another *rambla*: the Arroyo de Verdelecho, according to the map. A highway lies beyond – another reality away – and between the highway and the *rambla* there is a village.

There is something strange about it. No cars, no people. Squinting against the orange sun I make out wood-framed houses, a little chapel, a hotel. There is a rope-and-bucket well; whitewashed adobe buildings facing a dirt-floored plaza; a weather-bleached General Store; and is that a *gallows*? At a discreet distance stand four sad-looking tepees. I am looking at the film set of Western Leone.

Originally built as the main location of *C'era una volta il West*, or *Once Upon a Time in the West* – other scenes were filmed in Rome and in Monument Valley, Arizona – Western Leone now appears distinctly down at heel. In fact it looks largely derelict, one flash flood away from collapse; the adobe neighbourhood might stand (I'm guessing that's Old Mexico) but the wood-framed houses (Anglo-Saxon) seem to be made of matchsticks. For a second I see myself as anyone alive down there might see me, if they happened to glance up: a silhouetted figure on the ridge, with his wide-brimmed hat and his thousand-yard stare, ready to rob the mail wagon. But the sun is almost down. I leave America behind and retreat to my gully.

~

Breakfast is a raw white onion, eaten as I walk. It's strangely refreshing in the heat, like a hot chilli pepper; the trick is not to eat too much, peeling one layer at a time, only breathing through the mouth. God, I must stink. With three litres on my back, which ought to last for several hours, I am following the Arroyo de Verdelecho to the north.

The morning started strangely cool, a thick haze in the air. Having hidden my belongings under a screen of torn-up scrub – from whom or what I do not know – and followed the map I sketched last night back down the canyon's twists and turns, I tried to locate Western Leone, but could find no sign of it. It might have been a mirage or a displaced memory. Now I am back underneath the desert, where the only view is of the layered walls on either side, cross-sections of geology sandwiched horizontally, vertically and diagonally, a parade of forms: honeycombed and organ-piped, rippled into spreading fans, concertinaed, cracked and slumped or eroded like rotten fangs. Suggestive god-rocks, like the one that stands guard over Agüilla Salada. Further north, *caña* grows as if along a dried-out Nile. The riverbed turns to grey sand. It is an ashen landscape.

A rattle of falling stones pulls my eyes upward. Three ibex

– an adult and two young – are moving with impossible calmness up a perpendicular rockface, ascending somehow vertically, a motion that cannot be described as walking and is not exactly climbing but seems closer to levitation in its sheer uncanniness. A type of wild mountain goat, extremophiles drawn to live in arid, inaccessible places, ibex are widespread in Arabia, Egypt and the Middle East, with a small population in the Alps; the animals floating up that cliff are from the Iberian species, numbering fifty thousand in the Pyrenees and Spain. The one in front is a male, from the great size of his horns – ungainly, backward-curving things like thickly ridged scimitars, almost half his body's length – like the one that ambushed me with a rock-attack yesterday morning. The lines of those horns are archetypal: black and yellow ibex appear, drawn with fingered dots, in twenty-thousand-year-old Paleolithic cave art.

Their history in this part of Spain is long and mixed with magic. Near the town of Vélez Blanco, sixty miles north of here, is the Cueva de los Letreros, the Cave of the Signs. Its paintings and petroglyphs, dating back four and a half thousand years, depict the stylised forms of ibex, men and women, archers, hunters, birds and deer, as well as geometric shapes like interlocking triangles. The most famous of the signs is the iconic Indalo, which seems to show a human figure with splayed legs and outstretched arms holding a rainbow in his hands – thought to represent protection – which, painted on the walls of shops and houses for good luck, has been adopted as a symbol of Almería. But more potent is the figure of the Brujo.

Brujo means 'sorcerer'. His body seems to be mid-dance. He has an elongated head, either a tail or a penis dangling between his legs and an object in one hand, perhaps a vessel or a heart. His arms end in sickles. From his head spread what are unmistakably ibex horns, mirroring the sickles' curves, either a shamanic headpiece or an act of shapeshifting. Part human, part animal, the figure flows between the species as ibex flow up and down the rocks, a traveller between dimensions.

Whatever system of beliefs this Brujo might have represented, long before the Romans, the Christians or the Muslims came, is as vanished as the water that shaped the land. We don't know what ibex meant to the people who daubed their likeness. But with their agility, their mastery of different planes, and their ability to thrive in harsh environments – and, perhaps, the crafty, knowing, strangely human-looking eyes that later religious prejudice would come to associate with the devil – it is easy to imagine that they might have been worshipped. Like the reindeer in the Cairngorms or the bison in Białowieża, they are a totem animal for the Tabernas Desert.

As for the other creatures here, several species are more commonly found in North Africa, stranded from their wider range by a hundred miles of water. Red-beaked trumpeter finches and elusive Dupont's larks are native to the arid regions of the Maghreb and the Middle East. Algerian hedgehogs and spiny-footed lizards, resident in Morocco, Algeria and Tunisia, are unknown in the rest of Europe outside the Iberian Peninsula. In terms of its arachnids, too, Tabernas has the sense of being a northern protrusion of Africa: yellow scorpions, tarantulas and black widows hide among the rocks. 'It feels like a double bee sting,' said Laurence of the scorpions. 'Hurts like hell, but it won't kill you. You get a warning with them too – they go *click click click*.' It doesn't bode well for sleeping outside, or for the open-toed sandals I'm wearing, but for now the only clicking is debris rolling down the cliff as the ibex ascend.

Lulled by the morning's relative cool, I walk for hours northwards up this sunken valley, never quite able to resist the mystery of the next bend. Each corner is a plot twist that promises revelation. The place-names on the map are invitations to dark adventures: Cortijos de Haza Blanca, Farmsteads of the White Haze; El Tesorero, The Treasurer; Rambla el Cautivo, Ravine of the Captive; Barranco del Infierno, Ravine of Hell; and the horrifying Quemado del Muerto, Burnt of the Dead. I wonder what their stories are and if anyone still knows them. The Arroyo de Verdelecho, Gully of the Green Bed, runs the length of Tabernas to a hamlet of the same name, and in a flight of fantasy I imagine walking on, past noon and into night, to emerge on the other side of the desert like some nineteenth-century explorer crossing the Empty Quarter. '[I]t lures a man on and on,' writes the American writer and eco-activist Edward Abbey in *Desert Solitaire*, about his time working as a ranger in Arches National Park, Utah, 'from the red-walled canyons to the smoke-blue ranges beyond, in a futile but fascinating quest for the great unimaginable treasure which the desert seems to promise. Once caught by this golden lure you become a prospector for life, condemned, doomed, exalted.' But I only have half an onion and a swallow or two of water left. This is not the age of great explorers. The Ravine of Hell and Burnt of the Dead will have to remain vague nightmares.

The *rambla* narrows, squeezing tightly into a claustrophobic gorge, before widening out again to a waste of scree. Suddenly the air turns solid with the stench of death. My next breath comes out as a retch. The smell is like a wall. Exactly as I turn my head, the haze that has covered the desert since dawn shockingly peels away to reveal a raw blue sky. The white explosion of the sun sends me fumbling for dark glasses. The events seem ominously connected: death and the sun. I am hours of heat and light away from shelter.

Knowing that I have come too far, taking my last swallow

of lukewarm, plastic-tasting water, I start to retrace my steps back along the Green Bed, misnamed in both instances. There is no resting here. The ground is white, encrusted in a crystal scurf of salt, which has the effect of escalating the quality of my thirst from nagging to insistent to quietly desperate. At one point, where the *caña* grows, I come across a brown puddle in the middle of the track – leaked, perhaps, from some irrigation failure far away – and dip a hopeful finger in. But it is foul and brackish. At least I can use it to dunk my hat, cooling my head and hanging a dripping curtain around my face, which feels briefly wonderful. It is bone dry in a minute.

Bone dry, bone dry, bone dry: a marching step. Bone for the left foot and dry for the right. Repetition breaks the phrase apart – it is one I have never considered before – and in the context of this heat the words turn sinister. Bones, when situated where they should be, are enwrapped in wetness, only taking on that description when they are removed from flesh and left in places such as this, a land of moistureless remains. The desert resembles parts of a desiccated body. The path is a rubble of pinkish quartz, pale rock like marbled fat. Baked vehicle tracks here and there in the mud look fossilised. Miles on, the carcass of a tractor tyre lies like a monument to a vanished age, which it might be before long. The sensation of thirst is as placeless as cicadas.

The warning signs of heatstroke include dry skin, headaches, rapid breathing, dizziness, slurred speech and confusion. I do not have the worst of these symptoms but I have the least of them. Or do I have all of them? In this heat, this unreal glare, it is hard to know what feels normal. In my mind is a simple, brutal fact: above a certain temperature the body's cooling mechanisms no longer work effectively and the system shuts down. It is no great mystery. The heating can be external or internal – a result of environmental conditions or overexertion from exercise – or a combination of both. The damage starts once the body's core temperature reaches forty degrees Celsius, which is the same temperature as the air around me now.

At forty degrees and above, the transpiration of sweat is no longer enough to cool the skin. A positive feedback loop is tripped: as they malfunction, systems designed to reduce the body's temperature effectively make it hotter. Forty-one degrees brings seizures. Forty-two degrees brings vomiting and diarrhoea, massively exacerbating dehydration. The emergency redirection of hot blood away from vital organs deprives the intestines of oxygen and puts strain on the heart, leading to a risk of strokes and cardiac arrest. At forty-three degrees increased pressure in the skull causes the brain to swell and the body literally starts to cook: blood vessels haemorrhage; liver and kidney cells are destroyed; perforated intestines leak and toxins flood into the bloodstream; proteins disintegrate; muscle tissue melts.

There are fewer than six degrees between the body's optimal core temperature – 37.7 degrees – and the 'critical thermal maximum' that brings absolute collapse.

I think of the colour map of Europe, the livid scalds and blotches that resemble haemorrhages, outward signs of the heatstroke that is raging through the continent. A core temperature has been breached and systems are breaking down, positive feedback loops are kicking in everywhere. As climates aridify, evapotranspiration from foliage – as with sweat from the human body – no longer helps to cool things down. The hotter it gets the hotter it gets. Aquifers dehydrate. Like overheating body cells, individuals and species die.

I will find out later that this week's heat killed one and a half thousand people, the vast majority in France. A heatwave in 2003 killed seventy thousand across Europe.

It will only intensify, according to the forecasts. Climate models show heat-related deaths increasing year by year as record-breaking temperatures become ordinary events. Manual and outdoor labourers – farmers and construction workers, the fruit-pickers of the Plastic Sea – will be especially vulnerable; in the worst-hit regions such work will become physically impossible. One point five degrees of warming is predicted to increase the average length of droughts in the south of Europe by three months, and the area burned by wildfires by forty-one per cent. With two degrees of warming this rises to six months and sixty-two per cent. Three degrees is exponentially worse.

Globally, there are fewer than four degrees between an optimal climate and absolute collapse.

Bone dry, bone dry, bone dry. My saliva has formed a solid. An itching heat-rash has spread across my arms and chest, my skin blotched with pricks of red. My eyeballs feel exhausted. But ahead is a fork in the road and in the sky appears an aura of dancing specks that coalesce, the closer I get, into the shapes of sand martins. I recognise rock formations, the walls of the ruined *cortijo* that marks the entrance to my hide.

It seems I am delusional because I hear voices as well, an animated conversation or an argument. No, it is a single voice, either angry or ecstatic, echoing off the rock walls around the next bend. The hallucination progresses from the aural to the visual: here he comes, a kind of heatstruck demon materialising out of the air, a manifestation of all the fears that are in my head. The figure takes shape as a ragged man in a green shirt and tattered shorts, his skin scorched a reddish brown, his dust-caked mass of frizzy hair piled in a towering afro. He is kicking up dust and waving his arms, shouting at the sky, the sun, the rocks, the desert or himself – I understand '*mierda!*', 'shit!', followed by '*Dios!*', 'God!' – striking out determinedly in the direction I have come from.

'*Qué tal?*', 'How's it going?' I ask as the apparition nears.

The question really answers itself. His bloodshot eyes stare through me. For a moment I think he might attack but instead he makes a dismissive flicking gesture with both his hands, as if he were chasing away a fly, and when I look back he is doing a bouncing, limb-jerking dance, a kind of defiant jig of performed nihilism. On his back is a small knapsack. Off he goes around a rock. Minutes later I can still hear the echoes of his rage.

'The desert drives people crazy,' said Laurence.

Either that or I have just met the Brujo without his horns.

~

My hands are so thirsty that they can hardly work the lid. When I get the jug to my lips the weight of it makes it tip and water pours down my face, unforgivably wasted. I catch a mouthful, two, three. I can actually hear it sloshing around inside me, as if in an empty drum. I drink until my belly is tight. Then follows a wonderful calm.

The blue flame of the gas stove roars. One packet of instant noodles floors me; overwhelmed by MSG, I can only lie on my back, carb-drunk, staring at the sky. There are peculiar drifting sobs coming from somewhere far away, perhaps the ragged man in green or perhaps another desert djinn.

After a while I pinpoint the sound as my own breath.

My sleeping mat has a slow puncture, nicked by a razor-sharp gypsum shard. At 2 a.m. I wake uncomfortably moulded to the lumpy ground, my back full of divots. Inflating it gives me three more hours and then I'm on the ground again. The sky at dawn is the same weak blue as it was seven hours before.

The elliptical canyon walls look like eyelids made of rock. I lie inside this bare socket watching the faintest cataract of a morning cloud inch across the emptiness until the heat smears it away. Then there is only blue, an infinite depth of field. An hour passes, two, three. Here comes the sun again.

I do not repeat my foolish misadventure of yesterday. Apart from pre-emptive shifts to keep my body from exposure I spend the afternoon motionless, guarding my core temperature. From now on I will only venture out in the mornings and the evenings, when the heat is tolerable, the radius of my wandering determined by my water supply: never more than a maximum of three hours' walk from camp. I cannot walk in a straight line but must orbit this fixed point, as if on a tether.

I spend the next five days and five nights in this gully, a miniature wilderness quest for a miniature wilderness.

By the end of the second day I am talking to myself.

Time passes strangely here. The long, hot hours of the afternoons are measurable only by the slow migration of shadows on rocks and by my diminishing litres of water, which I count obsessively. Lying with my eyes half closed, not quite asleep and not quite awake, in a heat-stunned semi-siesta, I occasionally leap awake with a feeling of alarm: I should *do* something! But when I rise dizzily to take a step into the glare, that hostile medium, the lesson comes back to me. Doing is dangerous here.

I drink rehydration salts to make the water I have go further and begrudge the wasted steam that rises from the cooking pan.

Urine evaporates. Shit I carefully bury.

By the end of the third day a host of flies has discovered my camp, seething in a happy swarm around my rubbish bag. I imagine them wandering in the desert, lost for mosquito years, before picking up my trail. My waste is their oasis.

The cicadas make a sound like steam escaping from a pressure valve. Every evening I attempt the meditation of trying to catch the moment it starts – it must begin with an individual spark from which the rest catch fire – but it is impossible. No matter how hard I concentrate, straining my ears for the first whirr, the sound is suddenly everywhere and has apparently been happening for some time. There is never a first.

I play the same game with the stars and fail at that as well. They go from nothing to everything, like the monotheistic God.

A short walk above my camp, where the canyon equalises with the desert's surface level, is a black, shining hill that looks almost vitrified. Its sides are slick with stones that slither under my boots, meaning I have to scramble up on my hands and knees. It is only five hundred metres tall but a mountain in this landscape. I make a ritual of climbing it after dawn and before dusk to see the spectrum of desert colour – purple-grey, purple-orange, purple-red, charcoal, ash, crimson, kidney red, yellow, dun, terracotta – emerging and submerging, a memory that the heat destroys.

To the north is blasted white, all colour scorched away.

I have one-sided conversations with the beetles that trundle through the dust, infinitesimal pioneers wandering *ramblas* of their own. One, a frequent visitor, is a devotee of the parmesan sauce that spills from the ready pasta meals I cook once or twice a day, its mandibles working excitedly as it feeds on the congealing lakes. Having eaten, it returns to its own small canyon, full of cheese. I wonder what it dreams of.

At night the sky is bright with suns. The *Vía Láctea*, the Milky Way, spills across the universe, and eking out the contents of a one-euro cardboard box of astringent red wine – yet another litre on the liquid weight I carried in – I think about the radiation burning its way through space to catch me lying here, exposed. No sooner has the sun gone down than a billion more suns rise.

By the end of the fourth day my camp is overrun. Beetles, flies, spiders, mites and millipedes – though no scorpions, yet – have made the place their own, converging on this point from every direction. Legs as thin as hairs scale my face as I sleep. My pasta is full of big red ants, boiled to death in hot cheese sauce.

It feels like that might be the fate of all of us some day.

~

Sometimes in the mornings and evenings, if the wind blows a certain way, I hear volleys of distorted pings and ricochets echoing down the canyons, a noise that makes no sense to me. It takes me several days to identify it as gunfire.

At first I think it must be hunters – the Virgin of the Sea Hunting Society venturing down from the sierra, perhaps, in search of trophy ibex horns – but it is something far more surreal: the twice-daily cowboy gunfights taking place at Texas Hollywood. In the clear desert air the sound carries for miles. As a dependable marker of time it becomes strangely comforting, a reminder that I am not alone with the insects and the sun. There are other humans out there, even if they are acting out a deranged fantasy.

One late afternoon, returning from a walk down Arroyo de Verdelecho, I come across a tall red cliff that appears to be singing. The notes of an ethereal voice are emanating from the rock, soaring and falling against waves of swelling strings. To my amazement I know the tune: it is the wordless, operatic theme of *Once Upon a Time in the West*, composed by Ennio Morricone and sung by Edda Dell'Orso. The melody must be drifting from the film set of Western Leone – invisible to me, at the foot of this ravine – echoing off the opposite cliff, surely inaudible from anywhere else but here. I am the only listener in a stone auditorium.

The echo is not the only refraction that the music has made. Scored by an Italian composer to evoke a reimagined frontier on a distant continent a century after it ceased to exist, and now playing on a loop in a derelict theme park in Spain, it is many degrees removed from historical foundation. Grandiose, melodramatic, tragic, absurd, heroic, it is utterly unlike anything that was ever heard in the nineteenth-century American West, and yet it has become emblematic of that time. It is a Wild West fairy song, an electronic haunting.

Morricone's other compositions haunt this landscape too. Back at camp I expend precious battery life listening to some of the themes downloaded on my phone: *A Fistful of Dollars*, *For a Few Dollars More* and other scores written for Leone's films. In some ways Morricone – a childhood friend of Leone's who, like him, spoke no English and had never crossed the Atlantic – had an even greater effect on the public imagination. The pistol shots, the cracks of rawhide whips and particularly the famous whistle from *The Good, the Bad and the Ugly* – a trilling of notes that has become synonymous with thousand-yard stares and trigger fingers twitching over the handles of holstered guns – are now inseparable from conceptions of that era. The music provides a soundtrack not only to the cowboy myth, in all its machismo and its camp absurdity, but to America at its most aggressive and confident, the ever-expanding frontier of Manifest Destiny.

Never has a genocide been scored so lovingly.

After a while the faraway shootouts lose their unreal sense, becoming as natural to this place as the clatter of falling pebbles. Sometimes I hear a mournful howl, elongated by distance, that turns out to be the brakes of trucks on the A-92 to Gérgal. I practise my Morricone whistle, the gunslinger's call and response. It echoes off the gully walls as naturally as birdsong.

South of the singing rock lies a different dream. An hour's

walk brings me close to the foothills of the sierra, where –
against the backdrop of a lumpen mountain that has the
appearance of a deformed head or a rotting root vegetable, a
blanched celeriac slumping in the heat – there is a patch of
desert quite unlike the *ramblas* further north. From the base
of the butte stretches a playa of dazzling sand atomised from
the slopes above, almost too white to look at, ending in the
surprising green of an oasis.

Apart from the occasional eucalyptus or black locust tree,
a brief encounter with a fig, these palms are the only trees I
have seen for days. Just the rustling of their fronds, rummaged
through by the wind, feels enough to take degrees off my
body temperature. Pushing into their shade is like being
absorbed. Through a screen of serrated leaves I look back out
at the glare. Secure and calm, under cover, I am back in
Białowieża again. But these trees, unlike those ones, are not
supposed to be here.

Europe's only native palms are the European fan palm (also
known as the Mediterranean dwarf palm) and the Cretan date
palm. All the others have invaded or been introduced. But
the individuals around me are less invasive species than cinematic extras; like so many things in Europe's only desert, they
are shreds of a fantasy.

The English director David Lean came here in the early
1960s, before Leone had built the walls of his first saloon. The
filming of *Lawrence of Arabia* was an epic undertaking, involving
a cast and crew of over a thousand people, hundreds of horses
and dozens of camels imported from what was then the Spanish
Sahara. Many of the 'Arab' extras were played by local Roma.
The scene they filmed at this spot shows T.E. Lawrence (Peter
O'Toole) and Sherif Ali (Omar Sharif) reclining against a
background of paradisiacal plenty. Around a shaded waterhole
Arab tribesmen and their camels take a break from fighting
Ottomans. The severely handsome Sharif, dressed in an austere

black robe, sips tea and occasionally whacks a subordinate with his cane. O'Toole, blond and safari-suited, is the opposite end of the spectrum, bleached of colour from head to toe apart from his uncanny blue eyes. They evoke the 'white hat, black hat' scheme of the early cowboy films, except that neither is a villain and neither is quite a hero.

The palms were brought here from Alicante, 150 miles away. The scene lasts for less than three minutes of an almost four-hour film.

When it was done the production moved to a new location in Morocco. The actors left. The cameras left. The camels left. The palm trees stayed.

The water is long gone, presumably evaporated.

The original Lawrence, an archaeologist who became a key player in the Arab Revolt against the Ottoman Empire in the First World War, was part of a lineage of European desert travellers that went back to the nineteenth century. As pioneering homesteaders were crossing deserts in North America, seeking fertile lands beyond, British, French and German explorers were mounting expeditions into the arid zones of North Africa and the Middle East. While there were cultural parallels – the inevitable 'conquering' and 'penetrating'; the colonial obsession with filling in blank spaces on the map – these peregrinations in dusty lands had different purposes. In America no one *wanted* to trek across waterless wastes of sand and rock, regions that even the indigenous populations thought best avoided. They only did it in order to get to the other side. By contrast, the western explorers of the Sahara and Rub' al Khali, the Empty Quarter of Arabia, were drawn to such places as if by an obsession. The desert was not a means to an end but an end in itself. Like the Arctic and the Antarctic at the other extreme of temperature, these harsh landscapes – seemingly stripped of everything but heat – became natural proving grounds for a cult of imperial maleness.

The idea of deserts as crucibles, as places of purification that could somehow scour away the corruption of worldly influence, goes right back to the dawn of monotheism. Moses, Jesus and Mohammed, the prophets of the three Abrahamic religions – worshippers of the sky god and the all-consuming light – all received their revelations in BWh arid zones, as did the Desert Fathers (and the lesser-known Desert Mothers) of the early Christian Church. In *The Immeasurable World*, describing his travels in desert places, the writer William Atkins traces this association between desolate environments and spiritual attainment. The desert is 'solitary, godless, lonesome, deathly, barren, waterless, trackless, impassable, infested, cursed, forsaken – and yet, at the same time, the site of revelation, of contemplation and sanctuary. Amid its horrors, peace – peace *magnified* by those horrors.'

Unlike in North America, where pioneers showed little but scorn towards the native peoples whose lands they were passing through, or invading, in Arabia – faced with some of the least hospitable landscapes on earth – the attitude of white explorers was largely more respectful. While there was certainly racial and religious prejudice, they used Bedouin guides and sought permission from local tribes whose territories they wanted to cross; they ate like Arabs, rode camels like Arabs and dressed in Arab clothing. Perhaps a shared predilection for militarism and monotheism partly explained the affinity; there was also admiration for the toughness, asceticism and discipline of the desert people, qualities that also happened to be seen as imperial virtues.

Deeply embedded in Arab culture during his years of desert warfare, Lawrence, in the language of the day, went native. Fluent in Arabic and proficient on camelback, he was known as El Aurens, an Arabisation of his English name (in contrast with O'Toole, whom Arab extras nicknamed Ab al-'Isfanjah, Father of the Sponge, for his habit of lining his saddle with foam rubber). The immersion was profound and changed Lawrence utterly. '[T]he effort for these years to live in the dress of Arabs, and to imitate their mental foundation, quitted me of my English self, and let me look at the West and its conventions with new eyes: they destroyed it all for me,' he wrote in *Seven Pillars of Wisdom*. The desert crucible had worked, transforming him into something else, but he had not been made pure; his Arab identity was 'an affectation only. Easily was a man made an infidel, but hardly might he be converted to another faith. I had dropped one form and not taken on the other.'

His divided loyalties were not only cultural but, tragically, political. Having incited the Arabs to fight, and given assurances of British support for their independence after the war, he watched as the British and French proceeded to help themselves to the ex-Ottoman provinces, carving up the Middle East between their empires. For the Arabs it was a deep betrayal; for Lawrence it was a guilt he never recovered from. Traumatised from the war – he had been beaten and possibly raped by Ottoman soldiers in 1917 – he died at the age of forty-six in a motorcycle crash in Dorset.

The palm trees of this fake oasis, imported from hundreds of miles away to provide a backdrop for an entirely fictitious scene (the character of Sherif Ali was invented for the film), remain here as a monument that is entirely accidental. They are a tattered variant of the Stara Białowieża grove, the ancient Polish century oaks embodying national heroes. Like the man who became El Aurens, they are half one thing and half another; successful transplants that nevertheless do not truly belong. They have gone native too, in this false Arabia.

A sudden gust of hot wind. The palm fronds rasp like saws. Leaving the shade of the oasis I walk past deep cracks in the earth and the ruins of old stone walls, southwards under the booming archway of the A-92. Somewhere in the hills ahead is a spot known as Crocodile Rock where an iconic scene from *The Good, the Bad and the Ugly* was filmed. I could also seek the place where a German tank drove off a cliff in *Indiana Jones and the Last Crusade*, or where John Lennon starred in *How I Won the War* (his only non-Beatles film role; he also wrote 'Strawberry Fields Forever' in Almería).

But the prospect is ugly and uninviting, oppressed by white noise from the highway, and my invisible water leash is tugging me back to camp. I do not have the motivation to traipse in film directors' footsteps, lining up the angles from which they filmed this or that scene, like the nostalgia hunters who provide the tour guides of Tabernas with a steady income. I imagine that most of these seekers are men of a certain age: earnest, gently obsessive, with families that have stayed at home and modest internet followings. They come to the desert like fossil collectors, searching for memories.

Only once in my time in Tabernas do I see them, these movie devotees. I expected to encounter more but the heat-wave has kept them indoors. On my way back from Lawrence's oasis a muscular white 4x4 rolls past me in a cloud of dust, halting in the shade of the *rambla* wall. The sight of a vehicle, so close, feels slightly shocking. The doors open to disgorge two young men in shirts and shorts, bright and fresh, aiming camera phones. Their guide, an older man, points out some former location – perhaps a place where a lawman was ambushed or a Comanche raiding party bristled their head-dresses over a ridge – but, as I approach, their attention turns to me. I suddenly see myself through their eyes: grey with dust, streaked with sweat, unwashed for almost seven days, conspicuously alone. Have I been talking to myself? I'm pretty sure I have not been shouting – most certainly I have not been *dancing* – but it's more than possible that I have vocalised some thoughts, have made some utterances out loud, within the hearing range of this clean young pair.

I can imagine how it happens: a cautious '*Qué tal?*' from them. And then, unbidden from my lips: '*Aargh! Dios! Mierda!*'

Instead I tip my hat to them – the formality feels appropriate – and leave them to their memory tour, retreating out of sight. A few minutes later, hearing the engine, I jump behind a rock. Some Brujo instinct compels me to hide as the vehicle rumbles past, accompanied by an amplified monologue reverberating off the cliffs, and I only step back into daylight after it has gone.

A trickle of stones. High up the cliff, an ibex rising quietly. I tip my hat to it as well, thinking that it might understand.

~

I see him on one other occasion, the ragged man in green. The *loco*, the desert madman; perhaps a vision of what I might look like myself if I stay too long. He is on the opposite side of the Rambla de Tabernas, scrambling hand over foot up a steep hillside, still raving to himself, though less furiously than before. I don't know whether he's seen me or not, or if it even matters.

The impulse to follow him comes partly from curiosity and partly from concern. Does he actually live up there? Is he *okay*? The next morning I make my way cautiously up the same slope, pausing at its crest to scan the land ahead. The vista revealed is unexpected: a landscape of white, erupted mud entirely hidden from below, like the aftermath of a series of random explosions. The skin of the earth has peeled away to expose an interior world of crumbling arches and shallow caves, their ceilings partially collapsed, areas where the ground has slumped and fallen through. There is no sign of him but he could be anywhere.

An apprehensive trespasser, I descend into this weird terrain. The ground knocks hollow to the step, tunnelled out beneath my feet. Walls of mud rise on either side, kicking out refracted heat, their texture resembling cracked flesh or the pathways of a dried-out brain. There are ranges of repeating forms that have the appearance of limpet shells, alluvial fans created by sediment washed down from above, settling into identical pyramidal angles of repose. The combined effect is fractal, almost psychedelic.

It would be easy to get lost here; much harder to be found. The proper topographical term for terrain like this is 'badlands'.

No other landscape word is as brutally descriptive. It comes from *mako sica*, literally 'bad land' (in some versions 'land of bad spirits'), the no-nonsense name the Lakota gave to the striated canyonscapes of what is now South Dakota. French Canadian frontiersmen described it as *mauvaises terres à traverser*, 'bad lands to cross', and the term spread from there to describe similar territories across North America: from Badlands National Park, South Dakota, and Makoshika State Park, Montana, to Ontario's Cheltenham Badlands and the Big Muddy Badlands in Saskatchewan. New Mexico's El Malpais National Monument takes its name from the Spanish *malpaís*, 'bad country'.

Tabernas is not just Europe's only desert but its largest area of *malpaís* (others include Italy's *calanchi* and the *calanques* in the south of France). Desert is the climate and badlands the topography. The term is both cultural – synonymous with outlaws, runaway slaves and recalcitrant tribes – as well as geological: 'a region marked by intricate erosional sculpturing, scanty vegetation, and fantastically formed hills', according to a dictionary definition. With their strange replications and their twisted, tortured forms that take the shape of buttes and turrets, precariously balanced mushrooms and contorted phalluses, badlands conjure up a sense of deep uncanniness; such architecture must surely be the work not of an order-loving

God but of some diabolical, possibly demented hand. Common features of such landscapes are the irregular, spindly spires known as fairy chimneys or hoodoos, which are found in eroded regions from Utah to Cappadocia. Revealingly, the word 'hoodoo' is thought to derive from 'voodoo', an association (in Christian minds, at least) with malevolent supernatural forces and bad luck. It is a topographical version of 'Here be monsters'.

It is not monsters, though, that lie behind this weirdness. As it says in one of Kevin's travel books – my copy now coated with dust, like the books in Laurence and Bri's van-library – 'badlands are likely to occur if the following three key factors are present: a dry climate with occasional fierce downpours, soft rocks that are easily eroded, and slopes that allow fast flow of water over the surface.' The legacy of water is everywhere, a fluvial sculpting and smoothing that has given this land its shape. But water's influence here is older than floods and rains.

Eight million years ago – when the climate was warmer and the oceans higher than they are today – while much of northern Europe was grassland roamed by ungulate herds, this part of southern Spain was covered by a sea. Cliffs of fossilised coral reefs in the Sierra de los Filabres and the nearby Sorbas Basin indicate where the coastline was, far north of its present location. During this epoch, the Miocene, whales and other cetacean species were slowly assuming their modern forms. These shallow waters would have been rich in shellfish and crustaceans. For hundreds of thousands of years a slow rain of organisms drifted to the sandy floor, compacting into layers of calcium and forming the sedimentary rocks – sandstone, limestone, mudstone and marl – that comprise the twisted walls of today's *ramblas*.

When, seven million years ago, the Sierra Alhamilla was thrust up by tectonic shifts, the mountains acted like a dam, separating the Tabernas Basin from the open sea to the south. The region remained an inland sea for another three million years. In a strange climactic twist the same range that once trapped water in now keeps it out, preventing moisture from today's Mediterranean from reaching inland.

If the Cairngorms' Lairig Ghru is the negative shape of ice, this, Europe's driest place, is the negative shape of water. The name of the little museum in Níjar – Museo Memoria del Agua – takes on a deeper meaning, not referring to the memory of a few hundred years of watermills but to the absence of water that existed beyond memory. Or perhaps this desert is not memory but prophecy: as the planet returns towards Miocene heat the seas are on the rise again, claiming back the empty spaces they once filled. One day the dam wall of the sierra might burst and a saline lake flood back, lapping at the fossilised reefs and turning sandstone back to sand. Whales, if there are any left, might throw their shadows on these hills. These desert badlands were once water and they might be again.

But there is no sign of the *loco*, no sign of any life at all. No birds, no insects, not even plants; nothing can gain purchase in this brittle, flaking mudscape. I take one fork in the cracked maze and then another fork and each decision brings me lower, deeper into airlessness. Reeling with heat, awash with sweat, I make my way along a narrow ridge towards a cave sagging like a down-turned mouth. I half expect to find his den but there is nowhere to lie down, nowhere to even sit, just boulders of cracked mud and dust, dust everywhere. A tunnel leads downward and I stoop to follow it, mud-rocks breaking apart with soft thumps beneath my boots, emerging into another cave more rubbly than the first. In the floor a sinkhole leads to yet another lower level. Far above, a chimney opens to a blue dot of sky. The air is stifling here, the heat truly horrible, and I am sweating so

much that I can hardly see. What am I doing here? I clumsily retrace my steps, guilty at having come blundering into
his secret world, territory as disturbed and disturbing as a bad
dream. Is he watching from behind a rock somewhere, hexing
me from shadowed ground? A fugitive from the devil knows
what, he clearly does not want to be found. From the crest
of the *rambla* I pause to look back and see movement down
below: something dark lifting from a gallery of hoodoo forms.
A bird of prey – I think it's a kestrel – swoops low and
vanishes. Then the warren is bare again.

Tonight is my last night in this gully. Pointlessly inflating
my punctured sleeping mat yet again, I think of him lying
asleep – *does* he sleep? – not far away, nested in that ruptured
ground. The thought occurs to me: are there others like him
– others like me – somewhere out there too, watching the
billion suns rise, holed up in their private badlands?

~

I do not follow the *ramblas* back but leave my gully by another
route, over the top and into the higher desert to the north.
It is late afternoon and the heat today has breached forty
degrees; if that was replicated in my body, the differential
equalised, I would be into the seizure stage, my cells beginning to deform. But I have two litres of water left and the
confidence of having survived a week in the wilderness. I am
not done yet. For my last night in the desert I want to sleep
somewhere high, with a view over the dried-out seabed of
the Miocene, so I am heading towards the mesas – table
mountains – that rise to the north-west of the town and its
Moorish fort. They take the names of animals: La Tortuga,
the Turtle; Cabeza del Águila, Eagle's Head; guardian spirits
of the desert preserved in the living rock. Crossing a playa
of crunching salt, a mineral deposit washed down from the

hills above, I leave a line of perfect bootprints as if on a field of frost. Ruined *cortijos* are scattered about, abandoned attempts at settlement, foolhardy outposts of cultivation beaten back by harsh conditions.

A long hill of yellow grasses brings me to the top of the mesa and I follow its ridge towards the drop-off point. It comes suddenly, a plunge into open space like the edge of the Grand Canyon; I think of covered wagons halting and pioneers scratching their heads in despair. A shed snakeskin flutters on a rock, a flag marking danger.

A series of unwise manoeuvres brings me underneath the lip of sandstone that forms the mesa's edge, where I find an overhang. It conceals a bed of dust that lies several feet deep, scattered with ibex droppings, and after several minutes' work scooping the dust into shape I have made a hollowed space just the right size for my body. The rock is like a cresting wave of fossilised surf that curves above, folding me inside itself, hiding me from view. Suspended over empty space, it is strangely comforting. As evening falls – the ancient seabed flooding with dazzling orange light – a wind picks up from the canyon floor and rushes to meet me. It creates a dust storm that rages long into the night, a tornado of choking powder that has me as its epicentre, forcing me to cover my eyes and breathe in short, protected huffs. I cannot cook, cannot really move, can only huddle and wait for it to pass. In the morning my skin and hair are grey, my eyes full of grit, my nose blocked, my lungs clogged; my mouth fills up with sediment every time I cough. Descending the mesa the steep way down, following winding ibex trails, I slap at my clothes and it raises clouds as if from a climber's chalk bag.

The dust pours thickly from my body in miniature mudslides, cascading torrents, scouring the buttes of my ankles and the hoodoos of my toes. The thundering flash flood sweeps me clean, takes decades off my skin. I am in the same shower in the same one-star hotel and it feels like luxury beyond all imagining. The linen on the bed is crisp and the ceiling fan sounds like an old friend. I fall into a deep siesta and wake to the alarm of church bells.

Being back in this one-horse town is bewildering. The palm trees' shadows are too precise, the blue of the municipal swimming pool is unreal, quite unbelievable, and the people in the streets – more than they ever did before – look like extras playing parts in a film about Andalucian life: *Once Upon a Time in the South*. Old men in flat caps dress in woollen cardigans in plus-forty-degree heat; multiple generations of women drag their chairs into the streets to smoke together and cheerfully pass judgement on passers-by. In one café after another I down iced drink after iced drink until my urine, amber-brown, begins to run clear again. A single glass of evening beer gets me drunk instantly.

On the way back to my hotel I come across a travelling saint. He is being carried, with great solemnity and joy, at the head of a procession from the church and around the town, accompanied by a brass band playing a ponderous, melancholy tune. Little girls in their best lace dresses are scattering rose petals in the streets. Men and women are bearing icons and candles in red glass holders. The flow is irresistible; despite my tiredness my body is drawn along with it, through the maze of alleyways as narrow and steep as *rambla* walls, into the canyons of wider streets and the level plains of plazas. The procession ebbs and flows, gets caught in gossiping neighbourly eddies and picks up speed on downhill slopes, before eventually pooling in a tidy public square. The priest, who walks beneath a golden awning carried by four dark-suited men, swings his orb of sweet smoke. From where I stand his face is obscured by the item of sacred treasure he holds: a circular silver mirror in a glory of golden rays.

The patron saint, whoever he is, becomes an irrelevance. It seems to me that this crowd is following an effigy of the sun.

~

There is a certain vantage point not far into the desert – it should be marked with a plaque – where Tabernas offers up the two conflicting visions of itself. On one side the ruined Moorish castle stands as a reminder of a history that actually took place – eight centuries of Islamic rule and a cultural melting pot that influenced everything from language and architecture to the DNA of today's Andalucians – but which, since the Christian reconquest, has largely been brushed aside, overlooked and conveniently forgotten about. On the other, the mimicking letters of the Texas Hollywood sign symbolise a history that is entirely fake yet glorified; celebrated to such an extent that, for generations of movie-goers, it has become more real than reality itself. To scan the distance between these points is to travel a thousand years in time, from the landing of the army of Tariq ibn Ziyad at Gibraltar in the eighth century AD to the American wagon trains rumbling west in the nineteenth. In the middle of this history stands 1492: not only the year that the three ships of Cristoforo Colombo made landfall in the New World, claiming the Americas for the Spanish crown, but also – in a strange quirk of fate – the year that the last Moorish sultan, known to the Spanish as Boabdil, surrendered the Kingdom of Granada, turning once to look back from the Pass of the Moor's Last Sigh before sailing into exile in Morocco. In that year Spain finally severed its ties with the Islamic east to pursue unimaginable wealth and power in the west, dragging much of Europe along with it and changing world history for ever. This is the pivot point of the schizophrenic split between the desert's identities: Middle East on one side and Wild West on the other.

Tabernas itself, of course, is neither of these things. The memories and fantasies that people have layered on top of it carry a hint of desperation, a kind of furious denial, as if no one can bring themselves to admit that it is simply what it is: a desert – harsh, inhospitable, unproductive, alien – on the supposedly tame and cultivated continent of Europe. It has been made unreal.

But reality is catching up.

From Spain to Italy to Greece, across the European south, desert and semi-desert conditions are steadily creeping northwards. They have been for a long time, ever since the green and fertile hinterland of North Africa – the breadbasket of the Roman Empire – started turning yellow and brown a thousand years ago. In this age of climate crisis the thermogram of the world is shifting hues more rapidly than we have ever seen before. A recent article in the peer-reviewed journal *Scientific Data* features a comparison of two maps, one showing the Köppen–Geiger climate classification from 1980 to 2016 – the one I have become familiar with – and the other a projection, based on current trends, stretching from 2071 to 2100. In this future, much of France is not coloured green but yellow, recategorised from 'temperate oceanic' to Csa, 'savanna'. A sweeping belt of northern Russia is no longer considered 'subarctic' but 'humid continental', and a patch of Spain's south-east, projecting inland from the coast, is stained the red of BWh, 'hot desert', merging with the greater mass of the incarnadine Sahara.

Within the next three decades, says a recent report from ETH Zürich, cities in the Northern Hemisphere will start to feel more like cities hundreds of miles further south. By 2050, temperatures in Madrid will resemble those in Marrakech today; Warsaw will be more like Tbilisi; Stockholm more like

Budapest; London more like Barcelona. As this week's scalding spell suggests, fearsome extremes of heat will no longer be confined to peripheral arid zones. What we call record temperatures will soon be average summers.

In the Cairngorms and Białowieża I was walking into loss, but my immersion in Tabernas feels like something else: an unconscious acclimatisation to conditions yet to come. In these desert badlands I have stepped into the future.

~

Before I leave Tabernas, though, I cannot resist the afterglow of the reimagined past. At last the time has come to visit Texas Hollywood.

The gate is manned by a handsome young cowboy in a black shirt, six-shooters slung around his waist, his sheriff's badge flashing silver in the midday sun. The flags of Spain, Mexico, Andalucía and the EU flutter weakly on their poles, while the Stars and Stripes flies confidently above Fort Bravo, the stockade fort that serves as the headquarters of the 3rd US Cavalry; defending white civilisation, presumably, against the clear and present danger of the few pathetic tepees clustered on a nearby mound, daubed with unlikely sigils. I walk through the empty fort and into the frontier town, where a monkey-faced gunslinger is checking his smartphone in the shade. Tourists wander in pairs, taking turns to trundle up and down Main Street in a horse and cart driven by a black-bearded man with forearms thicker than my legs. I wait until the cart is free and climb aboard.

As Western Leone seemed to be, the film set is divided into two distinct neighbourhoods: the Anglo-Saxon settlement and the Mexican pueblo. We clip-clop pass a wooden school-house, the Doña Ana County Jail, a gunsmith's, gallows, hitching posts, the Sheriff's Office and the First Union Bank, which must surely be one of the most-robbed banks in existence. Mayfield's Timber Lumber Yard – from the recent film *The Sisters Brothers* – turns out to be a façade, held up by scaffolding. In the Mexican district are crumbling adobe houses built in colonial style and two magnificent agaves, perhaps the only ones left standing in Almería. Not even the weevil plague, it seems, can penetrate this fantasy, a protective celluloid bubble that keeps reality at bay. '*No hay muro! No Trump!*' is the brawny cowboy's line as we pass back into the United States, 'There's no wall! No Trump!' He has clearly said it many times before but delivers it with relish. When I ask how he came to work here he says, '*Me gustan los caballos*', 'I like horses,' in a quiet manner that is oddly touching.

After the ride I buy myself a cold drink in the saloon, where the barmaids are dressed as prostitutes with headpieces of red plumes, corsets and scarlet garter belts, looking significantly tougher than their cowboy counterparts. I recognise one from a café in town, and remember something Laurence said: 'There was a time when the chief of police in Tabernas doubled as the sheriff in Fort Bravo.' Laurence could probably get a job as the resident Native American, but expressed disdain for this place. A bloody Disneyland, he said, taking all the water.

On the wall above the bar is a mounted buffalo skull. It is identical to a skull you might find in an oak grove in Białowieża; buffalo and bison each iconic of the wild frontiers of America and Europe, and their exterminations – though carried out hundreds of years apart – emblematic of civilisation and dubious Christian progress. In the United States the buffalo herds were reduced, by the end of the nineteenth century, from thirty million to just a few hundred in the wild. The infamous 'Buffalo' Bill Cody boasted of personally slaughtering over four thousand of them, sometimes averaging twelve a day, in order to break the resistance of the Plains Indian tribes who depended on the hunt. In the words of a US colonel of the time: 'Kill every buffalo you can! Every buffalo dead is an Indian gone.'

Almost as soon as it was established, the American frontier became a self-referencing parody, enraptured by the image it had conjured for itself. Long before Texas Hollywood, it had turned itself into a product. By the 1870s Buffalo Bill, his Indian-fighting days behind him, was acting out a pantomime version of his own adventurous life in a travelling Wild West sideshow that toured the United States and Europe. A similar sideshow run by his former business partner Pawnee Bill featured another iconic name: Goyaałé, 'Yawning One', the defeated Apache war leader better known as Geronimo.

The man whose name has become synonymous with vainglorious defiance and death-defying falls from heights – yodelled by Dougie's acquaintance as he plunged off a Scottish mountainside – did not, despite his legacy, go out in a blaze of glory. After leading his people in wars against Americans and Mexicans, seeing his mother, wife and children murdered, and eventually being captured, Geronimo ended his life performing, under US Army guard, the role of the Noble Savage tamed, selling the buttons off his shirt for twenty-five cents apiece to curious townsfolk wanting to own a slice of American history.

Geronimo. Less of a dizzy drop now and more of a sinking feeling.

Dust swirls beyond the swing doors. The show is about to begin.

Here he comes, the handsome sheriff on his glossy chestnut mare. He hacks and spits into the dust. Morricone music swells. Three hard men ride after him, desperados – identifiable as such by their greasy hair and surly scowls – who have clearly come to town with the intention of causing trouble. A fifth rider appears, the smartphone-checking deputy on his piebald steed, and all of them gallop madly round the plaza, choking the audience with dust. As it settles they dismount and tether their sweating horses.

What follows – as in most Western plots – is less a storyline than a series of excuses for dramatic violent acts, with much thumbs-in-belt-loops acting and masturbatory gun-twiddling. The dialogue is in Spanish, too fast for me to follow. There are guns fired at dancing feet, goodies being pistol-whipped and lassoed baddies being dragged behind horses through the dust. There is comic drunkenness, a bank robbery and a breakout from the county jail. The shootout finale has everything – Stetsons flying off heads, a screaming man doing a somersault from a first-floor balcony – before the action culminates in the Old World ritual of the duel. Fingers tremble over holsters. Thousand-yard stares are held. Two rapid shots ring out. One man – the baddie – falls.

Later the bordello girls do the can-can, flashing their white bloomers, while the resurrected cowboys dutifully clap along. This leads to another display of jovial male violence: tequila shots slide down the bar; there is poker and a three-way brawl; punches are thrown; testicles are booted; the prostitutes scream; a child in the audience screams; someone is flung head-first through the swing doors; someone else comes in shooting; the child continues screaming and has to be taken outside; the last man standing is shot dead, pleasingly, by the barmaid.

Cue Johnny Cash's 'Ring of Fire'. The audience makes polite applause. The buffalo skull looks on, grimly unimpressed.

It is all ridiculous. And yet something in it moves me. This ritualised brutality, re-enacting the violent foundational myths of another time and place, are a kind of cowboy mystery play, a folk-memory upheld through unquestioning repetition. Its symbols, rites and superstitions are choreographed as perfectly as the gentle Catholic procession I followed through the streets last night. I can imagine it being performed, perhaps with a few distorted details here and there, a thousand years from now by whatever culture still survives in the greater Iberian desert, on the shores of a risen sea. Liberated from its claims to the slightest historical accuracy, it will have become what it wants to be: a true mythology.

The show is over. It is time to go. But I do not want to. With the heat of the day diminishing and the shadows growing long, the horses being rubbed down and softly crooned to in their stalls, these streets, and the illusion they create, are strangely soothing. An overwhelming melancholy has settled after all those deaths, the calm that follows violent acts; its atmosphere is a dream I do not want to leave. But the cowboys have retired and the entrance gate is closing. The cars of tourists overtake as I start the final walk – my bus to Almería awaits – in the softest evening light. Ahead of me, stretched into grotesque proportions on the earth, strides the shadow of a man in a wide-brimmed hat.

I follow him into the sunset.

HUNGARY'S STEPPE

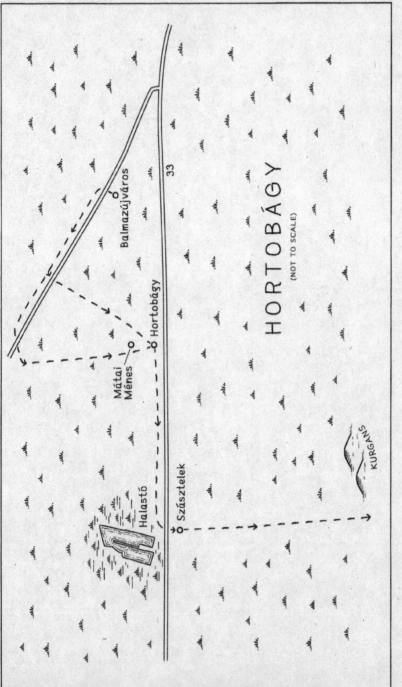

Once upon a time there were two brothers. Their names were Hunor and Magor. Their father was Ménrót, a warrior king – some say he was a giant – who ruled in the distant east: a land of enormous skies and ground as level as a sea, covered with rippling grass from horizon to horizon. The people tamed horses there and learned to ride them well. That country in the east is where horses came from.

Hunor and Magor liked to hunt, and on one of their hunting trips they surprised a stag that was unlike any animal they had seen before. It was white from head to hoof, with magnificent white antlers. They gave chase to it but the stag was very swift, swifter than their steeds, and they pursued the beast for days without catching it. The stag ran further and further west across the plains of grass and they galloped after it, away from their father's kingdom. At last the brothers reached another land – green, well-watered, plentiful – where the stag, having performed its role in the story, disappeared.

But they found greater quarry there: the beautiful daughters of Prince Dula, ruler of a people called the Alans, who were encamped by a lake. Hunor and Magor carried them off. They married them or raped them or probably both of those things. The descendants of Hunor became the Huns, the descendants of Magor became the Magyars, and the forceful union of the three nomadic tribes – Huns, Magyars and Alans – was the wellspring from which came the Hungarian people.

There is a low, mottled sky. The countryside looks drab. The moment the train pulls out of Munich my rucksack is thoroughly searched by a plainclothes officer who has a lot of questions. 'What is your business in Hungary?' he asks.

'Searching for the white stag,' is what I do not say. Instead I ask: 'Are you German police?'

'Bavarian,' he says sternly.

Later I realise that tomorrow is the start of a Budapest music festival and that the train is packed with dreadlocked German ravers. There are probably kilos of drugs on board, but none are in my bag.

Lower Austria blends smoothly into western Hungary, the same monotonous farmland and stuffy imperial architecture that recalls the time when both were joined in a Dual Monarchy. I drift off to sleep alone and wake, sprawled across three seats, to find that the compartment has filled with large, awkward-looking men attempting to allow me space. I'm sure I have been drooling. To my left is a glimpse of wooded hills. On the other side of the train is flatness stretching south. Budapest, when I arrive, seems to be oddly hushed for what I remember as a clattering, noisy city, but maybe that's just my brain, running on four hours of broken sleep, filtering out the stimulus. Multinational chain stores sit next to old-fashioned shops with dowdy displays of rope, brooms and fishing supplies. Drunks surround Keleti station, street people with fume-aged faces and expressions of long endurance. The Danube flows, grey and green, through the joined, divided city, half Buda and half Pest, spanned by iron bridges. The air is sticky; the August heat feels like an oven that has been left on too high and forgotten about. Squelching in humidity I climb to Buda Castle.

Here, from the imposing Habsburg barracks and the fantasy architecture of St Matthias Church, with its many-coloured tiles and its whimsical white follies, is a view towards the next outland I will walk. Beyond Pest's maze of grimy streets is a welling of open space that starts where the city ends and stretches for hundreds of miles to the east: this is the beginning of the Great Hungarian Plain.

In the morning that level ground is gliding past the grubby window of yet another train, and I have a brief, disjointed recollection of the miniature steam engine chugging across the Dungeness headland; a similar sense of setting forth into unfathomable space. Suburbs soon become fields interspersed with red-roofed houses and fenced-off garden plots, each with their careful rows of vegetables or grapevine. We rattle through Cegléd and Szolnok, then through smaller settlements with jostlings of consonants, the agglutinative jumble of Magyar, which is like no other language in Europe. Between occasional clumps of trees the land runs evenly away.

It bears a passing resemblance to Poland – the country-sized field of the Clearing – but there was never a forest here, or at least not in human time. The Great Hungarian Plain lies in the Carpathian or Pannonian Basin (named after Pannonia, an imperial Roman province), a vast depression bounded by the protective walls of the Carpathian Mountains and the Dinaric Alps. Like Tabernas it was once submerged, not by a sea but by the prehistoric Lake Pannon, which drained ten thousand years ago at the end of the last ice age and became a washland of the Tisza River. The resulting freshwater marshes have been drying out for ten millennia, aided by the drainage schemes of agricultural peoples. The fertile soil is called loess, a wistful and poetic name: powdery, fine and pale, blown across Europe on the wind to accumulate in great deposits. From China to South America, loess underlies some of the world's most ancient agrarian civilisations.

The fertility of this loess is what drew nomads from the east, initially for raiding and pasturage but eventually for farming. This has been farmland for a long time, at least since Hunor and Magor's descendants settled down a thousand years ago, converted to Christianity and started ploughing. Loess is part of the story that has drawn me here, but for the most part it is the land's uncanny flatness. The great plain rolling by – which Hungarians call the Puszta, a word that derives from 'barren', 'bare' – is the westernmost extension of the Eurasian Steppe.

'Steppe' is a term for the temperate, semi-arid grassland that forms when there is enough rainfall to keep the desert at bay and support a profusion of grasses, but not forests. One of the largest biomes on earth – known as prairie in North America, pampas in South America and veld in southern Africa – its Eurasian variant (from the Slavic *step*) stretches for five thousand miles from the Great Hungarian Plain through Ukraine, southern Russia, Kazakhstan, Mongolia and into Manchuria, connecting the east of Europe with the interior of China. End to end, this is almost a fifth of the distance around the planet. Throughout history the Eurasian Steppe has acted as a kind of conveyor belt for the migration of populations from the east to the west; it enabled both the Silk Road and the Mongol invasions. On a Köppen-Geiger map this girdle is coloured the dusty yellow of BSk, 'cold semi-arid'. Geographers zone this broad expanse of the world's largest continent into three: the Pontic-Caspian (Western) Steppe, the Kazakh (Central) Steppe and the Mongol (Eastern) Steppe. The Great Hungarian Plain, separated from the rest by the rampart of the Carpathians, is an exclave of the mother-steppe.

The Puszta is a piece of Asia stranded in the heart of Europe.

The few desultory attempts at hills are like waves that fail to break and slide back into flatness, leaving no ripple in the land. Fields of wheat and corn go past, and meadows that have been cut for hay. The light has a certain quality – a clarity, a lucent glow – that produces a feeling that I can only describe as 'bigness'. Beneath that sky, glimpsed details stand out with urgency: a crane landing in a field, as white and sharp as a paper plane; a flock of sparrow-like birds rising up above a roof; the spume of dust drawn behind a distant truck. Then, for what feels like hours, pass nothing but sunflowers, drooping their heads as if collectively ashamed.

The sight strikes me as ominous, but I have never liked sunflowers; have always found them sinister, ever since their appearance in a recurring childhood dream. Now I come to think of it, it took place in a land much like this. I was riding a red tricycle up a sandy hill. At the top was the vista of a vast, flat space that I knew went on for ever, and far away – but charging closer with impossible nightmare speed – were three enormous monsters reaching almost to the sky. I don't remember what they looked like, only the sense of dread. My wheels were bogged down in sand and I could not get away.

Every time I had this dream it was preceded by the image of a faded sunflower, like the title screen before a film.

Perhaps, unconsciously, I have come here for a showdown.

By train rather than tricycle I charge eastwards on the plain that may as well go on for ever, towards a horizon that never comes. A shadow of that dread returns; the old fear of being exposed, with nothing to hide behind. Is it the land, or is it me, or is it something else? I have been slightly edgy all day; Hungary, for all its eminent culture and civility, its *Mitteleuropa* courtesy, seems to me on this journey to have a sense of menace. From Buda Castle yesterday I looked down on the neo-Gothic splendour of the Parliament building and remembered that this is a country on the verge of dictatorship – or maybe it is past that verge – whose government has taken control of the press, cultural organisations and the judiciary, the first nation in the EU to dismantle its own democracy to the extent that the term no longer really applies. The undercurrent of fascism that is prevalent across Europe now is especially potent here, tugging on old injuries. The country's southern borders are sealed with razor wire. This knowledge seems present in the land, in the dizzying sense of range; open spaces often seem to foster closed mentalities, as if the scale turns people's minds inwards to seek shelter. The fields of sunflowers go by. I nod asleep for a while. No sky-high monsters appear on the horizon, but I wake with unease.

At Debrecen is a waiting hall in grand socialist style, with two faded murals depicting blocky workers toiling bravely. I buy bread, fruit and cheese. Then I'm on a local bus going west towards Balmazújváros.

At last my boots touch the ground in a small country town with ripe plums hanging from roadside trees and elderly farmers sitting on benches eating ice cream. It is a humid afternoon. No one seems to look at me, for which I am grateful. After hours – days – on transport, carried along with no exertion, walking does not come naturally as I follow a straight road lined with black locust trees. My feet have not found their stride. I feel like an impostor. But the rucksack on my back is the same bag I have worn through arctic snow and desert heat, discoloured with Tabernas dust. The wide-brimmed hat is on my head. My legs resume their rhythm. It is easier not to think and so I just walk, going west towards the sun. What could be simpler than this? The unease subsides.

Far away across the sky bends a flexing, flowing line that turns out not to be smoke but a distant murmuration, starlings that migrate from continent to continent.

After half an hour of walking a gap appears in the trees, like a window opening. Through it lies my first glimpse of the outland I have come to find.

Nothing but yellow grasses hissing in the wind.

Or almost nothing. There is a white-walled cottage next to a scattering of hayricks that have tufty, pointed tops, and the silhouette of a man working with a pitchfork. A cockerel crows and I hear the clanging of an unseen animal bell.

This is the boundary of Hortobágy, Hungary's largest intact swathe of uncultivated Puszta.

~

It may not be Outer Mongolia, at just over three hundred square miles, but to many Hungarians this protected cultural landscape – the country's first national park and a UNESCO World Heritage Site – has an almost spiritual resonance. As a region that preserves traditions of a herding way of life that go back to the earliest days of the Magyar settlement, Hortobágy is hallowed ground, a symbolic repository of the national origin story and a portal to the vaster landscapes of the east. Hundreds of thousands come to visit the park each year, astonishing numbers for a place in which – on first impression, anyway – there is nothing to see but grass.

For the older generation that grew up under communism, Hortobágy also has unhappier connotations. From 1950 to 1953 – three years before the failed revolution against Soviet Russian rule – between ten and fifteen thousand political prisoners from around the country were sent to do forced labour here, having been told to leave their homes with only hours' notice. They slept in cattle sheds and were beaten for the slightest misdemeanours, sweltering in the heat of summer and freezing in the winter. The spiritual homeland of the nation became a place in which the dream of independence was systematically crushed, through pointless, back-breaking work. This gulag was a central European variant of Siberia.

The murmuration is now overhead, a fluctuating river of birds pouring across the sky like the contents of a never-ending bottle. The road runs past a cattle barn pumping out the sewage-sweet stench of slurry, and I glimpse black and white heads nodding up and down inside. After that there is only grass in a rippling pale haze.

Something moves on the road ahead: an enormous rabbit. It bounds away, longer and leggier than any rabbit I have seen before, followed by another, and another; the Puszta is thick with them, leaping up from their crouching places in the yellow grass and thundering across the steppe like a stampede of miniature horses. Then I realise they are hares, multitudes of them. Minutes later another creature that I can't at first identify comes hauling itself in strange bunched movements across my path, some kind of giant hedgehog. As I stoop to look at it there is a sharp hiss, like the sound of escaping air, and its body bristles with untidy javelins. A warning display. I step away, surprised at so much life.

The animal overture goes on. Beside the road a flock of sheep advances across the grass in a determined front, like a Roman phalanx. A shepherd with a round-brimmed hat and a brown weathered face turns his head to watch me come; his dog barks once, curtly.

'Hortobágy?' I ask. It is not really a question. It is a way of letting him know that I am on my way somewhere – to the village from which the region takes its name, where I plan to sleep – that my purpose is legitimate; that I am not out to steal his sheep but am only passing through.

'*Igen*,' 'Yes.' He nods, holding up three stubby fingers that I take to mean three miles.

It turns out to be three hours.

After a couple of those hours comes a collection of cottages, weather-beaten and sun-cracked, where three chestnut horses gleam in a green paddock. A black dog rushes out in challenge, slathering ferociously, but it has the feel of a ritual more than an attack, as if performed for an audience that only the dog can see. When I look back to check that it has stopped trailing me, I see, to the north, a pile of fat cumulus clouds and the sky streaked with smears: extremely distant weather systems – perhaps as far away as the Carpathian Mountain range – that are entirely unrelated to this unclouded afternoon. It is possible to see a long way here, in weather as well as in time.

Suddenly the air is sweet with a comforting, breath-warm smell that precedes a herd, unfenced: a cattle murmuration. I stop in admiration, for these are not the yoghurt-carton bovines I saw earlier; ivory-coloured, marble-smooth, with outsized, gracefully curving horns that taper into black tips, they are more like animals you might see guarded by Masai warriors on an African savanna, possessions of great status. They are Hungarian grey cattle, the traditional breed of the Puszta, brought here from the east a thousand years ago by migrating Magyar tribes and once prized throughout Europe, herded on droving routes to the courts of French and German kings. The breed passed through a bottleneck of near-extinction in the twentieth century and now survive only here and in a few other spots in Hungary.

There is no sense of threat, despite their formidable weaponry, so I sit down to rest my legs. I close my eyes and listen. The sound is like a quiet machine: the multiple, muffled crunch of several hundred mouths at work, cudding the sugars of the grass, a kind of aural massage.

A whistle makes me turn to see their owner on the road: not a Masai warrior but an old man on a battered bike, accompanied by the same black dog that assailed me earlier. It has no interest in me now; its attention is focused on the task of rounding up the cattle into a desired formation, trimming the edges and turning them back, snapping playfully at the strays that lower their horns to challenge it, a series of negotiations of defended dignity. The cowherd, nodding at me once, shouts one-syllable cow-words (or maybe they are dog-words) to give direction to the flow. The herd moves back towards the hamlet, from where the voice of an old woman calls them home.

When they have gone I see, beyond, a smaller, darker herd. They are not cows but wild asses, small numbers of which still live, free-roaming, on the steppe. Crooked, ancient-looking things from an age beyond agriculture, from the undomesticated past, they seem both familiar and eerily unfamiliar. One lifts its head and starts to bray, a jerky, suffering sound.

Hortobágy is less a village than a sprawl of farmsteads, or houses that resemble farmsteads, each surrounded by its plot of fruit trees, paddocks and chicken runs. The campsite where I pitch my tent borders a field of foals. By the time I arrive there are swallows in the sky and a half moon; it has been a long walk and hunger stabs inside me. At the old cattlemen's inn by the famous Nine-holed Bridge that crosses the Hortobágy River, an icon of the national park, I drink spicy goulash soup as darkness floods the steppe beyond. The inn has white linen tablecloths, an arched terrace of whitewashed walls and red carnations in pots; a bowl of paprika peppers sits on every table. This must be a link to the east as well, for the condiment would never be found in Romania or Slovakia, and certainly not in Austria. Fiercely Hungarian, paprika is one of the signs – like the language and the nomadism – by which the country sternly sets itself apart.

This inn, known as the Great Csárda, is another icon of the park. It was an important stopping point on the ancient Salt Road that ran from Maramureș, in what is now Romania, across the monotony of the Puszta and into central Europe. It makes a virtue of that history, proudly informing customers that its cellars were used as a hiding place by a local *betyár* called Pista Sós, and boasting of a kind of safe known as a 'damage saver': 'used for the fragile belongings to put them in a safe place when the drunk guests started to smash things and fight with each other'. The establishment is more refined these days, which seems a shame, although some hope is aroused by the arrival of a motorcycle gang, with matching leathers and club patches, who park their Harleys by the road and troop inside for beers. But after half an hour they leave, with no sign of a brawl.

The folk-hero highwaymen popularly known as *betyárs* – the name comes from the Turkish *bekar*, meaning 'unmarried man' – were cattle-rustlers, horse-thieves, bandits, and the subject of rollicking ballads in the nineteenth century. A clue to their activities lies in the name of the county I'm in, Hajdú-Bihar County, and the names of nearby villages such as Hajdúnánás and Hajdúböszörmény; the *hajdús* were irregular soldiers garrisoned here to guard the herds from the *betyárs'* depredations. The dashing brigands of the steppe had an informal uniform consisting of cattlemen's stiff black hats and magnificent moustaches combed into points as fierce as the horns of the cows they robbed. The most infamous, and most celebrated, were Jóska Sobri and Sándor Rózsa, who died respectively in 1837 and 1878 – the latter in jail, the former by committing suicide when surrounded – but their legend was preceded by the Slovak bandit Juraj Jánošík who lived a century earlier, who became a symbol of resistance against aristocratic oppression. A kind of Puszta Robin Hood, he paid a heavy price for his lawlessness, executed by being left to hang from a hook driven through his side.

It all makes for a rousing yarn, but there are deeper under-currents to the highwaymen's romantic myth. Hungary has a bloody history of violent peasant uprisings, each followed by a predictably brutal aristocratic response; after the 1514 revolt that left a trail of impaled bishops, tax-collectors and treasurers across the Great Hungarian Plain, rebel leader György Dózsa was placed on a red-hot iron throne while his flesh was torn off with pliers and his comrades forced to eat it. Small wonder that when the Ottomans arrived, only twelve years later, the demoralised peasantry didn't put up much resistance. Many must have hated their rulers more than the Turkish invaders.

Three centuries afterwards, these resentments lingered on. The *betyárs* did not exist in a vacuum but operated at a time of profound social change, when the last great swathes of open grassland were being turned over to agriculture, divided up by fields, fences, canals and later railways and roads, dispossessing herders of their traditional grazing rights. Like the exiled Moors of Andalucía turning to piracy against Spain, the banditry was a counter-offensive as well as a means to survive; the ancient struggle between herders and farmers, between Cain and Abel, that has been playing out since the earliest human history.

If the steppe represented freedom, these outlaws were the last gasp of the old nomadic soul.

~

My original plan was to walk the Hortobágy steppe from north to south, but – for a land with no obstacles – this presents surprising difficulties. Like the UNESCO site of Białowieża, the national park is protected, much of it off limits outside a few permitted footpaths that take walkers in a loop back to where they started from. Furthermore, unlike the *puszcza* that conceals all trespassers, on this featureless Puszta I would be visible for miles. (*Puszcza*, Puszta: there must be a link. Checking the etymology I find that the latter is not of Magyar origin but a Slavic loanword designating 'wilderness'. It is strange that the same word should mean such different things – a place defined by the presence of trees and a place marked by their absence – meanings as fluid, in their ways, as those of 'desert' and 'forest'.)

Solving the problem of the walk can wait a few days, at least. At the park information office, near the haunt of Pista Sós, I learn that the Mátai Ménes Stud Farm, a mile north of here, hires out horses for half-day rides, and the romance of the idea draws me irresistibly. What better way to see the steppe than on the back of a Nonius mare, the quintessential Puszta breed? I call the stables in advance – 'yes, I can ride a horse' – and am told to arrive punctually for midday.

It is true, technically, that I can ride a horse. I haven't done it since I was a child but the knowledge, surely, is instinctive in my body. With utterly misplaced confidence I walk to Mátai Ménes along the bank of the green river, past walnut and black locust trees. Outside the stables beautiful steeds are grazing under oaks, their glossy coats chestnut or black. They exude an air of gentle power, like engines turning over. Horseshoes – downturned in Hungary – are nailed to the stalls for luck.

'I thought you said you had boots,' says the woman as she adjusts the stirrups.

'These are boots.'

'They are shoes.'

'They're boots!'

'They are not what we call boots.'

It is not an auspicious start but it does not set me back. Before she takes me to the steppe, which looms in a wobbling yellow haze beyond the green fringe of the farm, she wants to see me complete a few circuits around the paddock. Mounting smoothly, I sit straight-backed, in the manner I know to be correct, with the reins at the right length and my heels down in the stirrups. I touch my heels to the mare's sides and she starts an easy walk. After I have gone round twice the woman politely calls me back.

'You cannot go out,' she says.

'Why?'

She shrugs. 'You cannot ride a horse.'

Genuinely curious, I ask what I am doing incorrectly but she does not seem able to put it into words. Everything about it is just *wrong*; she knew it as soon as she saw me. I ask for another chance and she concedes reluctantly. 'All right, you can try a trot. Be *careful.*'

The trot is an unmitigated disaster. Unable to find the rhythm, I am jolted and bounced all over the place, immediately lose a stirrup and spend the rest of the time hanging on, my teeth crashing in my head, my mare seemingly intent on breaking into a canter. She knows full well that I am not in control and seems offended by the presumption that I ever was; this feels like equine punishment for my human hubris. We make it round two more times, watched by expressionless stablehands, and when the woman calls me back it is a relief. 'See?' she says without satisfaction. 'On the Puszta are deer, rabbits, wind. These horses are sensitive. You must know how to ride.'

Half humbled, half humiliated, I opt instead to see the steppe from the carriage tour.

Mine is the last of four carriages, each pulled by a pair of horses and driven by a taciturn driver in indigo shirt and felt hat, another Hortobágy costume. Apart from a solitary Japanese man, I am the only foreigner. Pitching on the dirt track we leave the stud farm behind and steer on to the range, trailing a wake of dust. On the horizon is a shack constructed out of yellow thatch. It looks close but takes a surprisingly long time to reach; the steppe does peculiar things to perceptions of time and distance.

Another indigo-shirted man emerges, stooping, from the

shack. He does not do or say anything, just watches, leaning on a stick. The tourists start taking photographs and I see what we have come here for: in a stagnant wallowing hole are a dozen water buffalo.

They are like living mud, elemental golems. They lie almost entirely submerged with only their nostrils, broad horns and the tops of their heads above water level, and the paddles of their ears beating flies away. Every part of them is the uniform colour of the mud; occasionally a grey tail lifts and comes down with a slop, or a grey tongue searches from a grey, cudding mouth. Their eyes are grey. Their teeth are grey. They look like bottom-feeding fish, stranded carp drowning in a slowly evaporating pond, regarding us with expressions of sullenness and indulgence.

'Ugh!' exclaims a toddler in genuine disgust.

The carriages keep a respectful distance. These beasts, notoriously grumpy, can outrun a galloping horse. Once again they arrived in Hungary via Europe's open back door, yoked to the baggage trains of the Avars – a nomadic Central Asian people who preceded the Magyar tribes – some time in the sixth century, during the period of the Great Migrations.

As we depart I turn to see the man stooping back inside his shack, the day's excitement over with. He is apparently their keeper, which looks a thankless task.

We jolt towards another point of focus in the vast space: a long, trapezium-shaped barn that seems to be all roof, with its reed-thatched eaves sloping almost to the ground. Hungarian grey cattle spread their majestic horns, impressive bladed architecture that looks too heavy for their heads, some standing and some lying down, unbothered by our presence. Here the tourists are permitted to disembark and walk about, poking at the metre-thick thatched walls of the barn, but this is really waiting time for a more significant arrival. We watch them come from far away: three dark horsemen sailing in like distant ships, heads bowed from the sun. They do not appear to be getting closer but getting larger.

These *csikós* are the traditional cattlemen of Hortobágy, cowboys of the Wild East, and their appearance is like something from a fairy tale. No denims or dusty chaps for them: they wear stiff black tricorn hats embellished with bustard feathers, black embroidered waistcoats and wide, skirt-like trousers of gorgeous indigo, below which gleam black boots of polished leather. The costume, some historians say, is a borrowing from Turkic nomads whom the Magyars encountered in their centuries of wandering, and who could blame them for stealing it? It is the epitome of dashing. They are here to perform – the clothes themselves insist on it – and the audience gathers around to watch in a tight horseshoe. It begins with the synchronised swinging of bullwhips that send ear-splitting cracks echoing across the steppe, ringing out like thunderclaps. Then, at a command, their horses sink to the ground and roll over on their sides, lying as if dead; the riders slip smoothly off and sit astride them, then stand on top of them, lashing their bullwhips in the air, a ritual of dominance. The horses endure this brutal-looking display uncomplainingly, sliding up to sitting position like dogs when it is over. There is meaning behind the performance, which, again, harks back to the era of *betyár* banditry: originally the bullwhips were cracked to accustom the horses to gunfire, so they would stay calm during raids, and they were trained to lie flat in order to merge into the grass when being pursued by *hajdús* or other law-enforcers. The saddles are elegantly simple, just a sheet of smooth leather, to allow riders to dismount in an instant.

Then comes the climax of the show, the stunt known as the Puszta Five, an act of gallantry so macho as to be absurd. A horseman stands with one of his feet on the back of one horse and one foot on another – shock-absorbing sponges on his boots to spare their backs – holding the reins of a further three horses tethered in front, going at a full gallop over the level ground. Unlike the cracking bullwhips or the trick of lying prone, this horse-surfing serves no purpose whatsoever but to look impressive. It is no time-honoured custom from nomadic days but a peculiar case of life imitating art. In 1923 an Austrian painter by the name of Ludwig Koch sketched this bizarre formation as an imaginary scene, a kind of steppe fantasy, and a Hungarian horseman called Béla Lénárd decided to try it. It took him years of trial and error to perfect the technique; the first successful Puszta Five was performed in the 1950s. Other riders learned the trick, and now it is part of the canon of *csikó* derring-do.

The performance comes to an end. The *csikós* pose for photographs and lead children around on horseback. I think of the Texas Hollywood show – the comparison is unavoidable – but these re-enactments are worlds apart. This might be tourism but it is also, unmistakably, a continuation of traditions founded in reality, not imported from a film. These tricks are performed by men whose grandfathers might have done the same (though not perhaps their fathers, in the years of communism) and they wear their outlandish costumes as if they mean it. Soon enough they ride away, doubtless to change into modern clothes and put the air-conditioning on, but that does not diminish the spell. On the way back to Mátai Ménes the driver is on his mobile phone, and in an incongruous way that makes the traditions safer.

Horses were first domesticated on the Western or Central Steppe between five and six thousand years ago – the date 3500 BC is often used for convenience – although a more recent study suggests it might have been much earlier, perhaps as far back as the end of the last ice age. The traditional steppe theory holds that pastoralists dubbed the Yamnaya migrated west around 3000 BC with knowledge of horse husbandry; another hypothesis points to the Botai, a people from what is now northern Kazakhstan, who left behind extensive troves of archaeological evidence – middens of horse bones and pottery that had once contained mare's milk – showing the centrality of horses to their culture. The truth lies in a web of archaeological counter-claims and mitochondrial DNA too complex for me to untangle. Most likely, perhaps, is that different people brought different strains of wild horse to different levels of domestication at different times, and that eventually the streams merged into one.

But there is a difference between domesticating something – farming or herding it for meat, drinking its milk, controlling its breeding and using it to carry things – and leaping on its back and galloping it around. There is further debate about whether horses were first used as draught animals, like oxen or water buffalo, or as rideable steeds. Larger breeds of reindeer, semi-domesticated at best, were (and still are) ridden by Turkic tribes such as the Dukha in Mongolia, but an order of magnitude lies between the cervine and the equine. Is it possible that reindeer were ridden first and horses later? I like to think that the discovery was made by some daredevil, a Béla Lénárd of ancient times, someone with a death-wish or the need to impress a lover. How terrifying and exhilarating it must have been for the first person to grip those flanks between their thighs and cling on for dear life to the mane; a startling acceleration of human possibility, winding the horizon in at speeds never before imagined. Before them stretched an unbounded space of limitless horse-fuel. Who, with the wind in their hair, would not have had the urge to see what lay beyond the furthest point, liberated from their feet, a revelation as world-expanding as the discovery of flight?

Like any other powerful energy-harnessing technology, horses revolutionised every culture that adopted them, transforming hunting, herding, farming, travel, long-distance communication, trade networks, warfare and just about every other interaction between groups of people. Power structures were also changed as horses became high status symbols, their bones interred in the graves of chieftains, kings and warriors. Spoked wheels, developed on the steppe – another accident of level ground – enabled the invention of chariots, the use of which quickly spread to Europe and Mesopotamia, precipitating invasions and the rise and fall of empires. There were equestrian great leaps forward: the invention of the bit, versions of which the Botai were already using five thousand years ago; the solid saddle, by Eurasian nomads as early as the seventh century BC; and the stirrup, which first appeared in China and spread west. These innovations allowed for greater manoeuvrability and stability when wielding weapons; the stirrup, in particular, was crucial to the Scythians who menaced Rome from the Western Steppe, enabling mounted archers who could twist and fire backward from the saddle, perfecting hit-and-run attacks that confounded pursuers. The centaur myths of the ancient Greeks perhaps originated with them: man and horse grafted together into one fearsome fighting unit. These, and other horse-warrior cultures, were the precursors to the Huns – the bastard offspring of Hunor – who invaded Europe in the fifth century, by no means the last steppe nomads to devastate Christendom.

'On the fringe of allegory, dimly perceived through legendary mist and the dust of chronicles, these strangers have an outsized quality about them; something of giants and something of ogres,' writes Patrick Leigh Fermor in *Between the Woods and the Water*, his account of walking across Europe, including the Great Hungarian Plain, in the 1930s. 'A permanent nuisance to the West, their newly-invented stirrup made them more formidable still: a firm seat in the saddle ousted the bow as the horseman's chief weapon and replaced it with the spear, and then the lance which in its turn led to the heavily armoured knights of the Middle Ages and, in dim barbaric fashion, foreshadowed the tank.' As the geographical terminus of thousands of miles of level ground, Hungary bore the brunt of this rolling horseback invasion machine; almost as soon as they had arrived, on the heels of other marauders, the Magyars became Europe's bulwark against waves of further incursion by Mongols, Cumans, Pechenegs, Tatars and finally Ottoman Turks, who crushed the army of Lajos II at Mohács in 1526, a catastrophe that ushered in the partition of the kingdom.

There were also breeds of wild horse endemic to the New World – where the *Equus* genus started out, before migrating to Eurasia across the Bering land bridge – but they disappeared from the grasslands there at the end of the last ice age; either driven to extinction by climate change, or by human populations arriving in a reverse migration, or most probably by a deadly combination of the two. Spreading westwards throughout Asia, they were extinct in North America for ten thousand years. The European invasion that started in 1492, to which horses were militarily essential, was also, unwittingly, a species reintroduction. Plains Indian and other groups quickly took up horseback riding and adapted it to suit their needs, mastering the practice so naturally it was as if horses had never been gone.

Hortobágy preserves a link to the earliest equine history. Only two never-domesticated breeds survived into modern times – today's 'wild' horses are actually feral, having escaped human control and effectively rewilded themselves – tarpans and Przewalski's horses (named after the Polish-Russian explorer Nikołaj Przewalski). The last known tarpan died in captivity in 1909, while the Przewalski's horse, like Hungarian grey cattle, squeezed through the bottleneck to precariously escape extinction, partly through breeding programmes in Mongolia where their ancestors might have roamed. There is a small herd of them here in the national park: stout,

dun-coloured, bandy-legged, with stiff black manes like
brooms, as different from a thoroughbred Nonius as yesterday's
wild asses are from domestic donkeys. Everything about them
looks ancient; once again, their lines flow straight from
Paleolithic cave art.

On my way back to the campsite in Hortobágy village I
fill my hat with ripe plums that offer themselves from roadside trees. They are astonishingly sweet, with dusty golden
skins. A small boy walks down the road with a pair of riding
boots in his hands ('They are not what we call boots') and a
bullwhip slung around his neck, a *csikó* in training.

~

Prevented from crossing the steppe on horseback I make an
attempt on bicycle, a rented sit-up-and-beg fixed-gear with
fat, no-nonsense tyres. No one criticises my choice of foot-
wear or demands to see proof of ability; I pedal away and off
I go, master of my steed.

Taking the road towards Debrecen and then north almost
back to Balmazújváros I finally turn west again, with the
national park on either side. The day is close and squelching
hot. The grasslands roll away. White clouds cast shadows on
the sky, deepening its blue, and the horizon shudders in a
gelatinous haze. My passing stirs up small brown birds that
rise in twittering shoals. Ahead is the region of Darassa,
marshier and woodier than the rest of Hortobágy – a hunting
ground for imperial eagles, white-tailed eagles and saker
falcons – but before I get to it a dirt track tempts me off the
road. There is no one in sight in any direction; disregarding
the UNESCO signs I steer on to a narrow trail of heat-
hardened earth that runs away due south. Hortobágy village
must lie nine or ten miles ahead. Between me and my destination is only the uncut Puszta.

I may not be galloping on horseback but, suspending my disbelief, gliding across this open space with nothing ahead and nothing behind – only the sky above my head and the ground beneath my wheels – feels as close to perfect freedom as I ever hoped to reach. Much about the experience feels surreal, the horizon always receding smoothly at the speed I dictate, fleeing when I chase after it, stopping when I stop. The sensation of pursuit is addictive, as if we were playing a game. Chase and catch. Hide and seek. But perfect freedom does not last; once past an isolated farm – empty of observers but for a huge-testicled bull that bellows once, as if in warning – the track soon deteriorates into rutted earth. Cycling becomes less an easy gallop and more like that ignominious trot, a bone-shaking trial of endurance that makes my whole body ache. Suddenly the level of exposure, and the distance, feel much greater.

The colour of the steppe crawls from threadbare yellow into more complex tones, darkening and lightening with shrubs, sedges, grasses and flowers that I cannot name; as in Białowieża, my eyes are becoming attuned to a world of differences. But the horizon stays unchanged, as if by some vast inertia. I have eaten nothing but yellow plums and neglected to bring any water, and the reality of thirst returns like a bad dream. In the heat of the late afternoon I am exhausted and sweaty enough to dunk my face in a waterhole – the water is too foul to drink – before noticing that the earth has been mashed by hooves. The presence of water buffalo is something I did not consider, and the possibility is alarming; if they can outrun a horse they can certainly catch a fixed-gear bicycle over rough terrain. I suppose, if sighted from a distance, I could lie flat like a *csikó*'s horse, but I lack the bullwhip.

Here and there the endlessness of the horizontal plane is broken by vertical structures like strange gallows. These are traditional sweep wells, and their design – a tall pole hinged with a cantilevered arm (or 'sweep') on which a bucket is suspended to draw water from the earth – is unknown in most of Europe but is common to Central Asia, Egypt and India, known by the Arabic name *shaduf*, another echo of the east. Leigh Fermor saw them in the 1930s: 'These lonely uprights give an air of desolation to the plain: they resemble derelict siege engines by day and the failing light turns them into gibbets or those wheel-topped stakes in pictures by Hieronymus Bosch where vultures wrangle over skeletons spreadeagled in mid-air.' Somewhere in my notes I have a list of diagrams showing how, in times gone by, they were used as a signalling system to send coded messages, a form of steppe semaphore. Depending on the angle of the sweep and the position of the bucket they could be used as invitations – 'Come home, food is ready'; 'A travelling tradesman has arrived' – or as emergency warnings: 'A death has occurred'; 'The water is poisoned'; 'Government officials in area, hide your cattle'. A woman's shawl hanging on the end might mean, to a lonely herdsman: 'A prostitute is here'.

Here comes a lonely herdsman now, beside a distant wedge of cows, a black shape materialising from the emptiness. Knowing I am supposed not to be here I walk, which feels more respectful. Wheeling the bicycle towards him, sweat running down my face, I see him grow in surprising propor- tions: a huge, heavy-headed man carrying a carved stick in the crook of his elbows, wedged tight behind his back. I greet him with a '*Servusz*', a salutation more courteous than the more familiar '*Szia*'. He rolls large eyes upon me, their whites the same pink as his skin. I try not to stare at his belly, which is of astonishing size, a purple, mottled bag that spills out from the bottom of his T-shirt and hangs between his crotch and his knees, undulating as he walks. He might be hiding his cattle in there. The yellow dog at his heel has eight long swinging nipples.

He envelops my hand in his and wags it solemnly, betraying no visible surprise to see me here, so far from a road. His placid curiosity has a vaguely bovine feel, as if, by some shamanic transformation, he has turned half cow himself in the isolation of the fields.

'Your cows?' I ask, indicating the herd that is blowing and stamping nearby.

'*Nem.*' He shakes his head, nodding to somewhere else on the steppe – another herd must be out there – that I can't even see.

'Hortobágy?' I ask, pointing south.

'*Igen.*' A single nod.

Jolting and bouncing away from him, I feel his eyes, and the eyes of his dog – even, perhaps, the eyes of the cows – following me for a long time, but when I look back all of them have been swallowed by the distance.

Miles of muscular punishment pass and I'm becoming concerned by the position of the sun, swiftly tilting towards night. The sky is glowing in the west. The grasses throw precise shadows. By the time I think I recognise the nub of a distant grain tower and the band of foliage that hints at my first sight of home – though the village must still be hours away – the distorted orange ball is teetering on the horizon, melting at the edge of sight. It is now, for no reason whatsoever, that the track comes to an end. Somehow, deep inside, I always knew it would. It has led me all this way to terminate in nothingness, with not even the faintest trace of a pathway through the grass beyond; there is nothing for it but to dismount and push. The bicycle, once liberating, becomes a liability, its heavy frame a burden I have to half drag, half carry over uneven ground and welters of shallow marsh. Boggy streams criss-cross the land. My boots splash ankle-deep. The grass grows taller, wilder, until it is up to my knees, my waist. A cloud of gnats follows me, driven to ecstasy by my sweat, but I do not have the energy to wipe them from my face. The sun is below the skyline now, on the far side of the world, and soon it will be too dark to see. Then – when it seems this will never end – my feet are on smooth ground again. I am in a meadow where the grass has been cut for hay.

A ruined farmstead sits nearby, overgrown with ragwort, its thatch split down the middle like a lightning-struck tree. This little house on the prairie is a landmark I have seen before, and just beyond lie a drainage canal and the tarmac of a road. My knees are wobbling from exertion, my body as battered and depleted as if it has climbed a mountain. But the road leads to the Nine-holed Bridge, the goulash of the Great Csárda and a bottle of strong beer, as it has for others returning thankfully from the steppe.

~

As in the Białowieża *puszcza* everything revolved around trees – the harvesting of them, the defending of them and once the worshipping of them – Hortobágy is centred upon the economy of grass. This Puszta is not a primeval bubble but designated as 'semi-natural', influenced over thousands of years by humans, and the livestock of humans, altering the composition of the steppe's original plant life. Grass not only gives sustenance to the drifting herds of cows and sheep, whose dung has been acidifying the mostly alkaline soil for centuries, but is harvested for fodder and fuel, either stacked into the upward-thrusting hayricks I saw earlier or baled by machine. Each morning from my tent I watch a slow cavalry of old men on bicycles pedalling towards the fields with strimmers balanced on their shoulders, like quixotic jousting knights, to do battle with the blades. (Later they gather outside the inn to smoke and drink Zwack, a black herbal liqueur that tastes extraordinarily foul.) The smell of cut grass is everywhere, sweetening the air.

Grasses are, by some measures, the world's most successful colonists, and certainly the most successful colonising plants. They propagate their seeds by wind, so can spread across vast distances, and, like pioneer birches, are among the first to colonise newly cleared ground, thriving in deforested or fire-ravaged areas. Around twelve thousand species of grass cover over a third of the planet's land surface. These species are, if looked at closely, as multiple in their forms as trees: feathery, hairy, slender, coarse, tinged with silver, purple or blue, as unassuming as meadow-grass or as towering as bamboo. From the cereal crops of the Fertile Crescent – the foundational trinity of emmer, einkorn and barley – to the ancient civilisations of China and Mesoamerica, consumption of various types of grass has fuelled the rise of cities. Wheat, oats, rye, rice, millet, maize, teff, sorghum and sugar cane are all domesticated grass; around a dozen strains of *Poaceae* feed over nine-tenths of the world's population today. When people are not eating grass we are eating animals that eat grass; apart from hunter-gatherers, who were never enslaved by the grains, humans have effectively become a grass-eating species.

More subversively, perhaps, domestication goes two ways. Grain supplies, stored as insurance against future scarcity, may have allowed human populations to expand exponentially, preparing the ground for the large-scale agricultural civilisations that followed the Neolithic Revolution, with their attendant hierarchies, social stratification, monumental building works, technologies, innovations and wars. But in service to grass, humans have spread its seeds far and wide. From Asian rice paddies to rolling fields of American wheat – not to mention the perfect lawns and golf courses, irrigated by precious water, that artificially green desert lands from Saudi Arabia to Nevada – our deification of grass has massively increased its range, ensuring the survival of its species (or a select few of them, anyway). Perhaps it is the other way round and grass is growing *us*.

In John Christopher's 1956 novel *The Death of Grass*, apocalypse comes in the form of a virus that sweeps across the world wiping out grass species one by one, beginning with rice in East Asia. Within a short space of time civilisation has collapsed; hundreds of millions have died of famine; China and the Soviet Union have relapsed into armed chaos; starving hordes from Pakistan have invaded Turkey; the Americas and Australia have imposed strict quarantine in a vain attempt to delay the inevitable. Beyond the outskirts of London, England has become a nightmarish landscape plagued by warlordism, with gangs roaming the countryside fighting and pillaging grain supplies. In Christopher's disturbing vision, as bleak and merciless as the aftermath of nuclear holocaust, grass is the thin veneer that stands between civilised humanity and barbarism. If it dies, we die.

On the subject of barbarism – in the historical, non-pejorative sense of the word – grass might also have been the cause of the ancient migrations westwards. Some theories point to changes in climate that had the effect of increasing humidity on the Eastern Steppe, reducing the amount of pastureland available for the herds of cattle and horses that were the backbone of nomadic barbarian economies. (The term 'barbarian', from the Greek *barbaroi*, is pure linguistic snobbery, deriving from the 'bar-bar-bar' gibberish languages spoken by the uncouth, uncivilised tribes beyond the Classical world.) Mounted climate refugees moved west in search of more favourable conditions, displacing other groups, who displaced other groups, a domino effect that reached Europe and eventually led to the collapse of the Roman Empire. In its various strains this innocuous plant has been the cause of some of the most profound developments, and disasters, in human history.

Near the Nine-holed Bridge is the Pásztormúzeum, the Herders' Museum, with its displays of folk costumes and waxwork models of Puszta life. Always a sucker for dioramas, I keep being drawn back here. Herders slept on the steppe in seasonal shelters made from reeds and cooked their meals behind thatched windbreaks, upright nests made of grass. A tree trunk, its branches chopped back to provide steps like a ladder, would serve as an observation post (or surely, in storms, a lightning rod) allowing them to see approaching horsemen from far away. They smoked foot-long tobacco pipes and wore elaborate baize gowns hemmed with red and blue and embroidered with tulips and other flowers. To propose, a herder would leave this expensive garment, called a *szűr*, outside a woman's door; if his overture was accepted it would be taken inside, if rejected it would still be hanging outside the next morning, damp with dew, to be humbly reclaimed. Modern Hungarian retains the phrase *kiteszik a szűret*, 'to sling one's *szűr*', for the rejection of romantic propositions.

It wouldn't surprise me if this is how Albert wooed his wife, Judit, the couple who own the guest-house I move to for my final night, before – it is my intention, at least – setting out on foot at last to walk across the Puszta. He is surely of *betyár* blood, a piratically noble man with a long grey ponytail and a black and grey beard combed into impressive moustaches. The downstairs room into which I am led is dominated along one wall by a ceramic stove, its tiles arsenic green, which thankfully is not lit; it is the hottest day so far and my clothes cling like a wetsuit. Dripping puddles on to an ornately carved, high-backed wooden chair, I sign the registration forms. By the time the process is over the paper is blobby with my sweat. Like someone regulating an engine, Albert cheerfully lowers my core temperature with a *fröccs* – not a spritzer, he insists, which is an Austrian plagiarism – yellow Tokaj wine and fizzy water from a SodaStream. He has lived on the Puszta all his life; his wife comes from the nearest town.

'In the summer we farm,' he says.

'What do you do in the winter?'

'We sleep and make children.'

In the evening Judit leads two horses into the yard and Albert appears in clothes that could have come from the Pásztormúzeum: a white shirt and a worsted waistcoat embellished with black knotwork, elaborate silver buttons in the shape of acorns and a grey felt hat with a bustard feather in its brim. He looks more natural wearing these than in his other clothes. The horses are hitched to a trap; sitting up in front, Albert guides them with a light, flicking whip on the end of a stick like a fishing rod. Ribbons in the national colours of Hungary – red, white and green – hang from their harnesses.

In the trap are two other guests, a couple from Germany on their way back from a bird-watching trip in Transylvania. We go eastwards through the village, past animals grazing in paddocks that are really extended gardens. Outside one of the houses is a field that holds two great bulls, one Hungarian grey and one water buffalo, that are as different from each other as barley is from maize; the grey keeps himself smooth and aloof, a sturdy block of ivory, as the buffalo rises with a primordial groan from his wallowing hole, festooned in dripping grey mud. I wonder what they think of each other.

Albert steers into the Puszta, guiding the horses by quiet whistles and the sound of air through sucked teeth, as fluent in the language of Horse as he is in German and English. His whip flicks this way and that to indicate encroaching tree species such as black locust, Russian olive and desert false indigo, invasives making inroads here in the warming climate. His costume might be frozen in time but the land around is changing. There are longer, drier summers now – the Carpathian Basin is one degree hotter on average than it was thirty years ago, a temperature anticipated, as with everywhere else, to climb – and droughts and water shortages are exacerbating the problems caused by human interference. 'In the long run, the draining of the puszta and the 19th century regulation of the Tisza may have damaged the puszta ecosystem in a serious way,' notes the Crossbill nature guidebook I have been using for reference here. 'The drop of the alkaline ground water as a result of these measures may mean that the alkaline salts cannot reach the surface anymore and may thereby result in a desalination of the puszta.' This ongoing desalination is changing the character of the steppe; migratory birds are especially vulnerable to this change. Like the waves of human invasion that have swept in over the years, threats to the grassland's serenity come from far over the horizon. 'National Parks do not exist in a vacuum,' says the guide again. 'Despite protective measures, the populations of some breeding birds are slowly, but steadily, declining. Many of them winter beyond the Sahara. The expansion of the Sahara Desert due to climate change and the use of pesticides on the African continent take their toll on the summer residents of the Hortobágy.'

The desert again: always there, a looming yellow reminder of death, a *memento mori* as present as the melting ice. On the sliding scale from damp to dry, temperate to hot, the steppes – these semi-arid grasslands – are a few small shifts in temperature from the truly arid zones to the south, where the soil turns to dust and not even grass will grow. The semi-arid becomes the arid, according to climatological wisdom, when annual precipitation falls below a certain mark, and desertification can be caused by climate change or human activity (though the boundary between the two is meaningless these days). The example of the dust bowl on the American prairies in the 1930s, or the spreading of desert conditions on the steppes of communist Central Asia throughout the twentieth century, offer uncomfortably recent examples of how quickly grass can die.

Albert gestures again with his whip: a red-footed falcon – which has flown here from Central Asia to breed on this shrinking island of uncut grass – is hovering out above the steppe as if it were treading water. I think no more of pesticides, global heating or other invisible horrors; it is easier to believe that this bird will always be hanging there, suspended in unchanging time, an immutable feature of the air. The German man beams as he watches it, as enchanted as a child.

Our destination is the house of an old farmer, a friend of Albert's, who has clearly made these visits part of his daily routine. The reason for his enthusiasm becomes apparent when the *pálinka* appears, clear spirit distilled from mirabelle plums, poured into five pewter cups decorated with hunting scenes. We toast '*Egészségedre!*' and drink. Curly-haired pigs grub around the wheels, and a flock of Racka sheep tug on yellow grass nearby, another traditional local breed, with horns like someone has gripped the ends and not stopped twisting. The scene seems held in time again, an illusion of changelessness that I am happy to indulge, especially when the cups are refilled. Our sunset journey back to the village is accompanied by a honking fly-by many hundreds of geese long, heading towards their roosting grounds in the wetlands at Halastó.

Back in the yard more *pálinka* and home-made wine is poured. The sweating horses have been fed green apples from the tree, rubbed down and led to pasture at the end of the village. Darkness comes suddenly and coincides with a drunkenness that no one seems quite ready for; it carries Albert and Judit to bed, perhaps to make more children, and soon after that the German woman trips off into the darkness. Only her husband and I are left, refilling each other's glasses. My attention is drawn more by the death-dance of moths in the candle flame than by the words he is saying – something about being a dental technician, about his love of birds, about the rightwards drift in European politics – but then his voice goes dark. 'I am in despair,' he says. 'They are all vanishing.'

I wait. Something has shifted but I don't yet know what.

'The birds. The insects they depend on. You heard this report from Germany? Three-quarters of insects have disappeared in the last twenty-five years, in nature reserves. In *nature reserves*. Is it climate change? Chemicals? No one knows. But every year, less of them.'

The candle is burning low. In the darkness I cannot see his face, only shifting planes of light and the black hollows around his eyes. He can only see the same of me, which makes this easier.

'Tomorrow we go to Halastó so I can look at birds, but it will not make me happy.' It is as if he were at confession. 'How can I tell this to my wife? I will smile and say nothing. We come here to see what we can no longer see in Germany. Soon we will have to go somewhere else to see what we cannot see here. Then that will be gone as well. There is so much beauty in the world but we are in a dark place.'

His face is almost entirely gone, a black, anonymous shape. Two strangers sitting in the dark, we are surely too drunk to remember this; but I do remember the boyish young man from the beginning of these walks, mourning unseasonal daffodils and the lack of snow. How many more small griefs like this are quietly being shared? 'I do not have hope any more,' he says, this previously smiling man drinking *pálinka* in a horse-drawn trap. His voice is getting quieter, guttering with the candle. 'These places . . . these places on the earth . . . there are getting less of them. And no one seems to care. The birds are all leaving and no one cares. What can we do?'

I feel something yaw inside me, an unexpected slippage. I manage to hold myself together until the conversation has reached its end – 'We will not solve this tonight,' he says with a smile (but if not tonight, *when*?) – and he pours away the rest of his drink and vanishes into the night. I wish him '*Schlaf gut*', 'Sleep well', and then I am alone in the dark. There is half a litre of wine on the table and the chirruping of crickets.

It wells up with astonishing force and makes me shake and crumple. I put my face in my hands and weep, as quietly as I can, half wishing that he would return – this stranger whose grief for the world touches mine – and half thankful that he is gone. In its shock and inevitability it feels like an iceberg calving or the crack running up a tree moments before it falls; a slow violence and release that has been coming for a long time. Gradually the noises I am making resolve into words. They are not clever words but they are all I can give at this time, or perhaps at any time, and I say them over and over again.

'I'm sorry. I'm sorry. I'm sorry.'

Geronimo. Below me, nothingness.

Afterwards I wipe my face, clear the table and go to bed.

In the morning Judit lays out breakfast: eggs, fresh bread, cheese, sausage, plums picked from the tree. The German couple and I eat well, commenting on the home-made jam, and neither the bird-watching man nor I say a word about last night. They pack their binoculars and drive away in their hired car. I never even asked his name.

Drained, I leave Albert's house to walk across the steppe.

~

Yesterday, using online maps, I identified a thin white line snaking south from a place called Faluvéghalma, which I assume to be a village, into the widest and emptiest swathe of the Hortobágy National Park. In the middle of nowhere this line terminates – this seems a theme with Puszta paths – and nothing but trackless grassland stretches ahead for miles; ashen grey on the satellite map, it looks less like rolling grassland than the skin of a pockmarked moon, blotched, threadbare and exposed. On the far side of the range, south-east, lies a town called Nádudvar. Ten miles away? Maybe twelve. A long way to walk across open ground where I am not supposed to be, but – in the spirit of nomadism and *betyár* devil-may-care attitude – I have made up my mind to try.

After last night's collapse, walking is all I can do.

To reach Faluvéghalma I must follow the railway line west for two hours in the direction of Halastó, the wetlands where the German couple have gone to look at birds. I pass the lightning-struck house on the prairie that was my sign of deliverance on that ill-fated crossing by bicycle, its roof now covered with crows. A battered blue train goes by, and takes a long time to diminish in the distance ahead of me; by the noise it makes, it was last oiled when the communists were in power. Ahead, a fringe of rushes marks the boundary of Halastó. Centred around a complex of fishponds dug by prisoners in the First World War – a modern extension of the age-old campaign to force the Puszta to be productive – this is now an important conservation area, home to three hundred species of birds, eighty per cent of Hungary's total. If I were here a month later I would witness the epic arrival of tens of thousands of cranes, a stopover on their annual migration from Scandinavia to Spain. Now a Brownian motion of starlings swirls above the reeds and I wonder if the dental technician is watching them through his binoculars, smiling and saying nothing. I hope that he has forgotten last night and can be happy.

The morning's fierce heat is cut by a tepid underflow. From the edge of Halastó I follow a road branching south through a hamlet called Szásztelek, past grey ponds and water buffalo with only their flattish skulls and unimpressed faces protruding above the slime. They seem untroubled by my intrusion. Szásztelek is empty of life but for a giant curly hog rolling underneath a tree. Half its houses are in ruins, their roofs collapsed, its humans seemingly in hiding or having long since fled. A derelict well stands with its sweep lying horizontally; in the old code, 'Be careful'.

An hour's walk after that, Faluvéghalma turns out not to be a village but a large, modern cattle farm. The road I am following ends here, in acres of aluminium barns and slurry; tractors in the distance pile up pyramids of hay bales. I dither uncertainly at the gate, trying to keep out of sight. This unexpected industry is not a reassuring prospect and there seems to be no way around. Just as I am turning back, deciding this route isn't possible – my roving spirit pathetically diminished at the first obstacle – a car pulls up and a white-haired man sticks his head out questioningly. I ask how to get to Nádudvar on the far side of the national park.

'Puszta,' he says simply, angling his chin south.

'*Tilos?*' I ask. 'Forbidden?'

His face makes several noncommittal expressions at the same time, a series of diplomatic contortions that are clearly intended to mean, 'It is and it isn't', or 'If anyone asks, you never met me'. He points to the farm's perimeter fence and tells me to follow it around; his finger sketches the suggestion of a path on the other side.

Pushing through waist-high grass and jumping snags of marsh, I slink guiltily around the farm's periphery. The path is there, as the finger advised, the insubstantial white line I identified on the satellite map. My trespass has attracted no attention from the clanking machines, though nerves have dried my throat. Open grassland lies ahead.

Turning my back on the agricultural, I walk into the pastoral.

After walking for fifteen minutes I could have been walking for an hour. I look back: the farm is gone, but I have the impression less of progress and more that the buildings have detached and floated away, like objects across a pond. I walk for an hour and I could have been walking for no time at all. For the rest of the morning, the rest of the day, through the pale heat of the afternoon, the experience of this journey only changes insofar as the muscles of my legs and feet pass through small escalations of pain; the repetition of flat ground, the metronomic jolt of each step, is as unexpectedly punishing as hiking up and down hillsides. But the effort brings about no change. I seem to be making no distance at all, just walking in place as the hamster wheel of the world rolls back beneath my boots, the same view sliding past once more. The only thing that alters is the passage of the clouds.

When the track comes to its end, a betrayal for which I was forewarned, I set my compass south-east and plunge into the uncut grass of a vast, untended lawn. Now all I have to do is keep going in a straight line.

Internally battered from last night, with the fumey ghost of *pálinka* still hovering inside my bones, having nothing to do but put one foot in front of the other brings a familiar rhythmic peace. With the farm behind the horizon now, my mind becomes serene. The old fear of being exposed beneath an all-seeing sky does not manifest as I thought it might; the level of exposure is so extreme, with no possibility whatsoever of cover, shelter or respite, that it brings about a paradoxical sense of privacy. No one can see me here because there is no one here to see. I might be alone in all the world, or walking in a dream.

On level ground, or at sea, the curvature of the earth means that the horizon is always about three miles away (from the top of a decent-sized mountain it might be up to a hundred). At a walking pace of three miles per hour, I know that the furthest visible point will take me an hour to reach; the problem is that there is nothing to tell me when I've got there. The lack of features makes it illogical to stop in any one place. Why this patch of grass and not the next? Why not three miles further? But I do stop, frequently; not with any particular intention but simply finding that my body has slowed and drifted to a halt, like a sailboat when the wind has dropped. Becalmed, I loiter motionless. Sometimes I lie down. Sometimes I revolve, travelling the slow circumference of the skyline with my eyes, the axis of a turning wheel, until they are back at the same point. Without my compass it could be a different point that looks the same.

When I lower my gaze from the horizon flowing away on every side, my eyes adjust from the hazy whole to a world of detail: small changes are happening at my feet, at the scale of blades and grains. Matted among the rough stalks are sedges, plantains, tiny wildflowers three or four millimetres across, invisible from standing height; there is dusty yellow tansy and a sprinkling of larger white flowers that I later discover are nicknamed 'summer snowflakes'. The elusive purple bloom of Hungarian sea lavender splashes across the range, a misleadingly named plant for a landlocked country.

Or maybe not; for hours on end I am more at sea than on the land. Occasional barns loom in and out of view like passing ships – not industrial but traditional now, with deep thatched roofs and whitewashed walls, each with the sweep of its well angled differently – before leaving me alone again. Fleets of trees slide away, en route to distant shores. In the shifting currents of the wind the grasses move like tides.

The Mongol born as Temüjin, whose empire of the steppes

was far from any sea, styled himself as Genghis Khan: Oceanic Ruler.

Dust devils of powdery loess dance far out across the plain. White butterflies skip above the grass. The fathomless blue sky soars like an upturned bowl.

That blue bowl has a name: the sky-father Tengri. It is not a Hungarian name but, again, Mongolian, having spread across the steppe in the prayers of nomadic Turkic tribes, Huns and pre-Christian Magyars; *tenger* in Mongolian simply means 'sky'. The religion known as Tengrism prevailed across much of Eurasia before the adoption of monotheism, or of Buddhism further east; before the nomads settled down and the shamans lost their power. A sky god faith, which the cultures of the Clearing might have recognised, it also contains an element of dualism, balancing the worship of light – so often a masculine archetype – with reverence for Etügen Eke, the dark and fertile earth-mother. It is still practised as a minority religion in Mongolia, Central Asia and Siberia, partly in opposition to Buddhism and Islam and partly syncretically entangled with their beliefs. As I will discover in the next few days, it survives, even thrives – like so much of the culture of the steppe – in modern Hungary also.

Now I walk between the two, the sky-father watching over me and the earth-mother supporting my feet.

Their cosmic harmony doesn't help. Over the course of the afternoon a nagging ache in my left shin evolves into needling pain, which I compensate for by adjusting the stride of my other leg. Before long there is pain in my right shin too. There is nothing to be done, so why stop here? Why anywhere? All I can do is carry on, my strides devolving into limps, maintaining my course south-east and waiting for something – anything – to emerge on the skyline that might indicate an end.

After another hour of this there comes a modulation in

the land: a grassed-over hump of earth, around the same height as me and perhaps ten metres long, lying a little to the west. Soon afterwards, another. They are unmistakably man-made, the burial mounds known as *kurgans*, which can be found from the Great Hungarian Plain to southern Russia. It was not sky-worshipping Tengrists who built them but a much earlier culture, a people almost as mythically distant as Hunor and Magor. The so-called Kurgan Hypothesis postulates that a prehistoric wave of westward-moving groups, with a shared Proto-Indo-European language and funerary culture, spread from the Western Steppe between 4000 and 1000 BC. They included the Yamnaya, the people who might have tamed the first horses, and certainly horses were pivotal to *kurgan* culture. These tumuli are the only physical evidence that remains of that ancient migration, whether – like the culture shift from hunter-gathering to farming – it was an invasion or a more complex process of assimilation, but its influence lives on in the spoken word. The Indo-European language group, which galloped at the speed of a horse not only into Europe but eastwards over the Himalayas, went on to diverge into several hundred tongues as apparently different from each other as Sanskrit, Persian, Russian, Greek, Latin, German and Gaelic. Perhaps ironically, Magyar has nothing to do with this great Eurasian family but derives from Uralic, an entirely unrelated group that also includes Estonian and Finnish.

This part of the Puszta is *kurgan*-rich; they are popping up like molehills. It takes mere seconds to climb one of them, which, at around two metres high, is the greatest altitude that I have gained all day (in fact, apart from my brief, inglorious time on horseback, the highest point above sea level that I have been for a fortnight). From this desultory vantage point I rest my aching shins and imagine that I can see marginally further, perhaps another fraction of a mile to the horizon.

Millennia lie beneath my boots. Perhaps there are skeletons foetally nestled in the earth, warriors or shamans whose significance is long since lost. There might be horses' bones down there, a residue of mare's milk.

The word *kurgan* comes from a Turkic word meaning 'fortress', reminding me of the Celtic link between prehistoric barrows ('fairy castles') and the *sídhe*, the little people believed to descend from a vanished race driven into extinction – or into the otherworld – by subsequent waves of invaders. Are there similar beliefs on the Puszta? In folk-tales, are Hungarian cattlemen drawn irresistibly underground by music playing from inside these mounds – the ghostly shades of the Yamnaya – emerging hours later to find that hundreds of years have passed and everyone they knew and loved has gone, like the music? I have not come across any stories like that, but, from atop this barrow, I am witness to an effect that does seem supernatural.

Far to the south, a line of trees has become detached from the earth and is apparently floating, trunkless, a short distance above the skyline, with clear space flowing under it. I glance away and look back. It is still there, levitating. This is the Hortobágy's equivalent of the Brocken spectre of the Cairngorms, the mirage known as the Fata Morgana (an Italian derivation of Morgan le Fay, the sorceress from Arthurian legend), caused by rays of light bending through a temperature inversion, with a warmer layer of air on top and a cooler layer below. From far away the effect is often mistaken for water shimmering in the heat, and I think of the westward-journeying people who must have been tempted for thousands of years to spur their horses after it, in pursuit of an illusion. Perhaps it wasn't a white stag that led Hunor and Magor west.

But then I turn the other way. Something altogether more real is coming across the steppe.

The grasses have an ominous roll, like a swell at sea. The sea lavender is rippling in fierce purple waves. Towering stacks of white clouds are boiling up in the north, thunderheads heaped vertically, augmenting almost as I watch. It is impossible to say how far away they are or how fast they are moving but they are gaining ground, throwing their shadows on the plain, collapsing and restacking themselves. There is no shelter of any description for miles and miles and miles. Descending from the burial mound I hurry towards the floating trees but there is no hurrying here; the distance eats my footsteps. The tallest thing from horizon to horizon, I am a walking lightning rod, a conductor from Tengri to the earth. The pain increases in my shins, reducing me to hobbling. I glance back every minute to see the storm huger, closer.

A rising wind. The roll of drums. And suddenly there it is, the childhood dream-familiar fear: the monster taller than the sky thundering across the plain, my footsteps dragging nightmare-slow, an infinity of emptiness and nowhere to run or hide.

~

In a storm of hooves the black-armoured cavalry breaks upon the plain, gleaming spears thrust ahead and silken banners fluttering behind. Long-moustached horsemen in pointed, fur-fringed iron hats twist in their saddles to fire backward as they ride. Next come columns of infantry clanging swords on shields; a man with a falcon on his wrist; a woman in a gold-embroidered tunic swinging a battle axe; Bactrian camels with double humps and jouncing scarlet pompoms; a wooden cart pulled by water buffalo; a carriage full of children. Finally two shepherds steer a flock of Racka sheep, mopping up the hoof-churned grass.

I have just witnessed the Arrival of the Magyars.

An encampment of yurts is going up, flags adorned with crescent moons and grinning wolf's-head profiles, while sturdy ponies graze on the pastureland beyond. White and black horse's tails hang from sinister scaffold-like entranceways – white for peace and black for war – and warriors in leather armour sip from drinking horns. Family groups browse stalls of spiked, serrated ironmongery and every few seconds the crack of a bullwhip splits the air. From speakers drones the doomy sound of Mongolian throat singing.

It has been three days since the storm. Lightning did not strike me. By the time the thunderheads broke I was safely off the steppe, sheltering in Nádudvar, watching the downpour turn the roads into rivers. Then followed days of rain; a campsite in the down-at-heel spa resort of Püspökladány; clattering train rides west across the Great Hungarian Plain; a night in a city called Kecskemét; a smaller, local train south; a five-hour walk from Kiskunfélegyháza to the village of Bugac on the outskirts of a smaller swathe of open Puszta. Signs along the road announced –

Ősök Napja

41ᴶ4꜀ Ꝋˣᴧˣ

– the familiar Latin letters followed by *rovásírás*, a runic script descended from the Old Turkic alphabet, promoted by Magyar nationalists harking back to ancient glories. It translates as Ancient Day, a weekend-long celebration of steppe identity.

Arriving here was much like the approach to any festival – rucksacks, long-haired bearded men, instruments, brightly coloured clothes – only with the addition of alarming quantities of medieval weaponry. I have never attended a festival that is so heavily armed. A man clutching an enormous curved sword is chatting to a police officer; everyone, including children, seems to carry at least a hatchet or a sheathed stabbing knife. Outside the camping area, signs warn against excessive drunkenness, nudity and the risk of getting shot by a horseback archer.

The attendees pitched next to me are welcoming, if a little puzzled by the appearance of a lone and swordless Englishman. On one side is an elderly couple who offer me rough home-made wine that produces an instant headache; my other neighbours are a group of Székelys – a Hungarian minority from what is now Romania – wearing white linen blouses and trousers, tall black boots and straw hats, drinking shots of *pálinka* and occasionally breaking into song. People are camped with their horses under a nearby line of trees, hay bales stacked between their tents. Water buffalo graze to heavy metal, which suits them.

Ősök Napja is an offshoot of the Great Kurultáj, which happens every other year, a gathering of steppe-dwelling peoples from more than forty nations stretching from Central Asia and Siberia to China. Ancestors Day is a scaled-down version, but there are still delegations from Mongolia, Turkey, Kyrgyzstan and a smattering of Russian republics, as well as ethnic Hungarians stranded outside the motherland by the vagaries of geopolitics, like my Székely neighbours. History is keenly remembered here, or perhaps never allowed to die. It is some-where between a hippy folk festival, a medieval re-enactment fair and, as I will discover, a far-right nationalist rally.

As the sun goes down the whine of goatskin bagpipes drifts from the festival site, a looping and maddening sound – less of a tune than an incitement – and, with my headache intact, I make my way towards it. Security guards whose uniform of black shirts and forage caps recalls interwar fascism patrol in twos and threes, checking for camping infringements. The real muscle here, however, appears to lie not with them but with the massive-chested, bare-armed men in voluminous robes and *csikó* hats, bullwhips wrapped around their waists, whose task it is to keep the public from being gored or trampled. These crowd-herders block my path as a column of Hunnic horsemen trots back from the arena, and then the way is clear again. Ahead is music, glaring lights and the rising steam of food stalls.

I drift towards a crowd watching the band on the main stage; not goatskin bagpipe music but angry, snarling punk. The singer, his shaved head dazzling, is wearing a black T-shirt emblazoned with gothic script, while the musician next to him – a mild, bespectacled flautist in a moleskin waistcoat – seems to come from a different band or a different century. Thrash guitar slips into twiddling flute solos and then into distorted feedback, a sound as confused as the audience, dressed variously in folk attire, buckskin and chain-mail armour. The shirtless man in front of me displays a full back tattoo depicting eagles, howling wolves and a crescent moon. An elderly couple draped in Turkish flags are talking to a smiling man with broad Central Asian features and a tall silk hat; he turns out, when I ask, to be an ethnic Kyrgyz. He is part of the Kyrgyzstani delegation whose yurt is pitched nearby, and when I shake his hand he touches his cheek to mine. The Turks understand his language, though he does not speak theirs. 'We are brothers!' he shouts before I lose him in the crowd.

Hours later we meet again, our hands clasped, spinning round and round, as the entropy of the mass becomes collective movement. The goatskin bagpipes are at work with their jerky, rhythmic wail, stitching together individuals into a patterned whole. I am dancing without knowing how, drawn into a democratically simple repetition of steps – two stamps forward and one stamp back – with each person gripping the hand of the person two along so that our arms, behind our backs, are almost plaited. The faces of the smiling Kyrgyz, a Mongol warrior in furs, a Székely woman with braided hair, blur past and vanish into the night. Disorderly and unrefined, it is a binding ritual.

I return to my tent at 2 a.m. The 'no excessive drunkenness' rule has been comprehensively ignored; collapsing *csikós* and hammered Huns litter the journey home. Only the gentle horses stand calmly beneath their trees, nodding their heads in the dark.

It is all baffling. I will work it out tomorrow.

~

'This is the only place where, after midnight, you can find a conservative Muslim dancing with a skinhead.'

He is one of those from the revels last night: a young man with a bushy beard, rather uncertain amber eyes and a horse-tail-tasselled hat. I bumped into him over a breakfast of *lángos*, fried dough sodden with sour cream, and asked about the awkward balance of multiculturalism and nationalism. Where are we exactly, on the spectrum of folksy to fascist?

'It's a hypocriticism,' he says. 'Or maybe a duality. Hungarian nationalists can't decide between being Christian Europeans and this Magyar identity, which comes from outside Europe. They admire the culture of the steppe, even though most steppe cultures are in Muslim countries now. The nomadic Muslims are okay, but not the non-nomadic ones, and definitely not the migrant ones. It is all confused.'

'What have you come here for?' I ask, and his amber eyes light up.

'Because I feel part of the east! I can talk with someone from Yakutsk and know he is the same as me. We are all Turanic people. And everyone hates the west . . .'

He is the first self-identifying Turanist I have met, though references to it are everywhere at Ősök Napja. The Romantic nationalist movement started – in the way of most Romantic nationalist movements – in the nineteenth century, when Hungary was the junior partner in an Austrian empire. With Pan-Germanism and Pan-Slavism rising in the countries around them, and among Hungary's own unassimilated minorities, Magyar patriots turned away from corrupting western influence and towards their fellow Uralic language-speakers in the east. After being linguistically isolated for a thousand years, the discovery that they were not alone but part of a family of related tongues that spanned the world's largest continent must have felt like an opening door; at the same time, ethnologists drew connections between Eurasian groups from Hungary, Finland and Estonia to the shores of the Pacific. Turanism was born from this blend of linguistic theory and dubious racial science; the name comes from the Turan Depression around the Caspian Sea.

After the disaster of defeat in the First World War, Hungary lost two-thirds of its territory. This severance is still felt today; a popular T-shirt at this festival depicts the country's former map, extending from Transylvania to the Adriatic Sea, being torn apart by the skeletal hands of its thieving neighbours. The feeling of being betrayed by Europe increased the attractiveness of the east, giving Turanism an emotive boost that shaded into 1930s fascism. After the Second World War it was suppressed by the communists, but now – as Hungary's right-wing government turns away from the EU and seeks renewal in nationalism and a glorious mythical past – its popularity is growing again.

Clearly the costumes help.

In among all the visual confusion, it takes me a while to understand what it is that feels so strange. Most European nationalists tend towards an identity that is Christian and Caucasian; civilisation holding the line against the barbarian hordes. Here it is the opposite. These Turanists are proudly on the side of the barbarians.

Nowhere is this more apparent than on the enormous banner strung upon a great wooden frame at the entrance to the arena. The sallow, humourless features of Attila, tribal ruler of the Huns, gaze upon the festival; flame-yellow, presumably, from the light of a burning village. Throughout Europe this man, whose armies ravaged the Balkans, Greece and the Western Roman Empire, crossed the Danube and the Rhine, and ransacked much of northern France, is remembered as a bogeyman, the terror of Christendom, a curse inflicted by God to punish the unworthy. 'He was a man born into the world to shake the nations, the scourge of all lands, who in some way terrified all mankind', wrote the sixth-century historian Jordanes. The word 'Hun' is synonymous with savagery and desecration, applied by Allied propagandists to German troops in the First World War, conjuring visions of burning churches, looted artworks and outraged nuns. Here, Attila is celebrated as a culture hero.

The round, happy face of Genghis Khan is also paid obeisance to. In a richly decorated *ger* – a Mongolian felt-skinned yurt – I drink a glass of fermented mare's milk before a shrine to the great despoiler, father to sixteen million descendants, while a woman from the Mongolian Embassy feeds me mare's milk biscuits. Genghis never came to Hungary but his grandson Batu did, at the head of the Golden Horde; the 1241 invasion devastated Europe. The Mongols outdid even the Huns in their effectiveness; Hungary lost, by some estimates, a quarter of its population and much of the Great Hungarian Plain remained depopulated centuries later. With two-thirds of its settlements destroyed and hundreds of thousands dead, the whole region was emptied out, its fields reverting to pasture again. In the same way that 'desert' means a place that has been deserted, the word Puszta – 'barren', 'bare' – also translates as 'bereft'.

The area where Ősök Napja is held preserves a linguistic

clue that harks back to that time of shifting populations. 'Kun'
is common in place-names here, as well as 'Kiskun', 'Little
Kun' – nearby towns and villages include Kunszállás,
Kiskunhalas and Kiskunfélegyháza, while the region itself is
called Kunság – which testifies to the historical presence of
yet another steppe people, the Kuns or Cumans, who migrated
westwards in advance of the Mongol invasions. Initially invited
to settle by King Béla IV, who hoped they might form a first
line of defence against further hordes from the east, they
ended up raiding their sedentary neighbours and causing
almost as much mayhem as the Mongols. Little and Greater
Cumania survived as distinctive ethnic regions even past the
extinction of the Cuman language in 1770 (its last speaker
died in Karcag, a town just outside Hortobágy); the
nineteenth-century cultural revival finally united Cumans and
Magyars – not to mention the Mongols themselves – under
the Turanist banner.

The biscuits are chewy and strange. The fermented milk
is frothy, chilled, with a taste a bit like whey. Outside the *ger*,
twenty Mongolian dancing girls with perfect red lipstick
smiles, attired in purple, gold, green, blue, pink and silver
gowns, with hats in the shapes of cones and spires, perform
a synchronised routine as the crowd wolf-whistles along.

A very drunk young Hungarian man who has clearly been
up all night is sitting as if in prayer, gazing through the
entranceway. 'My soul,' he says when I talk to him.

'Your soul?'

'I have an Asian soul. I want to live like them, always
moving.'

According to legend the restless Attila never slept more
than a single night in the same place.

'Radiating from the Great Plain, sacking and enslaving half
Europe, they made the whole Roman Empire tremble', writes
Leigh Fermor with characteristic relish. 'When Attila died in

reckless bridebed after a heavy banquet somewhere close to the Tisza . . . the Huns galloped round and round his burial tent in a stampede of lamentation.'

Leaving the man to his dreamy smile, I make my way towards a contemporary version of this burial tent. On the far side of the site looms the Yurt of the Ancestors.

It is, by far, the largest covered structure at the festival: an enormous black dome like a malevolent flying saucer landed at the edge of the field. The queue to enter it is over a hundred people long, moving forward inchingly – men, women and children, in family groups or alone – enduring the baking temperature of early afternoon. It takes almost an hour before I am near the entrance, which is guarded by one of the giant *csikós* in his baggy black robes. The policy is one in, one out. A sign indicates that no swords are allowed inside. At last I step into the gloom, intensely curious by now, and at first glance there is nothing much to see at all; it mostly contains empty space, like the inside of a mosque. Then I realise that people are shuffling clockwise around the wall, reading and examining signboards and exhibits. The history of the Magyar people is here, in Hungarian and *rovásírás*, with maps showing their arrowed advances from the east; there are funerary offerings, potshards and jewellery; the reconstructed wax heads of prominent tribal leaders, men with narrow eyes, high cheekbones and thin moustaches. The centrepiece, set into the floor in front of a melodramatic mural of flailing hooves and sundered flags, enemies trampled into the ground, is a human skeleton buried with the jawbone of a horse, disinterred from a *kurgan* on the Western Steppe. People stoop to pay their respects, hushed and reverential. Lastly, the Yurt of the Ancestors holds a collection of skulls that are grotesquely modified by cranial deformation: the practice of binding the head of a child so that the skull elongates, producing a flattened, sloping forehead and a cone-shaped crown. This was practised by the Huns to set them apart from the people they conquered and confer the status of royalty; inside this black UFO, they might be alien beings.

Later the flags of the Turanic nations are galloped around the packed arena: the Székely banner, with its golden sun and crescent moon on a field of blue, gets the biggest cheer after Hungary's own. There are horseback archery displays, mounted belt wrestling conducted by bare-chested teenage boys grappling for each other's trousers while their horses brace and turn, and the Central Asian game of *buzkashi*, which involves two teams of horsemen jostling for control of a decapitated goat and dragging its carcass around the field. The audience, whose waves of clapping fall into and out of rhythm, as if they can't decide between collectivism and individualism – a Hungarian peculiarity, which I have witnessed nowhere else – are not so much spectators as participants, often dressed in more barbaric finery than the performers. Unlike at Texas Hollywood they are not pretending to be what they are not; rather, they are pretending to be what they imagine they once were. What strikes me is how naturally *right* so many of these people look – like Albert driving his horse and trap in waistcoat and bustard-feathered hat – wearing clothes that were last in fashion centuries ago.

'It is a hypocriticism,' said my friend with the amber eyes. In among the bright Mongolian clothes and the proclamations of unity are T-shirts adorned with Nazi eagles and the words 'Europe Belongs to Me'; ironically, for these proud descendants of the Great Migrations. Later that night, during another performance of thundering guitars, I watch – with a hollow, dawning sickness – the unassuming man beside me raise his right arm at an angle of forty-five degrees, palm down, and hold it there. No one pays him any mind. His wife and teenage daughter giggle, a little embarrassed but not ashamed, and then a younger man joins in, smiling happily. The two of them keep it up for song after song until their arms grow tired; afterwards they embrace, as if a special moment has been shared between strangers.

~

According to a thirteenth-century chronicle, the *Gesta Hunnorum et Hungarorum*, the legend of Hunor and Magor has a biblical origin. Their father Ménrót, the warrior giant who ruled the distant steppes of the east, was none other than the tyrant Nimrod, grandson of Noah, who offended God by building the Tower of Babel. This was, perhaps, an attempt to assimilate the pagan myth into the Christian one, but it makes just as much sense as a way of understanding linguistics. How else to explain the existence of Hungarian in the heart of Europe – a language utterly unlike anything spoken by their neighbours – than as a product of the cacophonous babble of tongues that flooded the world when the tower collapsed? Unintelligibility was God's punishment for hubris.

Before I leave Ősök Napja and the Puszta, something else about the myth of Hunor and Magor occurs to me. I keep coming across the emblem of the many-antlered hind.

It flutters on flags, is sold on stalls, and is worn on the waist in the form of belt buckles and intricate leathercraft sporrans. It appears in the iconography of the festival itself: a stylised golden deer with antlers like curling flames flowing the length of its back. Its intensity and gracefulness have the quality of prehistoric cave art, though it is from millennia later; Scythian in origin, it was common across Central Asia, that great intermingled goulash of steppe nomadism. Each antler is supposed to represent an ancestral tribe.

The cervine symbol, many-antlered or not, is clearly related to the white stag, the Hungarian totem animal that led the brothers across the steppe; only to mysteriously vanish, as if merging back into it (their mother's name, notes the chronicle, was Eneth, which means 'hind'). Deer were worshipped by Eurasian nomads from the earliest times, tracing the seasonal patterns of the migrating herds that could never be truly domesticated but only followed. The symbol of the white stag has magical and sacred connotations in cultures across Europe, from Celtic mythology to the conversion of St Eustace, who saw a vision of a crucifix between a white hart's antlers.

And suddenly I am out of Hungary, at the other end of the continent, back where I started from.

When I think of white stags I see reindeer.

Could the whiteness, possibly, be that of a reindeer pelt? That silver-grey fur that is warm yet cool, the colour of ice and metal? It is not impossible. Migratory reindeer-herding cultures – Evenks, Dukhas, Soyots, Tofalars, Tozha Tuvans and other groups – still adhere to the ancient patterns in north-east China, Mongolia and across Siberia, as they do in Sámi Scandinavia, connecting the steppe zone of the south with shifting northern permafrost. Could it have been reindeer that led the first nomads west?

And now I see past all this – the costumes, the macho games, the flags, the bewildered nationalism – back to the freedom of an empty space that stretches on and on.

There is the Cairngorms' arctic tundra, as frosted as reindeer pelts. There is the green of Białowieża, as dark as memory. There are the blasted minerals of Europe's only desert, badlands that were once a sea, in the earth-tones of a painted cave. Finlay's lines come back to me –

> how did we first come here?
> following behind the reindeer
> walking backwards into Spring

– and I see anonymous herds filtering through time and place, mass migrations in response to a rapidly changing climate. Like the shrinking glaciers, the rising seas, the spreading desert, the light and shade that lap across the continent in a tide of trees, these movements of animals and people are the living pulse of the planet. The frozen past recedes from view and the future is dark, unknown. We are all walking backwards now, unable to see where we are going, into the spring that is coming with the melting of the ice.

EPILOGUE

The Last Snow

On the day I return to the Cairngorms, a funeral service is being held 2,700 metres up in the Alps – attended by a chaplain, a delegation of scientists from the Swiss Association for Climate Protection, and mourners blowing alpenhorns – to mark the death of the Pizol, a vanished Swiss glacier. Over the last few years so much of its substance has ablated that, from a scientific perspective, it can no longer be classified as a glacier. It has lost its name. Soon it will just be water.

During the time that I was sweating my way across the Great Hungarian Plain, a small plaque was being installed at Okjökull in the west of Iceland, a glacier otherwise known as Ok. The Icelandic and English words, composed by the writer and former presidential candidate Andri Snær Magnason, read:

A letter to the future

Ok is the first Icelandic glacier to lose
its status as a glacier.
In the next 200 years all our glaciers are
expected to follow the same path.
This monument is to acknowledge that we know
what is happening and what needs to be done.
Only you know if we did it.

Ágúst 2019
415ppm CO_2

The bottom figure refers to the parts per million of carbon dioxide in the atmosphere. The last time it was this high was not only before recorded history, but before the existence of the human species.

At the end of my travels in Europe's outlands I return to Scotland's arctic to find the Sphinx.

It is the last week of September and I have been obsessively following updates from Iain Cameron, the man who documents the health of Britain's year-round snows. His latest, from three days ago, warns that only three patches are left: one on the mountain of Aonach Beag, neighbouring Ben Nevis, and two – the Sphinx and Pinnacles – in the glacial hollow of Garbh Choire Mòr. All of them, he says, can be labelled 'critically endangered'. He is far from hopeful that they will make it to the winter.

The wind flaps damp and warm. If glaciers in the Alps and Iceland have already ceased to exist, what hope is there for these stranded blobs? Perhaps it is already too late.

Aviemore looks more compelling by dawn than it did when I first came here, at night and in spitting rain; with its gloomy Victorian architecture and its dark pines draped in cloud, its palette of purples, greens and greys, it bears just a trace of the Walter Scott romance I expected the first time round. From the sleeper train I make my way past the closed mountainwear shops, past Happy Haggis, Royal Tandoori and the pub where I studied maps with Dougie, over the bloated River Spey and through the hamlet of Inverdruie. The mountains lie ahead, unclothed. A path leads through the first trees of the Rothiemurchus Forest.

Eight months ago, on that winter night, the forest floor was buried in white. Now the ground beneath the gnarled Scots pines is an unreal green: what I now recognise as a temperate rainforest of ferns, heather and stunted juniper, gleaming with fungal life and wells of moss so deep I could sink my arm up to the elbow. Scaly sleeves of lichen hang from the red limbs of the trees. Light reflects off a silvery blanket of blaeberry leaves. Rothiemurchus is one of the remnants of the once great Caledonian Forest that covered the north of Scotland after the Last Glacial Maximum; around nine thousand years old, it is almost, but not quite, as primeval as Białowieża. Of course it is the lack of snow that has revealed it to me now, a richness and complexity that only comes with great age, but it also feels as if Białowieża, and the attentiveness of the people who guided me through those trees, has given me different eyes.

When I see dark scat on a rock my heart actually jolts; then I remember, no wolves here, not for a long time. Maybe – probably – again, but for now we have filled the landscape of fear with other fears.

Water burbles underfoot, scours whitely through the trees, where the descending Allt Druidh rolls on its bed of pebbles. After the desert and the steppe, it feels an indulgent luxury to be so surrounded by water, knowing my flask will always be full. A frog back-kicks through a burn. I shock the sleep of travel away with a face-dunk in a stream.

The land gets higher and the trees get lower as I approach the forest's edge, the spaces between the trunks widening and emptying. Complexity diminishes: the ferns and mosses are reduced, the deciduous trees stripped away, leaving only contorted pines, heather and blaeberry. Biome passes into biome: in the space of half a mile, temperate rainforest turns to taiga and taiga turns to tundra.

I am making for the northern entrance of the Lairig Ghru.

The great glacial valley is streaked with stretch marks of scree, evidence of the ancient trauma wreaked upon the landscape. Sunlight probes in pale spots, catching the threads of waterfalls gleaming on denuded land. Free of snow, free of ice, it looks like a new world, or perhaps the future reaching back to meet the past. On the ascent into the pass I press against a powerful headwind thundering from the narrow mouth – the sheer wall of Creag an Leth-choin, Lurcher's Crag, to my left, the flank of Coire Gorm to my right – no longer claggy and damp but brisk with a nip of ice. From the valley's highest point the rubbly path descends again, past the clear Pools of Dee, the walls leading down to which have been gouged more recently by rock collapse or avalanche, leaving long violent furrows in the mountain-side. Red gritty soil shows within, the *ruadh* of the Cairngorms' Gaelic name. I cup my hands to drink. The water tastes of stone.

The going gets awkward now, navigating a moraine of heaped erratic blocks. Ahead lies ominous cloud, alternately flooding with yellow light and darkening to grey, as if an unseen hand is playing with a dimmer switch. It looks like a hallway filled with smoke – I think of the long summer of fires – cutting off the mountaintops above the height of a thousand metres; it occurs to me that I may never find Garbh Choire Mòr inside that murk, let alone two spots of snow, if they are even still there. But the cloud is billowing, allowing fleeting glimpses through. Ahead and below is the Devil's Point and the hump of Angel's Peak, much further away than I imagined; ahead and above is the ridgeline that I walked with Dougie.

And then something holds the light in a way that rock does not.

Two pale dots are there, gleaming in the gloaming.

'[S]now gives the impression of gathering light to itself', notes the writer Christopher Nicholson, another compulsive snow patcher, in his book *Among the Summer Snows*. 'It opens its arms and embraces the light. This phenomenon, known as the Purkinje shift, is in truth nothing to do with the snow, but results from the adjustment of rods and cones within the human eye to changing light conditions.' The word 'gloaming', he points out, has the same root as 'gloom' but also as its opposite, 'glow'.

Gleam, gloam, gloom, glow. But these patches are wordless things. They are as pallid as egg whites, moons. I hold their gaze but the cloud smokes back and soon they vanish again.

I walk towards their memory, setting a straight course up the mountain.

Off path; over heather; through bog; into mud; into sphagnum; over streams; into the living mountain. I am not walking on its surface but in a squelching ecosystem of inter-woven life, my boots and sometimes lower legs plunging to sudden depths. Over this spongy ground, by turns yielding and buoyant, I tumble every minute or two, on my back, my front, my face. Luckily there couldn't be a more cushioned landing. As in the Rothiemurchus Forest, without the concealing cover of white an astonishing richness is revealed, the densely entan-gled web that is the fabric of the tundra: seeping crimson rustwort like some bloody internal organ; alien jungles of fork-moss that pulses algal green; the fleshy lobes of monster pawwort; splatters of lurid lichen. Through the damper, darker swathes grows a delicate branching form whose colour is the palest green before green turns into white: reindeer lichen, the reason that the herd thrives here today. This is what reminded Mikel Utsi so powerfully of his home, in the Arctic north of Sweden, and it is like nothing else I have seen in Britain. Recovering breath after one of my falls, half sunk into moist terrain, I put my face up close and lose myself in an antlered maze; it resembles nothing so much as a diagram of a neuronal network, a synaptic flowering that interconnects with the other plants, weaving the tundra to itself and the reindeer to the tundra. Its rate of growth is glacial, just a few millimetres a year, a sluggishness well adapted for subzero temperatures and surviving months or years buried under snow; it is the reindeers' favourite food and their lifeline in the winter. Having picked a stem, I cautiously chew it as I bounce along. It has a fishy, fungal taste, a kind of tundra seaweed.

With my eyes on my feet I have lost sight of my objective. Cloud obscures the steep bowl of the corrie I am making for, but following a glugging stream, advancing blindly on, I come across a climbers' refuge halfway up the slope. Like the refuge at the Ford of A'an it is a small triangular shelter, floored in wood and walled in stone, with just enough space inside to stretch out flat and stand up straight. Inside – among the usual offerings of half-empty gas canisters, candles and foil-packed food supplies – a literary benefactor has left behind a copy of *The Living Mountain*, which, as I leaf through, falls open at a significant page. 'There was snow worth seeing in those old summers. I used to believe it was eternal snow, and touched it with a feeling of awe', writes Shepherd of this place. 'But by August 1934, there was no snow left at all in the Cairngorms except a small patch in the innermost recess of the Garbh Choire of Braeriach. Antiquity has gone from our snow.'

In the visitors' book I find an entry from Iain Cameron, dated two months ago. 'As I write the situation looks bleak. I expect them to melt sometime in September. If it happens it'll be the first time it's all melted in three consecutive years. Historic!'

A pang of urgency. Dumping my rucksack on the floor I carry on, unburdened.

Garbh Choire Mòr is an amphitheatre gouged in the body of Braeriach, a bite taken out of the mountainside, the primordial gnawing of the winter-bringing Cailleach. Scrambling up the loose wet scree, at times on my hands and knees, effectively humbles my approach; it is like ascending the broken steps of a temple. The rocks are slippery, slimed with strange black moss and smears of mouldy greenery watered by the melt above, surviving in the terminal dribble of their own tiny glaciers. Bitter rain begins to fall. The light gets ever greyer. All I can do is climb to where the rock meets the clouds, towards the hidden points of snow, the earlier manifestation of which is starting to feel like an illusion. Were they a Purkinje Fata Morgana? The Brocken spectre at his tricks? Or did I glimpse them moments before a sudden, fateful melt?

Then the cloud gives way again and there they are, as real as rock.

The Sphinx and Pinnacles: the last snow in Scotland.

It is the Sphinx I come to first, breathless from the final climb. It is the smaller of the pair, despite its greater fame. Its shape is roughly circular, ten metres in diameter, and its edges are not smooth but scalloped like knapped flint, its serrations highlighted in grime. Its surface, pitted and eroded from ablating and refreezing, is matted with a coarse pelt of pine needles, twigs and blades of grass, like a roughly moulting beast; discolourations of pinkish soil, either washed down from above or blown here by the wind, give it the appearance of internal haemorrhaging.

It is thicker than I expected, standing at least a metre tall. Its bottom edge lifts from the rock in an upward-curling snarl, as if in recoil from a hostile surface. Until its first recorded disappearance in 1933, its mass was composed of untold generations of accumulated snowfall, but in this post-industrial age that link with the past has gone. What I am looking at now is less than a year old.

Traversing a saddle of wet grit I pay a visit to Pinnacles, thinner and longer than the Sphinx, an irregular obloid curled into the mountain. Initially I had the notion of mounting an expedition across – I even brought my ice axe and spikes for that purpose – but now I am up close to it the idea feels disrespectful. I think of my great-uncle's ascent up the Khumbu Icefall on his way to the highest place on earth, and how that route is collapsing now; I think of that glacier in Kashmir, dissolving to slush beneath the boots of solemn scientists. My weight, or so it seems, might snap this clean in half. Instead I cross back to the Sphinx and use the axe's point to chop out a small hole – even that feels like a violent act – and reach into my pocket for the offerings I have brought.

One by one I drop them in, souvenirs from other outlands: an acorn from Białowieża; a fragment of gypsum from Tabernas; some blades of grass from Hortobágy. Then I tomb them in with ice.

But how long will they stay buried?

Not long, judging by the tune: a percussive drip, drip, drip, a trickle of singing water. Lying flat against wet rock I see the seeping underbelly, a vaulted ceiling of ice flowing in a hundred places. The architecture is unsound, held up by corroding pillars and buttresses becoming slush. Liquid moves unstoppably inside and underneath the ice, welling and scurrying, steadily bleeding out.

I follow one clear thread to where it forms a slow, fat drop and position my flask beneath. Breakfast tomorrow will be porridge with ice-melt and blaeberries. As the drops expand and fall, expand and fall, expand and fall, I close my eyes – milking the Sphinx like the Cailleach milking her herd of deer – and concentrate on the pulse.

It takes an age to fill.

By the time the water brims, my limbs are cramped from the chill. Rain is falling. Wind is rising. It is hard to tear myself away but I have to go. All that is left to do is wish these blobs of stranded time good luck – wish all of us good luck – and let my feet take me back to the refuge that is waiting.

Halfway down the mountainside I turn for a last look back. Two pale eyes watch me go. One winks. Both blink. Then both are gone.

Afterword

Against predictions the Sphinx and Pinnacles did not melt in 2019 but were reprieved by an early fall of snow a week after my visit. A heavier fall at the start of October narrowly secured their existence into another winter. The Sphinx survived 2020 but vanished again in November 2021 – symbolically melting during the COP26 Climate Change Conference in Glasgow.

At the time of writing, the year in which I did these walks was the second-hottest (after 2016, tied with 2020) in recorded history.

Since I visited Białowieża, the border I crossed and camped beside became the latest front line in Europe's migrant crisis. In autumn 2021 the government of Belarus, seeking revenge on the EU for sanctions imposed the year before, encouraged refugees from the Middle East and Afghanistan to cross the border into Poland through that remote forest region. Forced back by Polish border guards, thousands of men, women and children found themselves stuck between the two countries, sleeping in freezing conditions in the forest, living in fear of wolves and facing the threat of violent assault on both sides of the border. If I'd known that was to come – how different my experience was from that of vulnerable refugees camped among those very same trees – I would have written the Białowieża chapter of this book differently.

Acknowledgements

Dungeness: thank you to David Snoo Wilson and family for our stay in the hut. Cairngorms: *tapadh leat* to Dougie Strang, Chris Hammond, Iain Cameron, Tilly Smith, John Hunt and the Big Grey Man. Białowieża: *dziękuję* to Joanna my forest guide, Augustyn, Marianka, Asia, Adam and all the other brave activists at the house of the forest defenders, and *spasibo* to Natalya. Tabernas: *muchas gracias* to Kevin Borman and Troy Roberts, Laurence Burton (Standing Eagle) and Bri Hutchings. Hortobágy: *köszönöm* to Judit Rácz, Albert and Judit, and the German man whose name I never knew. Elsewhere: thank you to Bethany Ritz at *Emergence* magazine, whose edits helped craft part of the Białowieża chapter, Gregory Norminton and Mark Goldthorpe for their neologisms, my agent Jessica Woollard, my fine-eyed editor Joe Zigmond, Nick Davies for all his support and guidance over the years, Caroline Westmore, Morag Lyall, Howard Davies and the rest of the brilliant team at John Murray, Rosie Collins for the beautiful maps, (the original) Nicholas Brealey, my ever-inspiring friends and colleagues at the Dark Mountain Project, Ron Hutchinson, Alisa Taylor and Isabella Hutchinson, Caroline Hunt, Caroline Williams, Otto and the house on Gratitude Road.

The author would like to thank the following for permission to reproduce quotations. The excerpt from 'The Fall of Rome' by W.H. Auden, copyright © *Collected Poems* 1976, renewed, is reprinted by permission of Curtis Brown, Ltd. Excerpts from *Gathering* by Alec Finlay are reprinted by permission of Hauser & Wirth Publishers. The excerpts from *The Ascent of Everest* by John Hunt are reprinted by permission of Hodder & Stoughton. Excerpts from *The Living Mountain*, copyright © Nan Shepherd, 1977, are reprinted by permission of Canongate Books Ltd. Excerpts from *Landscape and Memory* by Simon Schama are reprinted by permission of HarperCollins Publishers Ltd. Excerpts from *The World Without Us*, © 2007 Alan Weisman, are reproduced by permission of The Random House Group Ltd., and by permission of St Martin's Press. All rights reserved. Excerpts from *Where Hoopoes Fly* and *Flamingos in the Desert* are reprinted by permission of Kevin Borman. The excerpt from *The Immeasurable World* by William Atkins is reprinted by permission of Faber and Faber Ltd. The excerpts from *Between the Woods and the Water* by Patrick Leigh Fermor are reprinted by permission of John Murray Press. The excerpts from *The Nature Guide to the Hortobágy and Tisza River Floodplain, Hungary* are reprinted by permission of Dirk Hilbers at Crossbill Guides. The excerpts from *Among the Summer Snows* by Christopher Nicholson are reprinted by permission of September Publishing.

Bibliography

Abbey, Edward, *Desert Solitaire*, Ballantine Books, 1994

Atkins, William, *The Immeasurable World*, Faber & Faber, 2018

Blackburn, Julia, *Time Song*, Jonathan Cape, 2019

Borman, Kevin, *Flamingos in the Desert*, FeedaRead, 2014

——, *Where Hoopoes Fly*, FeedaRead, 2017

Burton, Laurence, *The Astral Twins*, Eloquent Books, 2012

Campbell, Nancy, *The Library of Ice*, Scribner, 2018

Fermor, Patrick Leigh, *Between the Woods and the Water*, John Murray, 1986

Finlay, Alec, *Gathering*, Hauser & Wirth Publishers, 2018

Gray, Affleck, *The Big Grey Man of Ben MacDui*, Birlinn Ltd, 1970

Hilbers, Dirk, *The Nature Guide to the Hortobágy and Tisza River Floodplain, Hungary*, Crossbill Guides, 2008

Hunt, John, *The Ascent of Everest*, Hodder & Stoughton, 1953

Lawrence, T.E., *Seven Pillars of Wisdom*, Penguin Classics, 2000

McOwan, Rennie, *Magic Mountains*, Mainstream Publishing, 1996

Magnason, Andri Snær, *On Time and Water*, Serpent's Tail, 2020

Nicholson, Christopher, *Among the Summer Snows*, September Publishing, 2017

Powers, Richard, *The Overstory*, W.W. Norton, 2018

Schama, Simon, *Landscape and Memory*, Harper Perennial, 2004

Shepherd, Nan, *The Living Mountain*, Canongate, 2011

Smith, Tilly, *Reindeer: An Arctic Life*, History Press, 2018

Strang, Dougie, 'The Laird's Tablecloth', *Bella Caledonia*, 2018

Tokarczuk, Olga, *Primeval and Other Times* (trans. Antonia Lloyd-Jones), Twisted Spoon Press, 2010

Tudge, Colin, *The Secret Life of Trees*, Penguin, 2006

Watson, Adam, *The Place Names of Upper Deeside*, Paragon Publishing, 2014

Watson, Adam, and Cameron, Iain, *Cool Britannia*, Paragon Publishing, 2010

Weisman, Alan, *The World Without Us*, Virgin, 2008